". . . articulates in practical, real-life terms our movement's most deeply held beliefs."

Cesar E. Chavez, President,
United Farm Workers of America

"The potential for using this new form of currency is limitless. Communities and groups can now create their own services without having to turn to government or the vote for new taxes. A simple but powerful concept."

Milan Dluhy, Ph.D., Director, Institute of Government,
Florida International University

". . . should be on the agenda of government and private agencies everywhere. A straightforward and unvarnished account of the issues, the obstacles, and the opportunities of this new medium of exchange."

Carl Eisdorfer, Past President,
Gerontological Society of America

"People of our nation want to serve one another. Time Dollars help them do this while also providing the individuals with the security of knowing that a helping hand will be available to them when they are in need."

Christopher H. Smith, U.S. Representative

"Organized labor ought to take this currency very seriously. Time Dollars could mean guaranteed useful employment for everyone as long as there is another human being in need."

James Brunkenhoefer, National Legislative Director,
United Transportation Union

"I hope *Time Dollars* generates wide debate and huge sales . . . for raising important questions about the loss of community and neighborhood in contemporary society."

James Lengle, Ph.D., Department of Government,
Georgetown University

TIME DOLLARS

The New Currency That Enables Americans to Turn Their Hidden Resource-Time-into Personal Security & Community Renewal

EDGAR CAHN, PH.D., J.D.
JONATHAN ROWE

"A New Slant on the Golden Rule" on pages 248–250 is reprinted with permission from the September 1990 *Reader's Digest*.

EDITOR: Charles Gerras
COPY EDITOR: Lisa D. Andruscavage
DESIGNER: Adrianne Onderdonk Dudden
INDEXER: Ed Yeager
COVER DESIGNER: Acey Lee

If you have any questions or comments concerning this book, please write:

Rodale Press
Book Reader Service
33 East Minor Street
Emmaus, PA 18098

Library of Congress Cataloging-in-Publication Data

Cahn, Edgar S.
   Time dollars : the new currency that enables Americans to turn their hidden resource—time—into personal security and community renewal / by Edgar Cahn and Jonathan Rowe.
      p.   cm.
   Includes bibliographical references and index.
   ISBN 0-87857-985-0   hardcover
   1. Voluntarism—United States.   2. Barter—United States.   3. Informal sector (Economics)—United States.   I. Rowe, Jonathan, 1946-   .   II. Title.
HN90.V64C34   1992
302' . 14—dc20   91–35168
                                                                                              CIP

Distributed in the book trade by St. Martin's Press

2 4 6 8 10 9 7 5 3 1 hardcover

TO JEAN CAMPER CAHN

For in the fullness of time, I must believe
that the voices of love shall prevail over the voices of hate
and the forces of justice shall triumph over the forces
    of injustice and inhumanity.

                                                            This I believe.

But in the here and now, there can be no safety,
    no guarantees, and no easy way.
At each point, our faith will be tested and, when weighed in the balance,
    if we are honest, our best efforts will be found wanting.

                                            This is true, this I believe.

And so, all that we have, in the here and now, is
    our love for each other,
    our willingness to forgive each other,
    our willingness to come to each other's rescue,
    our willingness to stand by silent or passive
        in the face of injustice.

This is my belief, this is our joint belief, and this we shall try to honor
    so long as life and breath permit.

She did.
Her spirit quickens these pages and lives on in this book and its
progeny.

Contents

Foreword by **Ralph Nader**   *ix*
Acknowledgments   *xv*

PART I   **The Untapped Resources of Time**

1   A Way Out in Hard Times   *3*

2   Economics Beyond Money: How Things
We Did Became Things We Buy   *15*

3   When Money Doesn't Work   *26*

4   Elderplan Grows a New Currency
in Brooklyn   *44*

5   But Is It Really Volunteering?   *62*

6   Why the Taxman Didn't Come   *75*

7   The Health of Helping   *83*

8   Florida I: How the Bureaucracy
Almost Killed Time Dollars   *95*

9   Florida II: How Grass-Roots Groups
    Built the New Currency
    on Their Own   108

10 "Disabling Professions": A Way
    to Take Back the Right
    to Help and Care   120

11 A Money Supply for Entrepreneurs
    Who Build Community   132

12 Centro San Vicente: From Ability
    to Pay to Willingness to Give   142

13 Michigan and Missouri Let
    a Hundred Flowers Bloom   151

14 The New Politics of Time   162

15 Taxpayers into Citizens:
    How Government Can Spend Less
    and Help More   173

16 The Long Shadow of the Future   184

**PART II   You Can Start a Time
            Dollar Bank**

17 How to Plan the Network   193

18 How to Launch
    the New Currency   208

19 How to Sustain the Bank   216

    Appendix   229
    Index   263

Foreword

In every idea a multitude of new ideas is lying dormant.
—*Emmanuel Swedenborg*

Citizen action must rest on a new economic base: one that makes it possible for people to meet their own needs while working to rebuild community and revitalize democracy at the grass-roots level.

Now along comes the Time Dollar, an organized, inflation-proof currency that can provide as constant, as powerful, as reliable a reward for decency as the market does for selfishness. It has been tested and it works. Government does not control it. It does not need new laws to make it happen. It can spring up tomorrow in a thousand places.

Resources are always limited. In a period of budget cutbacks and recession, social problems are multiplying at a rate that outstrips the most creative fundraising. The Time Dollar represents a strategy to generate tremendous resources and to involve thousands of people on a sustained basis.

On a one-to-one basis, the Time Dollar movement has begun to revolutionize the production of needed services between people who can meet their own needs through the earning of Time Dollars by helping others. A retired secretary types poetry written by a neighbor with multiple sclerosis, and the neighbor repays her by reading the newspaper to the secretary's blind daughter. Elsewhere, a retired teacher tutors a 12-year-old boy in English, and he mows her lawn periodically.

The mixes and matches are endless. Some 3,000 service credit volunteers, most of them over 60, are already at work through programs administered by community agencies, schools, local hospitals, and community colleges. That means citizens can begin to address critical needs that otherwise would remain neglected. On this level, Time Dollars simply reward people helping people. Fortunately, the IRS has ruled such exchanges tax-exempt because they are not "commercial in nature."

But Time Dollars are far more than a tax-exempt, barter currency. When strangers start acting like neighbors, and neighbors start acting like extended family, communities are reinvigorated. In an age of mobility, family break-up, neighborhood decay, and wide-spread drug-related crime, that is no small achievement. Indeed, in an era of white-collar crime, S&L fraud, personal greed, and governmental default, the need for an innovation that successfully promotes basic moral values of mutual assistance is enormous.

Time Dollars do more than meet human needs; they do more than rebuild trust in a world of many commercial predators. They provide the kind of new economics that can support sustained citizen action on the scale society needs. In these times, many Americans are resigned to the status quo or are too busy paying bills to give the time needed to make democracy work as it could, to hold government officials accountable, and to check corporate lawlessness. Time Dollars could change that.

Imagine being able to pay part of your medical bill with Time Dollars earned by attacking sanitation problems and monitoring sources of water pollution that cause hepatitis. That's happening in El Paso. Imagine being able to pay part of your health insurance premiums by giving adult literacy classes or staffing a latch-key program for kids whose only parent has to work? That's happening in Washington, D.C., and Miami. Imagine paying for quality child care by being part of a driver's pool for senior citizens on evenings and weekends. That's happening, too.

This book is about a practical, tested new idea finely organized around the ancient pre-currency practice of mutual aid. It is so simple that people often ask, "Why didn't I think of that?" But it could spark a revolution. Time Dollars could sweep the nation to higher levels of care, compassion, and enjoyment—without any imperious bureaucracies. Time Dollar programs can mobilize the best in people on a sustained basis—just at a time when society seems least able to make any progress in these service areas.

The Time Dollar as a currency has been used with impressive success for the past four years. People still do not know its full potential. For here, as a starter, in Albert Einstein's words, "Imagination is more important than knowledge."

The power of the Time Dollar idea stems from four basic truths.

The first is that the real wealth of our nation is not money; it is the time of people and the willingness of people to use that time helping others. Time Dollar experiments demonstrate that there are substantial and valuable reservoirs of human time that neither the market economy nor volunteerism has tapped. Experience with Time Dollars shows that they are able to tap that vast potential resource. This book notes that other advanced industrial nations, Germany, Japan, and Sweden, all say that they, too, will lack the monetary resources to meet important needs of their citizenry. And that suggests that something more basic is involved than the current health of the economy or the rate of growth of the gross national product.

The second truth is that the United States has two economies, the market economy, which the economists all analyze, and the household economy of family, neighborhood, and community. The book argues that many of the serious problems our society faces come from the erosion of the second economy, the economy of the family and the neighborhood. The Time Dollar is a currency designed to reward time spent rebuilding that economy.

In describing how Time Dollars actually work, it becomes clear that many of society's needs for money are the result of the steady decline of the household economy. That economy has been taken over by the market economy; many families now pay for services their predecessors used to provide for themselves: from entertainment to companionship, from rearing youngsters to caring for the elderly. For a long time, the decline of that economy was masked by one fact: The unpaid labor of women kept that economy going. With their massive entry into the job market, the involuntary subsidy that women provided disappeared. Time Dollars may provide an alternative strategy for rebuilding that second, essential economy.

The third basic truth underlying Time Dollars is that people respond to rewards other than money. Since society lacks money to reward all the activity it needs and wants, society had better find another reward system. The reward system that Time Dollars provide is unique: It responds to a fundamental human need, the need to be needed and valued. It does so by providing a combination of additional purchasing power with psychological reinforcement. It turns out that the psychological reinforcement, the self-esteem, and the recognition may be even more important than the additional purchasing power provided by Time Dollars. The Time Dollar movement translates that insight into a practical strategy for meeting needs. As this book points out, society needs a currency that rewards the important values. To avoid offering the things society values to the highest bidder, the rules of the game have to change. If money continues to be the only currency and dollar price remains as the only factor, society will continue to run a social and civic deficit.

The fourth and final truth is that money does not buy complete substitutes for what the family, the neighborhood, and community used to provide. It does part of the job; it leaves people to do the rest as citizens, as consumers, and as family members. And whether the market substitute does 70 or 80 or 90 percent of the job, it turns out that the other 10 or 20 or 30 percent that is absolutely critical often is inaccessible.

These concepts haven't been put to the fullest possible use. The book is a blueprint on how to put this knowledge to work. It is extremely readable; the human interest stories and the case histories come alive. They are real. And they are compelling dramas. The book provides fresh, clear insights on problems such as economic theory, professionalism, the characteristics of money, the nature of social service delivery systems, and the nature of government bureaucracy. Yet, even when dealing with these complex social policy issues, the book makes sense. It is so clearly and concretely written that it invites citizens to tackle these problems.

This book includes a clear, concise how-to-do-it program, with exhibits and brochures and work sheets and instructions. Any group, organization, or institution that wants to launch a Time Dollar program will know how from that material. That boils down to empowerment— the book not only inspires action, it also provides the civic tools that facilitate action.

This book doesn't fit the usual conservative-liberal categories. It challenges the notion that everything in life must be done by specialists and professionals. It challenges the assumption that money really defines what society can do.

The media, congressional debates, economists' predictions, and political oratory all deliver the same grim message: Without more money society must accept more babies dying at birth, more homeless people wandering the streets, more old people alone and abandoned. Global competition, the budget deficit, the S&L bailout, and the price of oil all come first.

It amounts to gridlock—moral, fiscal, political. Now Edgar Cahn and Jonathan Rowe come with a book that describes a new kind of money, a fresh vision, and a way to break that gridlock.

—RALPH NADER

Acknowledgments

We owe this book to the men and women who are pioneering Time Dollar networks all over the United States. This is not ritual modesty but a statement of fact. These individuals—program leaders and participants alike—have taken hold of a new concept and made it real. They are meeting urgent human needs and helping to restore to American life something worthy of the name "community."

We have been amazed and inspired at every turn, and we have felt fortunate to get to know these remarkable groups of people. We mention some of them in this book, but because of space limitations not all could be included. We regret these omissions, and we thank all who helped us—especially those who took time out from their work to aid us with this project.

We owe special thanks as well to a number of others. Ralph Nader and his associate, John Richard, both saw the potential of Time Dollars early on. Their enthusiasm and support have helped make the movement—and this book—possible. Jay Acton took on the promotion of the Time Dollar concept because he believed in it. His only compensation is our thanks, and that he has many times over.

The late Bob Rodale infused this project with his practical idealism and vision. It is an honor to be able to make this contribution to his large legacy. The staff at Rodale Books believed in the book enough to shepherd it through some very difficult times. In particular, Charlie

Gerras, our editor, met every difficulty with unfailing patience and support.

Eve Bargmann, Matthew Goodman, Irene Kim, David Littlefield, and Lenore Cahn Zola provided wise counsel on the manuscript at crucial junctures. We thank them and others who suffered through some very unpolished drafts and who buoyed our (sometimes flagging) sense that something eventually might come of them. Our extended families of colleagues and friends are too numerous to mention. They know who they are, but they probably don't know how helpful they have been, nor how grateful we feel.

Finally, we want to thank Christine Solomon who brought her keen eye and judgment to many of the chapters and who endured the disruption of her home for weeks on end with patience and good cheer.

PART I

The Untapped Resources of Time

The potential benefits of the Time Dollar concept are limitless. It can touch every life in every community, ranging from an apartment complex to an entire nation, every facility, from a nursing home to a university campus. In each instance, it fosters a sense of financial independence, camaraderie, community spirit, harmony among age groups, races, religions, income levels, and even political adversaries. It turns the improbable into the reasonable.

Many such developments have already happened. Some are happening right now. The chapters in this section show how Time Dollars can fit into your life and improve every day of it—new friends, more and better services, increased self-esteem.

1

A Way Out in Hard Times

If Dolores Galloway had followed the *Washington Post* in the fall of 1990, she might well have felt depressed. For weeks on end, the news was about budget cuts and deficits—a pervasive lack of money. The president and Congress were locked in a dreary stalemate over the federal budget. The deficit was huge, an election was coming, and nobody wanted to take the blame for tax increases or budget cuts. States and cities across the nation were in a similar bind. "I think you would have to go back to the Depression to find similar anguish," said Henry Aaron of the Brookings Institution in Washington, D.C.

Official Washington had access to the best experts in the land. Yet for all their sophistication and cunning, they always came up against the same hard wall. Money defined the nation's sense of the possible. And money was always limited, so the possibilities for solving problems were limited as well, even in the best of times. Of course, as times got bad and needs got greater, the ability to meet those needs decreased even further. The wall of money loomed up on every side.

Congress was considering spending cuts and tax increases that would total half a trillion dollars over the next five years. The Federal Reserve Board was insisting on such cuts before it would allow more money to flow into the economy. In effect, the entire government was hostage to this keeper of the nation's money. Meanwhile, government agencies were working overtime to develop contingency plans for shutting down.

If the budget picture looked bleak for the near future, the outlook for coming decades was even more depressing. Everything seemed to be getting old: roads, bridges, and people— especially people. The Baby Boomers were beginning to face the prospect that time didn't stop for them. By the year 2040, one out of every five Americans would be over age 65—a total of 50 million people. The generation that once defined itself as under 30 would soon be joining the already-swelling ranks of the elderly; costs for nursing home care alone were expected to approach $140 billion a year. Even the good news was bad: "Longer Life to Boost Health Bills," one newspaper headline proclaimed.

HARD TIMES NOW, HARDER TO COME

The morass of money troubles in Washington could hardly have cheered Galloway, since those grim projections of growing need and sinking resources included her. Galloway lives alone, in a senior citizens' building, in the section of Washington called Anacostia. The area is best known for its boarded-up housing projects, drugs, and crime; most residents of the nation's capital rarely go there, black as well as white. Galloway can't go anyplace else. A host of ailments have confined her to a motorized wheelchair, and her hands are so weak that she can't unscrew a bottle cap. Just answering the door to her apartment can be a major exertion.

Galloway goes to the hospital often, sometimes for days at a time. Her building is federally subsidized, one of the last funded in Washington before the Reagan administration killed the program. Altogether, her life fortunes are closely tied to government outlays for social services of various kinds. But Galloway also remembers a time when the social safety net was much more than the programs enacted in Washington. She was a girl in Atlanta and day care meant parents in the neighborhood keeping an eye on one another's kids. If Mom had to go to the store, she would just deposit the children in a neighbor's living room. There was help for young new mothers, too. "If you had a baby, the neighbors came over and cleaned your house for you," she says.

That is the puzzling thing about the enormous budget gaps that loom ahead. Somehow, normal life stages called youth and age have become social problems of staggering dimensions. Yes, people are living longer. And yes, the Baby Boomers are going to enter the ranks of the aged in a big lump. Still, people have been growing old for eons, and somehow, society took care of them without the massive programs that people are talking about now.

At some instinctive level, Galloway understood that the old neighborhood held some answers. "Up here," she says, speaking of the North, "people don't care about each other like they should." Trying to remedy that, she had stumbled onto an answer that Washington's officialdom didn't even know about and probably would have pooh-poohed if they did. It was a new kind of money—a new way to bring back the old ways—and it was working right under the noses of budget experts who didn't have a clue about what to do next.

OLD WAYS, NEW "MONEY"

Galloway is an exuberant woman who defies her physical ailments with earthy humor and rambunctious street-corner jive. "I don't sit around and feel sorry for myself, and I don't want nobody else feeling sorry for me either," she says. Instead, she set out to turn her building into the kind of neighborhood she grew up in. The Robert L. Walker House, where she lives, is a project of the Greater Southeast Community Hospital. Galloway herself is only 48, but qualified for the senior housing because of her physical condition.

Many of her neighbors have health problems of their own. Elder Gaston, for example, is a retired minister who lives on the third floor. He is a shy and quiet man who lost a leg, and he's inclined to hole up in his apartment for days at a stretch. "I have to go up there and get on him," Galloway says. "I have to call him up and threaten him."

Galloway does laundry for Gaston. She also shops for him at the supermarket, which is over 2 miles away, riding the motorized wheelchair she jokingly calls her Cadillac. (Speedy Suzie is what the residents who pass the time in the lobby call her.) "He says, 'I don't want to bother you.' I say, 'Give me the money, man, and let me go to the store.' "

Galloway has organized residents in the whole building to help one another in this way. Everybody gets a knock on the door in the morning, to make sure things are okay. People do the shopping for one another, do laundry, clean house for those who aren't feeling well. There are parties and outings, and on election day, those with cars make sure everyone has a ride to the polls. Galloway has five lieutenants who oversee the system while she is in the hospital, just to make sure nobody falls through the cracks.

MONEY MADE OF TIME

Galloway could easily be a character from the cue cards of ex-President Reagan, a living testimonial that the answer to today's problems is a return to a Norman Rockwell world. What makes her more than that, what makes her experience a real response to the money bind, is that Galloway's system runs on money, too. It is a different kind of money—a kind that she doesn't have to go begging for, to Congress or foundations. A new administration can't shut this money off, and bureaucrats can't siphon it off for administrative expenses. The pushers can't steal it, and central bankers can't inflate it. Galloway and her neighbors at the Walker House produce this new money themselves—not with printing presses, but with their own time.

"Time is money," the old saying goes, and the residents of the Walker House are converting that saying into a thriving economy of helpfulness and good works. Every Saturday, Galloway steers her electric cart down the corridor to the building manager's office and stations herself in front of the office computer, which she taught herself to use. There, she enters the balances for the week—the credits each resident of the building earned and spent, either by helping a neighbor or receiving help. The system works on a principle of strict equality: 1 hour, 1 credit, whether the task is doing laundry or helping someone with his taxes. Every resident's time is considered just as valuable as anyone else's.

These credits are known by different names: Time Dollars, service credits, care shares. (We shall call them Time Dollars and service credits interchangeably.) The basic concept is like that of a blood bank, in which people donate blood to a central supply, and then can take that much out if the need arises. With Time Dollars, people bank time instead of blood. Give some time to help a neighbor, and somewhere down the line, a neighbor—probably a different neighbor—will give some time to help you.

There are no coins or bills in the computer bank, just credits. In the near future, Galloway will even be able to send out monthly statements, just as a conventional bank does. People who feel financially strapped will then have a monthly reminder of the worth of their own good deeds.

"We don't want charity," Galloway says. "It's one hand washing the other. I wash your clothing. Maybe you can wash my dishes."

CHALLENGE TO THE MONOPOLY OF MONEY

Galloway's bank in southeast Washington is part of a movement that has been growing quietly in the shadows of the official money system, a little the way private enterprise—in the form of black markets—grew up in the back alleys of the former Communist states. Where those challenged the monopoly of a state economy, the Time Dollar banks are challenging the monopoly of government money.

Just when the federal budget debate was reaching heights of frenzy, with limousines shuttling back and forth between the White House and Congress, leaders of this new time banking network were gathered in a conference room practically at the foot of Capitol Hill. Each headed a program to help the elderly and infirm—the very people most affected by the budget turmoil on the Hill. The groups had reached the end of a three-year grant from the Robert Wood Johnson Foundation, and they were in town to share their final reports. They had every reason to share in the prevailing gloom.

Yet the tone in the room was, if not euphoric, at least lively and full of hope. Even the end of the foundation money didn't dampen their spirits much. "We are empowering people to take control of a part of their lives," said Eric Berry, an official with the Michigan Office of Aging. Participants said they were besieged by inquiries, from all over the United States and from other countries as well. "We don't know what to do with the phone calls," said Carolee DeVito, Vice Chair of the Department of Community Health at the University of

Miami School of Medicine, and an official at the South Shore Hospital there. "What do you do about a phone call from Japan?"

Most of the participants were women, and this was not a coincidence. They had found a kind of Northwest Passage through the male economic assumptions that lay beneath the budget stalemate. These are the assumptions they *didn't* buy.

- That "real" work is only work done for money.

- That taxing this work is the only way to generate resources to address human needs.

- That the only alternatives in the budget debate are to spend more or to spend less—more government versus less government.

By rejecting these beliefs, they had found a way out of their own fiscal binds, and possibly the nation's as well.

SOCIETY'S "BURDENS" BECOME PRODUCERS

Naturally, the participants preferred more money to less. But for them, this was no longer the only question, because they were spending *something else*. As it had evolved, their system looked something like a market, but one activated by a desire to help rather than a desire for gain. It looked something like the old informal helping of families and communities, but it went far beyond nostalgia. It had elements that appealed both to the political Right and to the Left. It turned people that society labeled burdens into active producers. "We are giving life to people who live alone," said Lovado Bryan, a Jamaican woman who runs a Time Dollar program in Dorchester, Massachusetts, where she began as a volunteer. "We enable them to be useful."

The people meeting in Washington had seen Time Dollars take root in their communities. They tapped a pool of time that was sitting like an oil reserve just a few feet below the ground. At first, it was the time of the retired and "disabled," and those unemployed because of how the society defines "work." But they knew the same system eventually could tap far greater reserves: the time of young people who cruise the streets, for example, or the time of entire families who vegetate in front of the television. The time of others the society deems useless and burdensome could also be used.

This time represents a potential resource of untold magnitude. If the money-driven marketplace is letting this time go to waste (or, as in the case of television, encouraging it to do so), and if the market cannot generate enough in taxes to help those who need it, then why keep wishing at dry wells, these time bankers asked? Why not invent (reinvent, actually) a marketplace driven by a different kind of money that brings time and needs together in a new and more efficient way? A money, moreover, that is based on a type of wealth that individuals and communities already have? This money would be Time Dollars, which people would receive for helping others, and which they could spend when they needed help themselves.

Conventional economics says it takes money to activate time. This puts those who have money in the driver's seat, politically as well as economically. It guarantees, too, that much important work never gets done because it is not profitable by the calculus of the market. But these limitations of conventional economics just may be self-imposed. If one person's time can activate the time of another, without conventional money coming in between, then people can meet at least some of their needs by, in effect, exchanging time with one another. This is done not just by occasional favors or by barter, but by a system that turns time itself into a medium of exchange, which people can earn to the extent that they are willing to give help. Just possibly, such Time Dollar exchanges can start to reactivate the exchange and caring that are fast disappearing from the American scene. This would be community in the root sense of the word: a locality where wealth is shared.

A MIRACLE IN MIAMI

It does sound fanciful. Yet it was actually happening just 2 miles from Capitol Hill at the Walker House in Anacostia, and in upwards of 100 other communities, some of which were represented at the Washington meeting.

These programs are growing rapidly, in very diverse settings. In Miami, for example, the new currency has enabled black and Cuban organizations, often bitter political rivals, to come together over a Time

Dollar pie that gets bigger rather than smaller to the extent more partake. Nine hundred participants, most of them elderly, are putting in over 8,000 hours per month at 32 different sites all over Miami. Several senior citizen developments have organized in Miami, just as Dolores Galloway's building has in Washington.

In Boston, St. Louis, Brooklyn, San Francisco, and a number of other cities, similar efforts are under way. Michigan and Missouri, meanwhile, have launched Time Dollar programs on a state-wide level, to provide relief for family members who care for the elderly at home. (These respite workers, as they are called, get paid in Time Dollars, which they can use to buy help for themselves—or for elderly parents— when the need arises.) Both programs operate through grass-roots organizations, with the state serving mainly as coordinator and record keeper. The result is a kind of do-it-yourself Federal Reserve System, based on good works instead of money.

These programs have all begun with services for the elderly, because that was the focus of the early funding, most of which came from the Robert Wood Johnson Foundation. Yet several are already evolving into mini-economies that link generations. High-schoolers are mowing lawns or painting houses for seniors, for example, and contributing their credits to other seniors who need them. Several programs have woven Time Dollars into conventional medical care systems, to provide more than ordinary dollars alone can buy, and to involve members and patients as providers of care.

The South Shore Hospital in Miami Beach, for example, is using service credit workers to make sure that elderly patients, once discharged, get adequate help at home. (Often, due to lack of proper care, such patients must return quickly to the hospital, at great expense.) In ordinary medical settings, people get individual attention only by having something wrong. This leads many elderly to make extra demands on the medical care system, because it is the only form of attention available to them. With a Time Dollar program, by contrast, members get attention and rewards by saying, in effect, "I am well enough to help someone else. I have something to offer."

In an era of tight budgets, these Time Dollar programs operate on a relative pittance. Costs run from $15,000 to $120,000 a year, for programs that include hundreds of volunteers. This works out to less than $1.50 for each hour of service provided. Dolores Galloway's operation, which is a satellite of a much larger program in Washington, shows that people can run their own service bank for virtually nothing, at least on a small scale—which makes sense, since these banks function simply as expanded versions of the old neighborhood car pool or babysitting club.

WHY VOLUNTEERS COME OUT FOR TIME DOLLARS

As human needs escalate far beyond what governments alone can meet, these programs do what a decade of White House bromides about volunteerism have failed to do. They are drawing out a whole new group of volunteers, men in particular. Over half the participants in Time Dollar programs nationally had not volunteered the year before they joined, said Judith Feder of the Center for Health Policy Studies in Washington, who did an assessment for the Robert Wood Johnson Foundation.

The most interesting part was why these volunteers signed on. It was not primarily the lure of Time Dollars as a material reward (or *incentive*, to use the favored Washington term). Many volunteers don't even report their hours, Feder and the program leaders reported, while others donate their credits to more needy people in their programs. (Not surprisingly, the credits are more important to low-income volunteers than to those who are financially secure.)

Still, the evidence is compelling that the new currency adds a dimension that conventional volunteer programs do not have. People who had never done so before, were volunteering, and drop-out rates were much lower than for conventional programs. The program leaders couldn't define this dimension exactly; but it was clear that the Time Dollars are not simply a substitute for money, or an ersatz financial reward. Rather, they seem to tap a different spectrum of motivation and concern—the desire to help and the need to be needed—that market wages either ignore or repulse. Programs draw volunteers by providing "a way to feel good about themselves and perform a useful service," Feder said. "The credits are simply a symbol of that value."

This is uncharted economic territory—a currency that makes people feel good about themselves for helping others. As Feder and the program leaders described it, the new money functions a little like the pat on the back that people used to get in stable neighborhood settings, where their good deeds became part of a collective memory that would one day return in the form of kindness to themselves. Strange as it may sound, the computer records are a part of this effect; matching givers and recipients and recording the hours spent and earned, the records serve to replicate that social memory in a modern urban setting—"not as mechanized matching arrangements," Feder said, "but as communities of volunteers."

Freed somewhat from the limitations of money-based thinking, and freed as well from the grim assumption that people can be motivated only by a desire for gain, the Time Dollar bankers at the Washington meeting had something rare in the nation's capital these days: a sense of promise for the years ahead. Not that there aren't difficulties, and not that funding doesn't matter. But through the inevitable clutter of detail, one could feel a little of the atmosphere of great advances from small beginnings.

GREAT EXPECTATIONS

A new currency, with the potential to tap a vast new pool of time and motivation, opens possibilities that can be exhilarating. At a time when most social welfare groups are glumly cutting their losses, people at the Washington meeting were talking about expanding care for seniors at home and expanding the role of young people in taking care of seniors. Some programs already enable members to buy child care and transportation with Time Dollars, and they are looking for more services to bring in.

If governments and institutions ever embrace the concept of Time Dollars, the whole arena of public services can become a kind of bustling enterprise zone. Teenagers who earn credits helping seniors, for example, might use them to pay tuition at public colleges. Public housing tenants could use Time Dollars to pay part of their rents. People could defray part of their medical bills through Time Dollars earned by helping other sick people. Citizens could pay part of their local property taxes in Time Dollars, so they'd lend a hand as well as just passing a buck.

The result could be a society in which people discharge their obligations by helping one another, rather than just by exchanging pieces of paper or bits of plastic. There could be cohesion in place of the rootlessness and disintegration so common today. A heady prospect to be sure; but who would claim that the current money system is functioning so well that we should ignore a new one that is actually working.

DOUBTERS RAISE QUESTIONS

Whether in spite of this heady sense of promise, or because of it, the Time Dollar idea has provoked its share of detractors. Is it really volunteering, some ask, if people get a credit in return? Politically, some see the idea as a Trojan Horse from the Right, a way to justify budget cuts. State officials, meanwhile, worry about runs on the Time Dollar bank. Who will stand behind the credits, they ask, if all the participants who have earned them try to spend them at once?

To a Dolores Galloway, such questions are hard to fathom. What could be so bad about a concept that does so much good?

Like many participants in Time Dollar programs, Galloway had never done volunteer work before service credits came along. She didn't even think she could do such work in her condition. "I never knew I could help someone," she says. Now she has a conversation starter for the laundry room and the lobby. She's gotten to know her neighbors, and she's seen the whole building come together.

When Galloway putters home with her groceries, she's greeted by male residents at the door. "Come on, you old lady, you shouldn't be carrying those groceries," they'll say. ("I don't want to be bothered with you old people today," she counters.) Hardly anyone uses the new color TV set in the basement rec room at the Walker House. Instead, the lobby has become the social center. Once, Galloway was being wheeled into an ambulance and realized she hadn't asked anyone to take care of her fish. She made the attendants wheel her back into the lobby so she could enlist a service credit member. Mind at rest, she proceeded to the hospital.

"I love service credits because it's voluntary," Galloway says. "The way I explain it, you volunteer your time. It's *your* time, whenever *you* want to do it. The only reason you get credit for it is maybe you want to go downtown and don't have a car. You don't have to worry about how you are going to get home from the grocery store." No less important, Galloway doesn't have to worry about the isolation that comes from not being needed.

Galloway doesn't even claim credits for the work she does running the program. Most of her work for Elder Gaston she doesn't record either. For her, the big reward is having something to keep her going. "When you got the kind of diseases I do, a lot of times you don't want to be bothered. But you have to make yourself get out there. Sometimes I hurt so bad. But I get off that bed, get in that chair, and go up and see a friend. It makes you feel so good to know you are doing something for someone."

2

Economics Beyond Money: How Things We Did Became Things We Buy

In his book *Growing Up*, Russell Baker, the *New York Times* columnist, described the kitchen table of his childhood.

It was Belleville, New Jersey, in the depths of the Depression. Baker was living with his mother and sister in an extended family of aunts and uncles. There was no television, no money for going out, few places to go anyway. Yet Baker remembers those evenings with affection and warmth.

"Often, waking deep in the night, I heard them down in the kitchen talking, talking, talking," Baker wrote years later. "Sitting around the table under the unshaded light bulb, they talked the nights away, reheating the coffee, then making fresh coffee, then reheating the pot again, and talking, talking, talking." The family talked about Father Coughlin, Mussolini, the New Deal W.P.A. (which stood for "We Poke Along," according to Baker's Uncle Allen). They discussed ways to outwit the electric company, debated the merits of crooners Bing Crosby versus Rudy Vallee. They told and retold the old family stories—for example, the time two carpenters mistook "ancient" Aunt Henrietta for a ghost and jumped out a second-story window.

"I would lie on my daybed half-awake listening to the murmur of voices, the clatter of cups, the splash of water in the sink, the occasional burst of laughter," Baker recalled. "If my homework was done, I could sit with them and listen until ten o'clock struck. I loved the sense of family warmth that radiated through those long kitchen nights of talk."

A great deal was happening at that kitchen table, though few would have thought about it at the time. For young Baker, the talk was a school, a window on the adult world that kids today get mainly through the manipulated lens of television. For adults, the kitchen table was a crossroads of generations, a place where everybody belonged, and a refuge from the discouragement of those hard years. Today it would be called therapy or group support.

The kitchen table was also what economists might call an information system, where needs and resources were matched. ("Fred, can you take Aunt Mary to the store this afternoon?") To this day, the kitchen table survives as a symbol of social cohesion. Retired people who work in Time Dollar programs remember it as a reference point for family and community.

The neighborhood was an extension of that table. Betty Little, a worker in the Washington, D.C., Time Dollar program, recalls the lady in her Buffalo, New York, neighborhood whom everyone called Aunt Lizzie. She wasn't really an aunt, just someone who would stop by to make sure the family had something hot to eat. Then, too, there was Mrs. Jones up the street. Her husband hunted, and she had no children, so she made big pots of rabbit stew for the neighbors. "We were family with most of the kids on the street," Little recalls.

That closely woven world has unraveled for most Americans today. Aunts and uncles and grandparents and even parents live far apart. Parents often are reduced to the role of purchasing agents, procuring the day care, schooling, entertainment that define their children's lives. "In architecture, we're seeing demands for media rooms," a New York City architect told *Newsweek* magazine not long ago. "What ever happened to the kitchen table as a gathering place?"

The sources of these changes looked like 50 different things, the litany of forces that swept through the American household after World War II. Cars. Divorce. TV. The entry of women into the workforce. But underneath the blur was one big thing. The things the kitchen table represented—companionship, entertainment, security, intimacy, even gossip—turned into things people buy for money. Families and neighborhoods were taken apart function by function and sold back to people who missed the things these once provided. Massive social problems ensued, as the glue that held people together no longer seemed to be there. Then government was forced to try to patch up the damage with programs and services bought for money.

It happened in two main stages. First, enterprise became disengaged from the core of community life. Production moved out of the home and small workshop and into the large factory, owned by a corporate entity with no local roots. This disrupted the world in which commercial dealings were entwined in a web of larger community concerns. And then, the economy redefined people as consumers, so that things bought seemed more desirable and modern than the things to be had for free. The common denominator is that people came to relate increasingly through the medium of money.

COMMUNITY CUSTOM YIELDS
TO CORPORATE NEED

This process was especially marked in the United States, a new society established during the transition to a monetary age (commemorated in the Latin inscription on the dollar bill, *novus ordo seclorum* — a new order in the world). In the early colonies, money was a hodgepodge of currencies, bank notes, and the like. Most transactions were in barter or "change work," which is an exchange of labor between, say, two farmers. Money might be thrown in for good measure, because people needed a certain amount of it to pay taxes and deal with the world outside the community.

Such transactions tended to reinforce local ties. People saw commerce as a form of social connection as well as an avenue of gain. Prices, for example, were set by local custom, rather than by the market. As late as 1838, a farmer complained to the *Albany Cultivator*, a farm newspaper, that the local miller was charging 20 percent rather than the customary 10 percent. Wasn't there a law?

There wasn't, as far as the editor knew. But he thought there should be. "Custom, which in the absence of law has the binding force of law, seems to have settled the toll at 10 percent," this editor replied. "If the miller can with impunity take 20, he may by the same rule take 50 percent."

It takes a long stretch of the mind to envision a day, in America, when people considered community norms a legitimate check on the profit-making urge. Yet that was the world that greeted the industrial age and its chief engine of change, the corporation. Soon, these corporations were ripping commerce from its local base and redefining

America as a mass market. Dealings based on locality and trust gave way to dealings governed solely by the market and through the vehicle of money.

John O'Hara captured the essence of the change in a short story called "The Hardware Man," about two merchants in a Pennsylvania town. One, Tom Esterly, was a man of the old order, whose business dealings were of a piece with his community concerns. The other, Lou Mauser, was a shrewd and driven man, not dishonest but focused exclusively on making money. Instinctively (this was the 1920s), he seized upon aggressive tactics that drove Esterly out of business. He ran big ads, opened branch stores, sold at cost during promotional sales. He even hired away Esterly's help.

In the closing scene, Mauser is offering to buy out Esterly's stock for 20 cents of the dollar, fixtures and goodwill included. Esterly demurs. The fixtures he can have, but the goodwill is separate. "It isn't for sale to you," he says. "A week from Saturday night at nine o'clock, this store goes out of business forever. But no part of it belongs to you."

WHEN "GOODWILL" MEANT SOMETHING TO EVERYONE

Once the word "goodwill" had a very specific meaning: namely, the value of the good name that a business built up in a community. It had to do with honesty and fairness and kindred qualities. Today it is a shell, a neutered accounting catch-all for the difference between what somebody pays for a company and the physical value of the assets. The degeneration of the word typified the passage from a kitchen table world of relationships and trust to a world held together—or pulled apart—by money.

Tom Esterlys were common in nineteenth-century commerce. Even large manufacturers—when they were individuals rather than large corporations—felt a commitment to the communities of which they were part. Andrew Carnegie left a large legacy to the city of Pittsburgh. Factory towns all over the United States boast similar bequests in the form of schools, museums, parks, and the like. In the old mill town of Winsted, Connecticut, Ralph Nader's hometown, the local library and high school were gifts of a manufacturer who owned the

Gilbert Clock Company there. Today, by contrast, relations between corporations and localities consist largely of corporate demands for tax breaks, highway access, sewer hook-ups and other subsidies, with new plants going to the highest bidder.

While community ties were turning into monetary transactions, the work of caring for others was doing so as well. The factory took work out of the home and community, swept it into the vortex of the national and international marketplace. Soon, traditional functions of care were drifting out of the domestic sphere and into institutions supported by taxes. In the colonies, care for the poor was typically based in the home. "Whenever possible, [a community] supported members in their own families," writes David Rothman of Columbia University in his award-winning book *The Discovery of the Asylum*. "In extenuating circumstances of old age, widowhood, or debility, it boarded them in a neighboring household." That changed when mobility and large-scale industry forced people to resort to institutional forms of care.

WE DON'T PROVIDE CARE, WE BUY IT

The rise of industry was not the only thing, of course, that hastened the separation of community and care. Affluence further disposed the nation to want to buy care rather than provide it. Robert and Helen Lynd noted this in their classic study of Middletown back in the 1920s. Neighborhood and face-to-face charity loomed large among those who were less well off, they wrote. By contrast, "the more impersonal group methods of giving are, on the contrary, diffusing more rapidly among the business class."

These business leaders in Middletown took the lead in starting a Community Chest, which further converted the practice of charity into the contribution of money, useful as that may be. The Lynds compared this effort to a "high-pressure sales campaign," adding, "There was a minimum of Christian *caritas* about it."

Put another way, people were becoming purchasers of community and care rather than participants in it. Labor was dividing to the point that these functions were being contracted out to professional charities. Traditional community bonds had increasingly little function. This trend continued as Americans left the farm and swarmed into cities, along with immigrants, and the New Deal put the federal government into the business of social welfare. What the corporation did to the small town, bureaucratized social service did somewhat to the old urban neighborhood, displacing the local ward heeler and other forms of one-to-one service. These local systems were far from perfect, especially for those who didn't vote the right way. But with the rise of bureaucratized social service, nothing was done to replace the cohesion these old networks provided.

THE "MARIO BROTHERS" REPLACE THE FAMILY

After World War II, this process of turning bonds of locality and trust into monetary exchanges took a new and especially destructive turn. In the nineteenth century, people were wrenched out of traditional social roles to become employees in mass production. After World War II, their role was increasingly to consume the things produced, and consumption became a substitute for the many social ties that remained. In the 1950s, Ronald Reagan, corporate spokesman for General Electric, declaimed on the "G.E. Theater" every week that "Progress Is Our Most Important Product." He was talking about the very devices—televisions, dishwashers, and the rest—that undermined the center of his Norman Rockwell world.

Put another way, families turned over the functions of the kitchen table to corporations. Labor divided to the point that people at the table had little reason to be there. This is one change that retirees who work in Time Dollar programs feel personally. Esterlene Colbrook, who works in the Miami program, was asked to speak to a high school class on what it feels like to be growing old. Colbrook is a grandmother whose father lived to be 120 and whose grandfather was a slave. There was lots of storytelling in her household, and one thing she conveyed to the high school class was the isolation she feels because television has displaced this bond.

"Before, we didn't have the radio and TV," she said. "So you would always love to sit next to your grandmother so she could tell you the old stories. Or read you a story. It was like story time. Because you didn't have those other things.

"When you came in at night to go to bed, you would always cling to grandmother, because that was the best entertainment. But now it's the TV and [the kids] don't have time. They don't even see you. And then we feel real lonely. It's the gap between us now."

Ray Hughes, a retired merchant seaman who works in the Elderplan program in Brooklyn, put it simply. "My grandchildren would rather play Nintendo than come and visit me," he said.

"I OWE. I OWE. SO OFF TO WORK I GO"

Americans like to point the finger at government. But what we see is what we are, and there is a troubling similarity between the fiscal travails on Capitol Hill and the finances of businesses and families throughout the land.

The federal deficit has mirrored, for example, the growing mountains of private debt. From 1980 to 1987, while the federal deficit was reaching record levels, consumer debt doubled from $300 billion to $600 billion. Not coincidentally, the number of Americans going bankrupt more than doubled over roughly the same period.

The Reagan years brought a phenomenon unseen in America before: Not only were personal bankruptcies increasing, they were increasing in good times rather than bad! Often, the victims weren't people with too little money, rather people who were too inclined to spend. One study of personal bankruptcies in the 1980s found that a third of the families owed three months' income on their credit cards alone. That grim prospect helps explain the bumper sticker that became popular toward the end of the decade: "I owe. I owe. So off to work I go."

A RISING NEED TO BUY HELP

This spending was not just the result of yuppie self-indulgence, however. Americans found themselves in the distressing circumstance of running harder and harder just to stay even. Ease, security, the good life—the promise of American marketing somehow had become a frenzied pursuit. Rising home prices and other kinds of "inflation" were certainly part of it; the media reported on these in great detail. But the other, and perhaps greater, part was something beyond the ken of most economists and reporters. The problem was *need inflation* as opposed to *price inflation*. Not only were there so many more things that Americans felt they had to buy, Americans also needed to buy what the family used to provide for free. As social bonds turned into commodities, families and communities began contracting out their functions to the market economy.

Let Kindercare watch the toddlers. Let preschool open their eyes to life. Hire counselors for neglected, latchkey kids. Buy entertainment from Nintendo and the video store. For adults, turn time away from work into a "leisure industry," which sells camcorders and motorized treadmills in place of visits on the side porch and walks through the neighborhood. In virtually every corner of family and community life, the things people used to *do* have turned into things they have to *buy*.

Partly this was the effect of broken families and moving about and affluence itself. Visitors from other countries remark on how separate Americans are, shutting themselves into their living rooms with their private entertainment equipment. But effect turns into cause, as families and communities without functions have less centripetal activity to hold them together.

Put another way, the cash marketplace has been cannibalizing the old informal ways of doing, leaving families and communities helpless in the face of new problems coming to their doors. Neighborhoods in which people barely know one another don't have much connective tissue with which to resist drugs or crime. Security from crime no longer means the watchfulness of neighbors. Rather it means insurance policies, burglar alarms, and other devices (largely to protect the VCR and other expensive equipment) as well as greater demands for police.

These changes are so entwined in our lives today, that we hardly notice. In the public discourse, they are called progress and growth, leaving people in the strange situation of feeling more harried and pressed even as things supposedly are getting better. But if the process is rarely noted for what it is, the impact is all too apparent as an insatiable need for cash. The effort to get that cash—through two-worker families, for example—means yet more need for things like day care and extra cars that require yet more money to purchase. One congressional study found that the average two-parent family was little better off in 1988 than it was ten years before; more mothers were working, and working more hours, but the costs of child care, transportation, and taxes were eating up much of the gain.

The impact is also apparent in a greater need for government. Economists use the term *externality* to describe the process by which a cost of business gets shifted onto someone else. Industry has externalized the cost of pollution, for example, by dumping wastes into the air and water for government to cope with, instead of preventing the effluents or disposing of them safely. Something very similar happened as what economists call the division of labor invaded the household economy of family and community. The costs to government have been large, in the form of new needs for social services, education, police, and the like.

PRIVATE GAIN, SOCIAL DISASTER

It is not surprising that industry got on this bandwagon; after all, it is their wagon, and they were shifting the costs to government. But economists are another matter.

The word *economics* derives from a Greek word meaning the proper stewardship of the household. When the household falls apart, presumably it would concern the profession bearing that name. Yet this very profession was leading the parade. By a strange twist of history and logic, the breakdown of family and community became something to cheer about. The more the kids were schlepped off to day care, the more they played Nintendo instead of talking to their parents, the more seniors needed professional home care instead of soup from Aunt Lizzie—the more money was changing hands and, therefore, the more economists beamed.

To understand why, we need to go back to Adam Smith. Before Smith's time, there wasn't a subject called economics as that term is used today. Commercial dealings were considered mainly in light of ethics and religion. There was much debate over the concept of a "just price," for example. The underlying assumption was that prices should be governed by a sense of justice rather than—as economists today believe—whatever the market will bear.

That's where Smith, the father of free market economics, came in.

He posed a direct challenge to the medieval world view and the bonds of affinity that held it together. According to *The Wealth of Nations*, human well-being (the original meaning of the word "wealth") would arise if all sought to increase their personal, private gain. This pursuit became a virtue; economics was yanked out of the context of social and moral teachings and set free in a universe of its own, governed by separate laws.

Today, Smith's theories are favored on the political Right, which claims also the mantle of traditional family and community values. Yet these values are precisely what Smith's economics tend to displace. The kitchen table is not a place where people maximize their profits; the profit-maximizers invade the table with new things to sell.

This myopia is built into the lens through which economists see the world. The prime index of the national well-being is the gross national product (GNP), and the GNP measures nothing but transactions for money. The kitchen table economy, the whole realm of informal helping and caring, barely exists where the GNP is concerned. So when their functions are contracted out to corporations or to government, they enter reality as economists define it.

Few economists bother to ask whether this "growth" they hail is actually little more than this cannibalizing process—the economy growing by eating the flesh and sinews that hold society together. Nor do economists ask whether economic "slowdowns" are times when, in part at least, the destructive process has somewhat abated.

In sum, economics today isn't concerned with social health, except incidentally. Its sole focus is exchanges involving money. To raise questions about money, therefore, is to question some of the notions that economists most cherish.

THE THINGS MONEY CAN'T MEASURE

Economists protest that money is just a measuring rod, as neutral as a ruler. It's not fair to blame the ruler for what it measures, they say. If Kindercare or Meals on Wheels displaces Aunt Lizzie, then Lizzie must be inferior, so good riddance. The market decides, not us.

But then, who was left to look after the sick people on the block or to make sure the elderly actually ate the meals the programs dropped off? For a while, it seemed possible to simply tax the market economy further (or to stimulate it with tax breaks) to generate revenue for new programs. But then competition became global, limiting the amount that could be wrung out of the market economy in any one country, to help correct the damage it was abetting. And the programs weren't working that well anyway.

The nature of money was implicated in this fiscal gridlock. Money is not just a measuring rod. It is also the thing measured, that which defines the world that economists choose to see. A person who measures only by feet and inches misses entire dimensions of reality, such as time. Similarly, economists who measure only by money miss those dimensions of life that money does not and cannot measure. They don't understand the kitchen table world, and so are oblivious to how the erosion of that world contributes to the social problems that we face. Until now, this closed system has precluded insight or debate. One cannot think one's way out from a closed system to something bigger. One needs a viewpoint outside the system to see where it has failed. Time Dollars provides that vantage point.

3

When Money Doesn't Work

What we call economics today is really just the study of money and of the kind of society that arises from the increasing use of money. Economists don't seem able to think about the subject in any other way.

An example is the classic textbook on economics by Nobel Prize winner Paul A. Samuelson. Samuelson puts money on a pedestal; it is a basic fact of his concept of economics, beyond question or modification.

Samuelson allows that there are certain drawbacks to a money-driven economy. Specifically, such an economy is inclined to break down, leaving people high and dry. In less complicated systems, people are inventive in hard times, finding ways to barter what they have for what they need. "If I am hungry and you are naked, I can always sew your clothes while you bake my bread," Samuelson writes.

But when people start using money, this instinct seems to atrophy. Fewer people bother to sew clothes or bake bread. And the social customs that encourage such exchanges eventually disappear.

The Great Depression was a prime example. The productive energies of a goodly portion of the country came to a halt because people didn't have the pieces of paper (i.e., dollars) that they believed gave them permission to exchange. "In the richest capitalistic country in history, the banks failed," Samuelson declares. "Money was hoarded; people went hungry while other people went in rags." Food still existed and so did clothes and other products. But for lack of money, the process of exchanging these virtually ceased.

A NOD TO THE APE-MEN

Samuelson draws the obvious conclusion. People get hooked on the medium of exchange; what money gives, money can take away. This is a rather alarming admission. It raises important questions, to a mind inclined to entertain them: Are there other hidden costs to money that people rarely think about? Should the nation foster other, complementary forms of exchange as a buffer against these? Is it a good idea to put all our eggs into the basket of money?

But mainstream economics—liberal and conservative alike—view such queries as hardly worthy of discussion. To be sure, barter was a "great step forward from a state of self-sufficiency," Samuelson acknowledges. He offers a pat on the back to the "first two ape-men" who realized that they could better their respective lots through exchange. But to Samuelson and most other economists, self-sufficiency is a backward state, and barter a kind of Stone-Age relic. Those ape-men were taking only the first step in the great evolutionary march leading to humanity's crowning economic achievement—money.

Why do economists dote on money? For one thing, money is the measuring rod that defines their professional turf. They can't study what they can't measure; and because money puts numbers on exchanges, economists can deal with them. The idea of realms of exchange that are not measured by money is unsettling to economists. The possibility that values, which cannot be measured by money, can hold out powerful incentives or rewards, is even more disturbing. That would mean a large part of the economic world would be outside the economist's measurement and control.

SPECIALIZE, SPECIALIZE, SPECIALIZE

But the attachment goes even deeper; it goes to the division of labor, a view of society based upon money. According to the Adam Smith classic *The Wealth of Nations*, progress requires that each person serve a smaller and smaller role. When each does that one small thing he or she presumably does best, the whole will work together like the wondrous machines that were appearing in the factories of Adam Smith's eighteenth-century Scotland. The key cog is money.

"An elaborate division of labor would be unthinkable," Samuelson states, "without the introduction of a great new improvement—the use of money." The more labor is divided into small segments, the more money is needed to exchange the products and services produced. To the economist, life becomes better the more money is involved.

What Adam Smith didn't fully foresee, and what economists like Samuelson today still don't see, is that division of labor becomes something different as it goes on. No longer just a way of producing more efficiently, it now begins to affect the way people connect to one another. As people become more specialized in their spheres of competence, they also become strangers, because they have fewer channels through which to connect except through the medium of money. They become less able to do things for one another informally, as friends and neighbors, as these relationships recede and people become hooked on monetary rewards that come from specialized work in the marketplace.

HOW MONEY CUTS INTO PERSONAL CARING

This means much more than just the drying up of channels of barter. It also means the erosion of the functional bonds that hold families and communities together. Families and communities are, in one sense, intricate webs of reciprocal exchange. Help, support, and care go back and forth among the members; such informal exchange is one definition of social health. As people become more and more specialized in their work, and as they meet their needs more and more through money, this informal exchange gets displaced and destroyed by the ever-expanding commercial marketplace. Instead of connecting as family members and neighbors and friends who offer what is needed, people connect as strangers who buy and sell from one another their specialized functions of production, information, entertainment, and care.

Then people wonder why communities don't function and families fall apart. But economists seem oblivious to the connection between their high regard for monetary transactions and the decline of these other modes of exchange, especially the informal kind. Samuelson cites a hypothetical example of natives on Fiji, who have become hooked on the monetary economies of the industrial world. They "carry water in empty Standard Oil cans and clothe their infants in Pillsbury flour bags." But if a bank in Austria fails, the natives might lose their livelihoods and perhaps starve.

PROP UP SELF-SUFFICIENCY INSTEAD OF BANKS

Dependency has a regrettable down side. The answer, however, is not to boost the capacity for local self-reliance, Samuelson says. That would "turn back the clock to a simpler and poorer life." Rather, we need to make the world safe for dependency, by protecting the bank from failure.

It never seems to occur to him that there might be something in between: that we can strive to prevent economic breakdowns, while at the same time boosting the resilience and self-sufficiency of local economies. Encouraging self-sufficiency might even help to prevent breakdowns, on the principle that the mattress with many springs is sturdier than the mattress with just one.

More important, division of labor exacts a social toll that the economic textbooks ignore. Those oil cans and flour bags—and the cars and commercial bread associated with them—may wreak havoc in traditional relationships within families and communities. Even if the bank gets going again, the supporting webs of social exchange may be wearing thin. And this does not bode well for the market economy, since the informal bonds of family and community give rise to the literacy, lawfulness, health, and stability on which a market economy depends.

One doesn't have to turn back the clock to look for ways to promote those bonds, even as economists are promoting the market culture that tends to pull them apart. This is the role of Time Dollars.

Time Dollars are not simply a new kind of money. They are a way to revive the informal modes of exchange in the face of the money-driven market. In effect, this new currency opens a discourse on the ecology of money. It has been recognized for several decades that the natural environment cannot absorb forever the pollutants of industrial society (whether market or Communist). The air and water need to be protected. Now we have to recognize that the fragile webs of family and community life cannot absorb forever the process by which informal relations of trust turn into formal transactions involving money.

LIVING UNDERWATER

A fish is unaware of the attributes of water, being immersed in it. Time Dollars, as a new form of currency, offer a viewpoint outside the "water" of money-centered thinking. The concept makes it easier to grasp the limitations of that thinking and to see how it distorts reality. There are *consequences* to using money as an exclusive measuring rod, and not the least of these is the paralyzing belief that society lacks the resources with which to solve its problems.

When we cease to use money as our only ruler, we begin to realize that we live in a world of two economies, not just one. One is the formal marketplace measured by—and consisting mainly of—monetary transactions. This is the realm of supermarkets and shopping centers, offices and factories that the media calls the economy. The other economy is the informal networks of helping in families, neighborhoods, volunteer groups, and the like. What we call growth is often merely the transfer of a function from the informal to the formal economy—from an invisible pocket to a visible one. There is no net gain in output, and often there is a loss in social cohesion and well-being.

Parenting is a prime example. The first economy of monetary transactions has grown substantially over recent decades by assuming roles once filled by parents. Yet because economists look only through the lens of money, they see only one side of the ledger.

"In any other industry, if you remove a million employees without reducing the job requirements very much, nobody would deny that the industry is woefully shorthanded," observed Amitai Etzione, a leader of a movement called socio-economics and a professor at George Washington University in Washington. Yet that very thing happened when millions of women went to work in industry, replaced with a minimal amount of professional child care. As a result, "the parenting 'industry' is woefully shorthanded (and television sets and the streets are overworked). This is not an argument for women to stay home but for someone to do more of it."

Perversely, the loss to children appears as a double gain on the GNP accounts: the money these women earn in the marketplace, plus the money families pay for child care. When one counts only in dollars, the loss on the social and emotional side of the ledger doesn't get counted. Time Dollars bring this loss out of the shrouds, because they acknowledge the value of time that is not exchanged for money. Time Dollars give this time an economic identity if not an exact measurement. The full loss cannot be measured, of course; a parent's time is different from Kindercare's in ways that cannot be quantified. But as an alternative currency, embodying different values than conventional money, Time Dollars at least serve as a reminder that a loss side of the ledger exists.

WHEN MONEY DOESN'T MEASURE UP TO EVERY NEED

Time Dollars do more than expose the shortcomings of money as a measuring rod. Equally important, this new currency helps reveal how money falls short as money—that is, as a medium of exchange. It takes a while for the mind to get a grip on that thought. Money failing as money? What else is there? In grade school texts we learned that money is the fruition of an evolutionary quest that began with wampum and stones and ended with a dollar bill. Money is the pure article, streamlined and modern. You can carry it in your pocket, send it zipping between computers in San Francisco and Hong Kong, use it for anything you want, any time, any place—the perfect lubricant for the gears of commerce.

That's probably how a fish thinks of water: the perfect medium. Yet seen from a different viewpoint, the water can appear wet and cold. There are specific consequences to using money that we lose sight of when it's the only thing we know.

This is not a wholesale indictment of money. One might just as well offer an indictment of water. But there's a difference between using water and experiencing total immersion in it like a fish. Money is necessary for many things, but it is not adequate for all things, especially the helping and caring exchanges that society needs many more of and that money has tended to displace.

This problem is rarely discussed in economics texts. The inability of economists to think outside of their monetary water runs very deep. When the Time Dollar idea first began to circulate in the early 1980s, a number of economists were asked for their opinions. All were identified with good social causes, all were eminent in their fields, and all thought that Time Dollars violated some fundamental principle of money as they conceived it.

One worried that Time Dollar proposals included no prices. There *could* be prices, of course, but most time banks don't want them, because they want to operate like the kitchen table, where everyone's time is equally important. The economist thought such an evaluation would be like selling every item in the supermarket for the same price.

Another economist charged that Time Dollars were "parochial." Because the concept is based in a sense of family and community, mobility would be hindered and some people would be left out (as though they aren't now).

The third economist summed up these concerns when he called Time Dollars "an inferior semi-money at the state level."

Yet these "inferior" dollars seem to sustain endeavors that society greatly needs. They generate public service from people the market has no use for and who have not responded to appeals for volunteerism. They help produce a feeling of family among people who are strangers. Could it be that the deficiencies of Time Dollars are really advances over money, in crucial respects?

Economists regard such thoughts as heresy. Probably the exact sentiment of a fish contemplating the possibility of becoming amphibious. Yet when one looks at the supposed deficiencies of Time Dollars in more detail, they begin to make life on dry land look possible.

Here are seven major reasons why economists brand Time Dollars an inferior semi-money.

1. **A Local Currency:** Time Dollars are issued locally and honored locally. You can't earn one in San Antonio and spend it in Hong Kong (not yet, anyway). Conventional money, by contrast, has no local roots. It can move wherever the return is highest or the prices are cheapest.

2. **Membership Required:** Time Dollars are a medium for a defined group of people, such as the members of a senior center and those businesses that link up with it. Money, by contrast, makes no such distinctions. It provides all the identification one needs to spend it, under most circumstances at least.

3. **Limited Purchasing Power:** Time Dollars are a little like trading stamps. You can buy only those products or services offered in the program. With conventional money, by contrast, you can buy virtually anything (with a few exceptions such as Federal Express and car rental companies, which won't take cash).

4. **No Prices:** Most Time Dollar systems value every hour of service equally—1 hour, 1 credit—whether you help a retiree with his tax return or scrub his kitchen floor. To an economist, this equality is terrible. A basic function of money is to define prices, which limit products and services to those who can pay for them. According to the laws of conventional economics, high prices or wages attract more people to do the work, thereby increasing supply and benefiting all.

5. **An Inefficient Medium:** Time Dollars require back-office work for every transaction, recording the hours in a computer bank. Conventional money, by contrast, is elegant and simple, at least in theory. Hand a shop owner a dollar bill and that's the end of it. Banking and credit cards involve paperwork, but at least this paperwork generates income. Time Dollars involve paperwork without the saving grace of profit.

6. **No Government Backing:** Most Time Dollars aren't backed by a state or local government. They are only as solid as the organization that runs the program and the participants in that program. There is no guarantee anyone will honor them in five or ten years. Conventional money, by contrast, is as solid as the U.S. Treasury.

7. **A Weak Incentive:** Time Dollars tap such motives as a desire to help and a need to be needed. To an economist, these are low-horsepower engines compared to the desire for acquisition and gain. Given a choice between working for money and working for Time Dollars, people will take money, particularly if they have a specialty that commands a high price.

These criticisms add up to a strong indictment. If anyone were proposing Time Dollars as a complete substitute for conventional money, the case would never even get to court. But Time Dollars aren't a substitute for money. They are a way to do things that money can't do and to claim back the realm of community that money has invaded. Seen in this light, the weaknesses of Time Dollars turn out to be advantages.

Let us take the criticisms one at a time.

The Mobility of Money

Money is as liquid as water. It can flow between cities, states, even nations, seeking the highest return. It is unencumbered by loyalty or history, human affinity or roots. These qualities make it an ideal medium for a commercial society, economists say.

There is no doubt that money's mobility has value. Few people would want to be stuck where they are because they couldn't use their money anyplace else. But mobility has a dark side. A dollar put into a poor community can exit in hours, to a cigarette manufacturer or Japanese electronics firm or a drug baron in Colombia. Of every dollar the federal government puts into Indian reservations, an estimated 75 cents flows out to border towns within 48 hours.

Dictators like General Manuel Noriega of Panama and the late Ferdinand Marcos of the Philippines can loot their countries. Banks can launder money from drugs and the mob. More to the present point, the Rust Belt was left abandoned when American corporations decided to seek a greater return abroad. The kitchen table emptied as its occupants went off in search of market wages. South African apartheid was underwritten by dollars seeking the highest return unencumbered by moral constraints.

Professional sports is one of the few areas of American business in which this footloose quality is seen for what it is, because sports teams still have tangible roots in loyalty and tradition. (Customers don't root for a corporation the way fans root for a team.) Not so long ago, team owners were people who earned the loyalty of local fans. Tom Yawkey of the Boston Red Sox and Phil Wrigley of the Cubs are almost synonyms for their cities; their ball parks, Fenway Park and Wrigley Field, are almost European in their quirky sense of place.

Today, by contrast, stadiums look almost as much alike as the dollars that built them. Teams are owned increasingly by corporations and partnerships, which have no qualms about deserting a city in search of a more lucrative stadium lease. George Steinbrenner, former managing partner of the New York Yankees, once threatened to move that tradition-laden team (or "franchise," in the owner's parlance) to New Jersey. That Steinbrenner lives in Tampa and runs a business in Cleveland may have something to do with his pecuniary attitude toward New York. Pro-sports owners grow apoplectic at the possibility of permanent links between cities and teams, since this—like marriage—could impede their ability to play the field.

Mobility is one of those good things that has become bad through excess. There is no shortage of forces pulling people and institutions apart in this country. Is it really so bad to have an alternate currency that pulls in the opposite direction—that embodies the value of sinking roots, of building a community or business, of keeping a family together? In the long run, this makes economic sense as well. The state of Missouri enacted Time Dollar legislation in large part because the young were leaving and abandoning their parents to the state. Mobility has become an efficient producer of hidden social costs that Time Dollars can help to counter.

Franklin Delano Roosevelt once opened a luncheon address to the Daughters of the American Revolution with the salutation: "Fellow Immigrants." Our origins are in mobility, but the ideal that drew the New England settlers was the City on a Hill. There is little danger that Time Dollars will stifle the American genius for flux and change. But there is great danger that if we don't remember how to sink roots and build the city, the object of all this wandering may be lost.

Money Includes Everyone (Who Has It)

In theory, another virtue of money is that it excludes no one. Anyone with enough of it, regardless of race or class, can walk into a Mercedes-Benz dealership or airline office or any other place of business and purchase whatever he or she desires.

Put another way, money is an apt medium for transactions between strangers. It took hold in Western culture at the trade fairs of medieval Europe, for dealings between itinerant traders who might never see one another again. This quality of money has definite advantages. It helped free society from the grip of feudal hierarchies. Today, it will help peoples in the former East Bloc to break free from the strictures of the old Communist states.

With money, one doesn't have to belong to any tight circle or clique in order to transact business. Thus, it opens up channels of opportunity to outsiders and those at the bottom. In theory, that is. To this day, black Americans are not welcome in many real estate offices, no matter how much money they have. Besides, money doesn't always seem so inclusive to those who don't have a lot of it.

But more to the present point, money makes trust irrelevant. A medium for strangers tends to turn people into strangers, by drawing them away from relationships in which trust and reciprocity are involved. Time Dollars, by contrast, tend to restore such relationships. That a tradesman is being paid does not vouch for his character in any particular way. The very act of participating in a Time Dollar program, by contrast, marks one as a particular kind of person. Frail retirees open their doors to Time Dollar volunteers while barring them tightly against others.

Time Dollar programs do exclude, but so do families, friendships, and relationships of trust. By excluding the selfish and bigoted and uncaring, Time Dollars can help transcend race and age and other barriers that keep people apart. In Washington, D.C., groups of handicapped people testified in favor of Time Dollar legislation at the city council, desiring to be included in the "exclusive" circle of people with something to give. Church groups testified that Time Dollars would enable them to reach outside the confines of their own religious denomination. In Miami, Time Dollars have helped bring feuding ethnic groups together, because with this currency, when one group gains, the others do as well.

The anonymity of a money economy breeds a hunger to belong to something. American Express sells credit cards as a form of belonging ("Membership has its privileges") because in the marketplace of money, people feel isolated and without help. Time Dollars offer membership that is real and includes that help. And unlike American Express, Time Dollar programs do not exclude if you don't make enough money.

Money Can Get You Anything

Money can buy anything. To an economist, that means "efficiency" and maximum opportunities for trade. But in practice, it means a tree that brings forth bad fruit as well as good.

Yes, money can buy books and homes and tickets to a movie. But it can also buy our elected officials and our Redwood forests; it can buy crack and assault weapons or whatever else the unscrupulous buyer wants.

Clearly, people who earn Time Dollars don't get the same range of choices. But that's bad only if you think that bribery and drugs and the rest are essential life options; and only if you think that a medium of exchange that encourages friendship and care and trust is unduly restrictive.

There is probably no way to remedy the moral ambiguity of money. But one way to lessen it is to lean more on an alternative currency that has good works built right into its genetic coding. Time Dollars can't be offered on a street corner for drugs. They can't be dangled as bait to lure people into highly paid but socially useless work. They don't put our lives up for grabs to the highest bidder.

If that's inefficient, Time Dollar advocates will take the rap. But before economists press it too hard, they should stand on a street corner and try to buy caring and trust with those revered dollars in their pockets. Money has limitations, too; sometimes it can't buy the things that people need most.

The Invisible Hand of Price

There is no facet of the Time Dollar program that causes economists more distress than the absence of prices. In most programs, everyone's time is valued the same, regardless what he does or when he does it. One hour, 1 credit, end of story. (A few programs tried giving fewer credits for administrative tasks at the office than for helping work in people's homes, only to abandon the attempt as causing more problems than it solved.)

Prices are absolutely central to the economist's view of the world. They adjust the balance between supply and demand and serve to ration products and services in the most "efficient" manner—i.e., according to who can pay.

In theory, prices also send signals to producers as to when to produce more or less. High fees for investment bankers send a signal to college students to swell the ranks upon graduation, and so forth, and in this manner, society's needs are filled, so the theory goes.

Yet price systems aren't as efficient as economists believe. That investment bankers make enormous salaries is a dubious sign that

America's most urgent need is for more of them. Prices often don't include major costs; the price of a box of Cheerios, for example, does not include the cost of disposing of the empty box, so society gets a false "signal" as to how much waste it can produce. Then, too, prices are often more the result of corporate bureaucracies than of rational management. One recent survey found that more than half of all corporations change their prices only once a year—if that—despite constant changes in their own costs and market demand.

Most important, wages (which are prices for labor) often reflect social status and ancient hierarchies rather than the true worth of work. Investment bankers make much more than home-care workers, not because their work is more important, but rather because theirs is a traditionally male occupation, while home-care workers are traditionally female.

The absence of such ancient baggage is a strength of Time Dollar programs. It is liberating to the retired housewife to know that her time is valued as highly as that of the retired executive. Economists believe that the lack of prices will throw the whole system into chaos. Demand for rides to the supermarket will go berserk, if prices don't keep the demand under control. Yet the world doesn't always work that way. In families, for example, food at the dinner table isn't put up to the highest bidder; Mom doesn't set a higher price for the drumstick than for the other dark meat, even though the drumstick is in greater demand. Parents and grandparents have even been known to go hungry so that their children can have enough to eat.

Economists assume a world of strangers who need to be controlled by a mechanism of price. But in families, churches, sports teams—in situations of affinity and trust—people act according to other principles. Time Dollar programs establish such networks, with their own etiquettes of supply and demand. No program has had to face the issue of rationing scarce services yet; there have been plenty of workers to go around. But if scarcity did arise, then two groups would get priority: those whose need was urgent and those who had done the most to help others. Then, willingness to care would replace ability to pay.

The Efficiency of Money

Time Dollars require a certain amount of paperwork. Participants report their hours (although not all do, all the time). The credits must be added and subtracted for each transaction. Most programs are aiming to send out regular statements, eventually, like banks.

So what's new? Cash may be elegantly simple when it changes hands. But that simplicity often hides an accounting morass that makes Time Dollars seem paperwork-free by comparison. People who earn Time Dollars don't have to keep drawers full of receipts for the IRS; most participants do not consider that a loss.

The question of efficiency goes much deeper, however. It's not just a matter of record keeping. It's also a matter of the nature of money itself. Money is not just a medium of exchange. It is also a thing exchanged, a commodity in its own right. People hoard it. They lend it. They play the exchange rates between currencies of different countries.

When a car engine also must power an air conditioner, its efficiency in moving the car goes down. Similarly, when a currency does double duty as a commodity, this dual role can impede exchanges between people. It can even displace their needs. This was revealed suggestively in a study of the use of cigarettes as a currency in prisoner-of-war (POW) camps during World War II.

Cigarettes were a natural choice. They were in constant demand; they could be carried about easily and they came in small units like coins. With this currency, there arose a bustling market in tinned milk, writing paper, razor blades, and other items procured from Red Cross distributions and private parcels. Each Red Cross drop brought a marked increase in exchange; there was more to buy and more cigarettes to buy it with.

But the cigarettes did double duty as a commodity. As prisoners smoked them, the currency vanished, and the POW economy ground to a halt. People still wanted to buy and sell, but the currency had disappeared, and they had not developed channels or conventions for trading in any other way. This is almost exactly the situation in the Depression that Samuelson describes in the passage quoted earlier. People had become so hooked on one form of money that—with a few exceptions—they couldn't figure out how to do business in any other way. The POW study also shows what happens when money is more than just a medium of exchange.

There was another consequence. Because chain-smokers tended to trade much of their food for cigarettes, their health declined. And because medical facilities were very limited, their health problems meant fewer infirmary beds for other prisoners who got sick.

Something comparable happens in a money economy. When third world countries shift from subsistence crops, like beans, to cash crops, like coffee, to earn dollars to pay their debts to U.S. bankers, the goal of agriculture becomes raising money instead of food. Money as a commodity displaces food and the ability of rural people to provide for their own needs. People go hungry and a mass exodus occurs from rural areas to urban barrios.

This even happens in the United States. Out of each dollar the federal government collects in taxes to deal with the nation's needs, 15 cents ($110 billion total) are taken off the top to pay the interest on the national debt. The cost of money as a commodity literally takes food out of people's mouths, right here at home. And that's not counting the enormous cost of maintaining this system of money, a cost that is built into every transaction. The cost of a banking system and automated teller machines and Brink's armored delivery, for example. The cost of FBI agents and police and courts and jails, and of the federal regulatory apparatus that oversees the banks.

Time Dollars, by contrast, have none of these divergent uses or hidden costs. You can give them but you can't lend them, so they have no value as a commodity. They do one thing and that only: facilitate giving help and care. They cannot be stolen, any more than inches can be stolen, because they serve only as a measure of help given and received.

Time Dollars cannot be hoarded any more than inches can be hoarded, moreover, because there is no limit on the number that can exist at any one time. With conventional money, the amount you keep under your mattress deprives everyone else. But with Time Dollars you withhold only from yourself, because the number in circulation is limited only by the desire of individuals to be helpful.

The Legitimacy of Money

Money bears the stamp of the sovereign. It shows symbols of national authority and pride, heroes, and monuments. People trust it. That makes it solid and real.

Leave aside the confidence with which Russians currently regard their rubles. If you are a hearty soul, ask yourself how much that dollar bill in your pocket is really worth. The banking industry is tottering. The Federal Deposit Insurance Corporation is running out of money. The federal treasury is essentially a clearinghouse of IOUs, propped up by the Japanese and other lenders from abroad. If the citizens of the nation were to line up at the Treasury one morning demanding something for their dollars, they'd get exactly what they have now—IOUs.

In the end, little stands behind that dollar in your pocket besides the public's faith in it. (Economics stands closer to religion than most economists care to acknowledge.) Why can't people choose to have as much faith in one another as they have in a federal treasury that is over a trillion dollars in debt?

The economist says that Time Dollars are shaky because they are backed only by the goodwill of social service organizations and the like (except where a state backs them, as in Missouri). These could shut down the program or even close their doors tomorrow. Fair enough. Yet the government would have to do that, too, if everyone suddenly lost all faith in the system of money.

Service organizations aren't likely to take casually the commitments that build up in a time bank. Besides, those commitments really represent the obligations of individual members to one another. Should an organization fold, the bank would still exist in a computer record (Time Dollars cannot be embezzled), ready for someone else to continue the program a little the way Dolores Galloway does in Washington (see chapter 1).

In the end, it comes down to whom and what we choose to trust and the role of that trust in building the world in which we want to live. Is a currency inherently less worthy of our faith because it cannot be inflated or deflated or manipulated by a central command? Are our neighbors inherently less worthy of our trust than are the politicians and international bankers who preside over the system of money?

There is another reason that money seems legitimate compared to other kinds of exchange. Money is the handmaiden of contract. It involves specific legal obligations between buyer and seller, as opposed to the encompassing context of trust that exists in families and communities and Time Dollar programs. This protection seems solid and real, until one tries to use it.

Most who have had to hire a lawyer and go through litigation because of a broken contract will repeat the words made famous by Dickens in *Bleak House:* "Suffer any wrong" rather than be subjected to that.

It will impoverish you; the proceedings will paralyze you and force you to put your life on hold. Only the lawyers will profit. In the end, you are likely to learn what the great jurist Oliver Wendell Holmes noted nearly 90 years ago. "It is not the policy of the law to compel adherence to contracts," he said, "but only to require each party to choose between performing in accordance with the contract and compensating the other party for any injury resulting from a failure to perform."

In transactions involving dollars, the legal obligation is partly an illusion. Money and contracts are not about keeping your word; they are about getting out of keeping your word as cheaply as possible, by paying dollar damages, if the opportunity arises to make more money off some other sucker. And as many who have dealt with car dealers or home builders well know, getting even that much is a privilege reserved for those who can afford a lawyer in the first place.

By that standard, the informal reciprocity of Time Dollar programs doesn't look so bad. If someone is supposed to drive you to the supermarket and never shows up, you just ask for someone else the next time. Only those enamored of lawyer bills would find that a deficiency.

The Incentive of Money

Economics is psychology in disguise. It postulates a type of human and then projects an entire theory from the kind of person it posits.

The image of man in economics is "Homo economicus," the acquisitive and self-seeking man, who reckons every life decision upon an exacting calculus of loss and gain. This image is the ghost that inhabits economic theories and models. It is embodied in the sacred principle that people will work or produce only as long as they gain money and will cease at the point where they start to lose. (In economic parlance, this is the point where "marginal return" falls below "marginal cost.")

This image governs respectable thinking about incentives and rewards. Without the premise of a self-seeking, profit-maximizing person, who responds to incentives in predictable ways, economics would have no pretense to science.

Nobody disputes that people respond to money. But it is not the only thing they respond to. "Economists use a totally outdated model of human motivation," David McClelland, a psychologist at Harvard, once said. And he was corroborated by the defensive football coach of the New York Giants, who told the *New York Times* that "I don't think I've ever worked a day in my life. It's been a joy. I'd do it for a lot less money."

Endeavor is more than a series of conditioned responses to money. If this is true in the big-money world of professional sports, how much more in the realm of helping and caring work. Time Dollars tap the side of human nature that barely exists in economic thinking—the side that wants to help and be useful and simply to feel good. In mobilizing this important resource, money is not very good.

Leave aside Mother Teresa and Gandhi. Ask your mother if she would accept market wages to go next door and clean a sick neighbor's house. Then ask her if she would accept Time Dollars which she could give to Granny across town so that she could get a ride to the doctor. Subtle issues of self-respect are involved. Money can deter action as well as bestir it. One teenager from the Anacostia section of Washington, D.C., was earning Time Dollars doing yard work for elderly homeowners. The Time Dollars were important, he said, because otherwise his buddies would think he was a chump. Earning something he could give away was a token of status; market wages for the same work, by contrast, could have subjected him to ridicule, especially from acquaintances who could make much more by dealing drugs.

"For 10 dollars an hour, I wouldn't do it," said Herbie Fine, a worker with the Elderplan program in Brooklyn described in chapter 4, speaking of his 2:00 A.M. missions to help a 95-year-old man. "I don't have to go out and search for a job. I worked hard and I have a right to take it easy. If I'm doing something because I want to help, that's [another] thing."

4

Elderplan Grows
a New Currency
in Brooklyn

Frank Vuolo is sitting in his Pontiac outside the Key Supermarket in the Sheepshead Bay section of Brooklyn. It's cold, with a faint whiff of salt in the air, and Vuolo looks hale and dapper in his 1940s mustache and plaid wool hat. He doesn't seem to be doing much. But he's helping to bring about fundamental change in the way the nation thinks about medical care.

Vuolo came up the hard way: a political prisoner in Shanghai during World War II, a farm laborer in Brooklyn (which had farms until the 1950s), a dockworker in Manhattan. He owned a dry-cleaning shop and finally ended up with a union job running a freight elevator before he retired.

Vuolo has every right to sit back and enjoy his pension. But he can't. "If I keep moving, I feel like I did when I was in the Marines," he says. "If I sit down, I'm a dead duck."

Vuolo's need to keep moving has become the answer to Etta Goldsmith's need for help. Goldsmith lives with her husband in an apartment building nearby, and life has been a struggle. Her husband is very ill, and she's battling physical ailments of her own. Her eyes are going bad, and simple tasks like shopping pose a major challenge.

So every Thursday, Vuolo picks up Goldsmith at her apartment, loads her shopping cart into the backseat, and drives the mile or so to the supermarket. On this particular day, Goldsmith seems happily in her element as she scrutinizes the tomatoes like a customs agent and scans the bakery shelf for bargains. "I had a hard time," she confides, fishing coupons out of a rumpled envelope in the check-out line.

She doesn't care to elaborate. But the first time Vuolo took her shopping, she insisted he take a pen in return. "If it weren't for you, I thought I'd be lost," she told him one day.

Vuolo and Goldsmith aren't old friends. They aren't even neighbors. Instead, they are both members of Elderplan, a Health Maintenance Organization (HMO) for seniors in Brooklyn. Elderplan goes far beyond the typical HMO in its approach to care and need. Most HMOs mimic the conventional medical system in treating members as consumers of expert services, though at somewhat lower prices. Elderplan goes much further and enlists members as participants in one another's care—and their own.

It does this through a time bank, which is called Member-to-Member. When Vuolo drives Goldsmith to the supermarket or helps in some other way (Goldsmith has been dropping hints about a ride to the dentist), Vuolo gets a credit in the time bank. He can then use this credit to get help from another member, should he need it somewhere down the line. If he accumulates enough of these Time Dollars, he can use them to pay one of his quarterly HMO premiums.

TAPPING A LATENT POOL OF ABILITY

The concept is as simple as the old neighborhood babysitting club. But its impact on Elderplan has been enormous. Time Dollars have tapped a latent pool of talent in Elderplan's own membership, turning passive recipients of care into producers and providers. These members tend to stay more healthy because they are active and needed. The concept has expanded the care the HMO can offer and has changed an insurance relationship into a familial one. "It is not often that people volunteer at their insurance companies," notes Terrie Raphael, who founded the Member-to-Member program.

The irony is that Time Dollars, despite the name, don't work as monetary incentive. Rather, the concept touches a side of people that doesn't respond to money. "For me, the credits don't mean nothing at all," Vuolo says, in the inflections of his native Italy. "It's my pleasure, my enjoyment, if I can help somebody in need."

When Elderplan was founded in 1985, Health Maintenance Organizations were widely regarded as a disappointment. They were originally promoted as a way to control the medical system's voracious appetite for money. Instead, HMOs have mainly reaffirmed the limits of monetary incentives and management economies in dealing with human needs.

HMOs entered the American medical scene in a big way during the 1970s. In the previous decade, Lyndon Johnson had finally overcome the opposition of the American Medical Association in pushing through the Medicare program for the elderly. With the exception of the Japanese and Germans after World War II, few losers have prospered so well. The sudden infusion of public moneys fed an escalation in medical costs, which went up seven to ten times the rate of inflation. National expenditures on medical care jumped from 2 percent to over 11 percent of the whole economy!

Medical specialties proliferated: The more specialists who worked on a patient, the more separate times the government could be billed. Anesthesiologists and radiologists fared especially well, while family doctors and general practitioners came to be seen almost as a form of unskilled labor. And meanwhile, the Medicare program gave rise to a vast new paperwork industry to keep records and process claims. H. Ross Perot, the self-made millionaire and passionate defender of free enterprise, made his fortune setting up this record-keeping system.

While the industry prospered, the government and medical consumers were going broke. America's medical system had become twice as expensive as Canada's, while providing nowhere near the coverage. The hemorrhage of taxpayer dollars finally prompted the government to action, and the result was a new panacea: the HMO.

The basic problem, said the experts, is that doctors make more money the more treatment they provide. Their economic interest lies in the direction of disease and high-tech treatment, rather than prevention and better health. The HMO was intended to change this perverse economics in a fundamental way. Members pay a flat premium, no matter how much treatment they receive. From the doctor's standpoint, the best patient then becomes a healthy patient; doctors do better when the patient needs less attention.

HMOs have improved on fee-for-service medicine, but not as much as hoped. Doctors found that keeping patients healthy is just one way to boost returns; an easier way is to establish layers of red tape before members can get to a hospital. As a result, HMOs often reject those who most need to be members. On top of that, HMOs found that their investments in prevention don't really pay monetarily, since members often drop out and take their good health someplace else.

However, the real problem is more basic than the screening policies. Many members seek care at hospitals because it is the only kind their insurance pays for. The elderly are especially prone to use hospitals as temporary nursing homes; even when they really have no acute need, they often can't be discharged because there is no one to take care of them at home. The lack of daily care is often the source of their illness in the first place.

DOCTORING UP THE HMOs

A group of medical care reformers got to pondering this problem, and the result was the social HMO. The SHMO, as it's called, simply adds social services to the HMO's medical insurance, to cut down on hospital use and help seniors maintain themselves at home. This is the concept behind Elderplan. Through some adept bureaucratic footwork in Washington, Elderplan became one of only four experimental SHMOs in the country under legislation enacted in 1985.

It turned out, however, that the SHMO is less a breakthrough than it first appeared. Home care and social services take money, too—much more than is available from Medicare and other sources. So the cash bind simply got transferred to a new, social service front. An elderly member who needs significant support at home, for example, quickly runs through his or her yearly allotment. Plus, the social support is limited in the first place. An Elderplan member can visit a psychologist 15 times, for example, but mainly for drugs and what is called, in medical circles, management. "There's not much money for counseling," says Raphael.

Raphael and others at Elderplan realized they were confronting more than just a glitch in medical strategy. Somehow, the functions of family and community life—taking seniors to the doctor, making sure they have companionship and food in the refrigerator—were being dumped in their laps. There is not enough money in America to buy that kind of attention and care. So the task for an organization like Elderplan becomes much larger than medical experts ever imagined. Beyond finding new sources of money, and beyond getting retirees to watch their diets, Elderplan had to find a way to replicate the old informal systems of care.

In other words, it had to become a social HMO in the root sense of the word—"involving allies and confederates." Time Dollar workers pick up on this intuitively. "Makin' like a family," Frank Vuolo says.

THE QUIET BEGINNINGS OF A REVOLUTION

Elderplan headquarters seems an unlikely place to start a social revolution. Until a recent move, the office occupied part of the second floor of a nondescript bank building in the Borough Park section of Brooklyn. The neighborhood is an Orthodox Jewish enclave, where the men wear yarmulkes and austere black suits without ties, and shops sell Hebrew books and kosher foods. Except for the blasting horns and the electronics products in the shop windows, life here doesn't seem to have changed much over the last 50 years.

Yet this setting in a traditional culture is appropriate for a Time Dollar program. Despite the immediate neighborhood, Elderplan members are a diverse group: Jamaican, Irish, Italian, Afro-American, Jewish—virtually the entire span of Brooklyn's ethnic mélange. One thing they share is memories of families and neighborhoods where people looked out for one another.

Time Dollar participants talk about a Brooklyn that barely exists anymore. Ray Hughes, a retired merchant seaman, recalls how people pulled together during the Depression. "We washed windows, we beat rugs, but we never thought of using the money for ourselves," he says. "We just came home and put it on the table."

Rebecca Peters recalls the cohesion of the immigrant world. A small, articulate woman who wears her hair in a braided bun, Peters came to Brooklyn from Germany in the 1920s, when her family fled from Hitler and the rising anti-Semitism there. "People brought over their families and friends, and they lived in a pretty tight circle," Peters says. These circles were called Landsman Schaften and they provided a community of care to strangers in the new land. "One could always go to the synagogue. In the basement, the Landsman Schaften would meet. You could always find a family to take you home if you needed a meal."

Peters has been an idealist for most of her life. She married a black man in the 1940s, and in the 1950s, she was the plaintiff in a lawsuit that challenged (successfully) a McCarthy-era loyalty oath for public housing tenants. Later, she helped to run an interracial summer camp that was attacked by local residents.

But like many Elderplan members, volunteer work as such didn't appeal to her until now. "I have never done anything like this before, although people would come to me with their problems," she says.

Perhaps more typical is Dorothy Gochal, a Brooklyn housewife who had never worked outside the home and who didn't think she had anything to offer. But then her husband died, and she started losing friends to death as well. Her children live close by, but, as she puts it tactfully, "They have their own lives." Feeling a need for human contact, she signed up for the Member-to-Member program.

A FRIEND TO LOOK FORWARD TO IS IMPORTANT

Her first case was an old couple who were entitled to home health care from the city, but wouldn't take it because they didn't want welfare. Gochal was nervous at the start. "I didn't think I would like it," she says. "What was I going to talk about?" As the three got to know one another, the situation became more comfortable. "I did nothing," Gochal says. "I sat and watched soap operas, like a friend. They didn't have a circle of friends they could call on."

It may seem a small thing. But a friend to look forward to can provide a big boost to seniors who live isolated in their homes. In many cases, it makes the difference between normal functioning and serious illness or a nursing home. This is especially true when members like Frank Vuolo help other members deal with the outside world. "When people live alone, the first things they have trouble with are things outside the house—shopping, the doctor, getting the laundry done," says Mashi Blech, coordinator of the Member-to-Member program.

"But if they don't get proper food or medical care, they get sicker and sicker and sicker very quickly."

The Member-to-Member program started three years ago from scratch. Today, there are over 100 Time Dollar workers, out of some 5,200 members overall. These have reported over 13,000 hours of helping work; and since many hours go unreported, the actual total is a great deal more. Home-care workers cost at least $10 an hour in New York, so the Member-to-Member program has supplied well over $130,000 worth of caring work.

At this rate, the program has more than paid for itself. But it is far more than a way to provide home care on the cheap. The Time Dollar structure adds dimensions of care that professionals couldn't supply, even if money were available. And it changes the concept of health from a product to be consumed to an activity to be pursued.

For one thing, members seem more willing to ask for help when that help comes from peers. The reluctance of seniors to admit their needs is a major problem in the social service field. Some would rather live in dirty clothes than acknowledge that they are too feeble to go to the laundromat. Pride is part of it; many Elderplan members grew up in the Depression, when people learned to tough it out, and they aren't about to cry on the shoulder of some social worker.

SENIORS PREFER PEERS AS CONFIDANTES

But more, seniors just don't want to deal with people they don't know, especially in their homes. "When a couple take care of one another, they get used to that routine," Gochal says. They make their bed a certain way, put the food in the refrigerator a certain way. "Somebody else does it differently, so they reject it."

The age difference between social workers and seniors only makes the problem worse. Imagine what it's like to have to admit incontinence to a city worker young enough to be a grandchild. "They don't want to talk to some young girl in her thirties about the death of their husbands," Gochal says. "Most psychologists in the field are men. For women, that's a turn-off—they think of them as grandsons."

Gochal can understand such problems because she lives with them herself. She also understands why many seniors don't want to be a burden to their children, even when they live close by. The relationship may be strained. Years of emotional baggage can complicate the simplest act. Or else the parent senses where he or she stands in the new hierarchy of things. "It's easier to ask me for a favor than to ask a son-in-law or daughter-in-law," Gochal says. "With them, it's a big production. They have to take time off from work. If they have to sit in the doctor's office for more than 5 minutes, it's a calamity."

One of Gochal's clients had a lot of pent-up anger. It turned out she just needed someone to talk to. "The family didn't want to hear the stories, because they've heard them so many times. But I'm fascinated," Gochal said. "These people get a new sense of being alive."

Elderpartners—as they are called—can enter their clients' lives because they approach them not as professionals but as friends. Avis Rhodes is an example. A retired psychiatric nurse from Jamaica, she has the lyric inflections of the Carribean, and the knowing manner of one who can be trusted with secrets.

Rhodes's first Elderpartner was a woman who was strapped into a wheelchair at a nursing home. (Over half a million old people are restrained in beds and wheelchairs every day.) Rhodes eased her way into the woman's trust, bringing her fresh bread and a Jewish newspaper, and chatting about current events. Gradually, the woman opened up, and soon she was able to go home. Rhodes continued to visit until the woman died a year later; a niece said she only came to the house while Rhodes was there, because then her aunt was on good behavior. "I looked on her more as a friend," Rhodes says.

Her current partner is a woman named Wilma, who stays at a nursing home near the boardwalk on Coney Island. Wilma is of Hungarian descent; she was widowed at 39 and lived with her son until he moved to Florida. As is often the case, her first weeks in the nursing home were not happy. She insisted on wearing a badge to separate herself from the other members. It read "Hi, my name is Wilma. I like to do volunteer work." A staff person at the home says Wilma was "confused and aggressive."

Wilma still wears the badge. And she still refers to her fellow residents as "the elderly people." But she has become settled and almost cordial since Rhodes started to visit. Though she offers detailed critiques of the menu, she concedes the place is very clean. She brightens noticeably when Rhodes appears. "Anything I need, she is right here," she says, almost as though it is a personal accomplishment. "She is a very good friend."

Helpers like Rhodes can't be bought. They have time to sit and listen; no clock is ticking, no caseload lies ahead. Seniors trust them like friends with intimate life details, such as taking care of bills. Some Elderhelpers go to extraordinary lengths. One scoured Brooklyn for a synagogue without front steps so that another member, who is confined to a wheelchair, could attend services. The latter was so thrilled, he was up and dressed hours before it was time to go.

ELDERPLAN RESTORES SELF-ESTEEM AND PROVIDES WORK

The extra dimension of care probably isn't the greatest benefit of the Time Dollar program. Rather, it's the opportunity that members like Gochal have to feel useful and needed. This begins to change the role of the HMO fundamentally. Rather than merely provide psychiatrists to restore their members' self-esteem, Elderplan also provides work that helps members feel *worthy* of self-esteem.

Seniors in America don't have much chance to feel useful and important. Many are separated from their grandchildren, and so are deprived of an opportunity to play a role in their lives (beyond sending gifts for birthdays and at holidays). They don't have work or an active social role to boost their sense of worth. Even the things that are supposed to make seniors feel good, often do the opposite.

A sobering study at the London School of Economics looked at what happens when adults visit their aging parents. The adult child generally came away feeling better about himself or herself, the study found; but the parent came away feeling worse. The reason is very simple—though it is one people seldom stop to think about. The children would bring news of all the good things in their lives; the promotions, the acclaim, the travel abroad. They were saying in effect, "Look Mommy and Daddy. See what I have done." They were trying to give pleasure and show that they had (finally) lived up to their parents' expectations. It was a combination of show-and-tell and report card time.

The parents listened dutifully and maybe even said something like, "That's interesting." That enabled the child to come away feeling better.

But the aging parent wasn't feeling better. Listening to the list of accomplishments, the hustle and bustle that filled their children's lives, only made them realize how uneventful their own were. The promotions and raises were reminders that the parent was no longer useful or needed. "My life isn't nearly as full," the aging parent thought. "My child is now self-sufficient and even better off than I am. They don't need my food or my money; I don't even have anything to talk about."

The thing they most wanted was to feel important and needed. They didn't realize how all-important their affection and approval still were. Instead, the child's recitation made them feel that they had less and less to give.

Not that every parent suffers such humiliations. But many do. And the general sense of uselessness can be a source of great depression. Time Dollar programs help to counter this. They permit all participants to define themselves as having something to give—to make a difference in the life of another.

Participants in the Time Dollar program mention this often. An example is Ray Hughes, the retired merchant seaman. Hughes isn't the type of person one would expect to find in a group of home care volunteers. But he works with members whose problems are especially severe, and he speaks with honest self-awareness and insight.

"My first client had emphysema," Hughes recounts. "He was stuck in one room, couldn't go out. He was very lonely. We found a common ground—ships. He worked in the navy yard. I could help him. And in doing so, I helped me. When you give to somebody, you get so much in return. It keeps you young. You want to keep going."

This is a reason that Elderplan lets members like Hughes use Time Dollars to pay part of their HMO fee. When people are feeling active and needed, they are less prone to disease, so they require less care from the HMO. It works a little like a health insurance discount for nonsmokers; lead a healthy life and your insurance will cost less.

Hughes, Peters and Gochal have gone through a special peer counseling course that Elderplan runs to help the most committed Time

Dollar workers deal with severe emotional problems of other members. The course met for ten weeks, 3 hours twice a week, and there are regular monthly seminars. The peer counselors have some of the esprit of an elite corps, and they take an obvious pride in their work.

Peter's first client, as she calls them proudly, was a woman who was schizophrenic. The woman liked to play Scrabble, by her own rules, making up her own words. She had beautiful white hair, but she couldn't manage it. Peters took this woman to the beauty parlor for the first time in 20 years. "It cheered her up no end."

Now she's working with a woman with a very bad heart, who is never more than a few feet away from her pills. The woman sits alone for most of the day and is very depressed. Peters has been visiting the woman for four months, and now she is starting to paint and to take occasional strolls down the block to the luncheonette for tea.

Who wouldn't feel good? And for a woman who had to work most of her life, the peer counseling program provides other satisfactions as well. "Before I got involved in this, there were times I was lonely," she says. (Peters also helps run a folk dance group.) "Now I am very happy. It is like continuing education. Today we learned relaxation and pressure points. We practiced on one another. It's wonderful."

Peters, Hughes, and the others conceivably could get the same satisfaction from a conventional volunteer program, without the Time Dollars. But Time Dollars, and the underlying dynamic of reciprocal exchange, add something that conventional volunteer programs do not have.

For one thing, the time bank dynamic provides a big boost for staff, and this enthusiasm pervades the whole program. At a time when most people in social service work are overseeing the triage of their programs, people at Elderplan feel they are just getting going. "From the staff point of view, it is very exciting to be on the cutting edge of an idea with very solid appeal, and that can start to make the world a little bit better," says Raphael, whose mother has been pioneering the peer counseling concept in California.

But the main impact is on the members. For them, the time bank takes away the stigma of charity. Elderplan members who receive help are undertaking an obligation to repay the help if they can. "Ordinarily, most people are reluctant to ask for help," Blech says. "But when I tell them they can do something to help someone else, it makes them feel better about asking for what they need." Even housebound seniors can help another member, if only through "telephone reassurance"—a simple phone call to chat and make sure things are okay. One Elderpartner lost both his legs and was confined to a wheelchair. But he did a lot of work at the Member-to-Member office and telephone reassurance at home. "He was very active until the time of his death," Raphael says.

Time Dollars also boost the status of these workers within the organization. Volunteers in typical programs are the lowest people on the ladder; they are considered expendable and often no one takes them seriously. Time Dollar workers, by contrast, are not extra; they are real workers, whose work is taken seriously. They speak to assemblies of new members and meet with journalists and other visitors; this has included a delegation from Poland that was exploring Time Dollars as a way to combine free market dynamics with caring work.

Beyond all this is the simple fact that people who have never done volunteer work before sign up for Member-to-Member. Even members have trouble articulating why the reciprocal exchange aspect is attractive; it seems to have something to do with belonging to an organization that functions something like a family.

This much can be said for sure: The attraction is not the Time Dollars themselves as a material reward.

When it first started to recruit members, Elderplan stressed the value of the credits in providing for a rainy day. But people didn't like to be reminded that one day they might become disabled and infirm. So Elderplan took a leaf from the insurance industry, which figured out long ago, as Raphael points out, that they had to present their product as *life* instead of death insurance. So now, the leaders talk about the good feelings and personal growth.

Almost universally, the Time Dollar workers echo this view. "It's good to have the credits, but that wasn't part of the reason for volunteering," Gochal says. "I just wanted to start doing something. I'm enjoying myself now."

Peters, never without a viewpoint to express, was even more emphatic. When the delegation from Poland came to visit, she advised them to forget the notion that people can only respond to market incentives. "If you want to start this program in your country," she said, "the basis of it should be that you want to help somebody. Then the other benefits will grow out of that."

HERBIE FINE, A STAR WORKER, A PATIENT MAN

Herbie Fine keeps a small clipboard by the telephone in the kitchen of his Brooklyn apartment. On it are names and telephone numbers, written in Fine's rounded, somewhat shaky hand: Mr. Branca, whose wife of 50 years died recently; Mr. Baumgarten, whose health problems are legion; Mr. Goldwasser, whom Fine is going to see today. (These names have been changed.)

Fine is one of Elderplan's star Time Dollar workers, and the people on the list by his telephone are other members that he's helped. "They give me the oldies," he says proudly. "They say no one else can handle them. I'm a patient man."

Fine also represents a resource that the nation has in growing abundance—the time of retired people who are able and want to be useful. And beyond them, the time of others the conventional workplace doesn't need or want. This resource has never existed before to the extent it does now. And due to our way of economic thinking, we don't know what to do with it! The experts in Washington keep harping on economic "incentives" and rewards. But Herbie Fine isn't interested in those.

Elderplan offers to reimburse Time Dollar workers for transportation costs, but Fine won't take it. Often he doesn't even report his hours. Partly, it is a question of pride. Fine worked hard all his life. He earned his pension. And he's not about to grovel for a few dollars now.

"I'm not looking to get something in return," he says. "I believe in the old school. In Europe, the rabbi never got paid."

Then why does he work in a Time Dollar program, when he's never volunteered for anything else? To Fine, the Time Dollars credited to him are less a reward than they are strands in a network of care. "What is Member-to-Member," he says. "It's helping one another out. Like a family."

"I would be a lousy doctor," he adds. "I wouldn't charge anybody nothing. I'd say 'Call me anytime.' My name is Fine. I want to keep it fine. If I do something for somebody, I feel good."

Fine's apartment is neat but somber, lacking the warm touches that would suggest a woman's presence. Fine's wife died more than 20 years ago, and he has lived alone here ever since. There are family pictures on a table and a white yarmulke that shows signs of recent use. But Fine doesn't talk much about religion—recoils from any display of virtue. "The whole thing is ask what you can do for your country, not what your country can do for you," he says. "Wasn't there a president who said that?"

Fine lives in the Orthodox Jewish enclave of Boro Park, where the tree-lined streets have the odd atmosphere of a comfortable American shtetl (or enclave). People call him mayor of the building because he's always helping out. "When we call, there is always somebody there," says Blech, of Elderplan. "When he comes to the office, he brings cake or sweet rolls. He gives. He's a giving person."

His first case was Arnold Baumgarten, a wealthy man in his nineties, who did not part easily with a dime. Baumgarten was a legend around Elderplan for his demands on volunteers. He would call with his complaints at all hours of the day and night, issue demands seemingly without end. Most volunteers begged off within a week or so. As a last resort, Elderplan gave Baumgarten to Fine. The demands continued. Herbie had to take three buses to get to Baumgarten's apartment, yet Baumgarten would insist that he stop at Waldbaum's supermarket on the way over; prices were too high at the market near his house, he said. He called frequently in the early hours, and Fine would take him to the hospital at 2:00 or 3:00 A.M.

Once Fine spent all night with Baumgarten in a hospital emergency room. "A problem with his stomach," Fine says delicately. "He couldn't go."

The problem became a major undertaking over the next several months. Trips to the doctor. Calls late at night. Then one morning the phone rang at 3:00 A.M. It was Baumgarten. " 'Herbie,' he says. 'I got good news for you. I did beautiful business.' "

Eventually, Elderplan got a paid helper for Baumgarten (though he wanted Fine back). But Fine holds no regrets for his two years with the demanding gentleman. "I figure I'm going to get old like that, too," he says. "It's my job to take care of him. When he called to tell me he did some business, I was very happy. He's showing me how much he likes me. He wants me to be part of his glory."

Like most members of Elderplan, Fine grew up in a world in which ties of family and community were much stronger than they are today. He was born in Lithuania, in the second decade of the century. His family came to the United States around 1920 and settled in Hammond, Indiana, where his father opened a grocery store. The senior Fine was a religious man who spent most of his time studying Torah. So Herbie helped in the grocery and went to work in a department store as soon as he was old enough, to send his brother through college. "Until the day I got married, I gave my father my pay envelope," he says. "I believe it should be that way."

After World War II, Herbie settled in Brooklyn, where his wife was raised. He wanted to go back to Chicago, but his wife wanted to be close to her family. "She started crying. I hate people crying. I can't stand it." On the basis of a little experience in a home darkroom, he talked his way into a job as a developer of movies and into a union that usually didn't admit Jews. He worked two, three jobs to send his daughter through Hebrew school and college. This didn't leave any time for organized volunteer work, apart from his informal attentions to neighbors and friends.

Fine almost didn't make it as a service credit worker. Like most programs, Elderplan trains these workers before sending them into people's homes, and Fine fell asleep during all of the sessions. But he aced the written test at the end, and now he's one of the most active members.

"He's had more *boychiks* than just about anyone," Blech says. *Boychik* is a Yiddish term of affection for a young man or an old friend. Fine uses it where a professional social worker would use the term *client* or *case*. His current *boychik* is Hyman Goldwasser, 95 years old, an Orthodox Jew whose dietary observance is very strict. He won't let Fine shop for him for fear he'll slip something that isn't kosher into the bag, so he buys his own food. "It's hard to get hold of that son-of-a-gun," Fine says in his gentle Brooklynese. "He's always running around."

This day, Fine is walking with a hesitant shuffle, his face is a bit tight. He is a small man with a sad face and gentle blue eyes and trousers that ride up high on his belly. Fine favors a sporty look: black vinyl jacket, baseball cap, and white sneakers. The sneakers are not tied, but this is not to fit in with the teenagers on the subway. His feet are swollen from diabetes, and he's been fighting a losing battle with his waistline. ("I'm a nosher," he shrugs.) If he's in pain, though, he keeps it to himself.

"A PRETTY SMART BABY"

When Fine arrives at Goldwasser's apartment, the latter is sitting at the table of his narrow kitchen, reading a Hebrew newspaper with a magnifying glass. He is a spry little man whose large ears and nose give him the appearance of an elfin rabbi; in fact, he is a *chazzen*, a man who leads the prayers, in his synagogue. On one wall are pictures from a special party to celebrate his longevity in the temple. Goldwasser wears thermal underwear under a white shirt and a black yarmulke over limp strands of hair. He is sharp and alert, though talking with him can seem at times like shouting down a long tunnel.

Fine is gentle with Goldwasser, almost paternal. There is close to 20 years difference between the two, and in this setting, Fine becomes the young man. With his vocabulary he brings Goldwasser back into the stream of life and makes him one of the guys. "He's a pretty smart baby," he says. "He's been in all sorts of business."

Goldwasser was born in Poland, in the 1890s. After two years in the Polish army during World War I—he lived on potatoes and vegetables because the Poles wouldn't provide kosher food—he came to the United States in 1921. "It was quite a few days ago," he says with a twinkle. "I didn't have a trade in my hands. I was studying to be a rabbi." So he worked a pushcart on Orchard Street, got a small grocery store, scraped together enough to enable his sons to become a lawyer and a surgeon ("One of the best," he says.).

The family pictures are in the living room, and Goldwasser invites his visitors to take a look. The room is surprisingly tidy, except for shirts that hang from various perches. But Goldwasser has forgotten something: The lights don't work. The bulbs in the chandelier blew out, and he couldn't get up on a chair to change them. Like many older people, Goldwasser holds tightly to his shreds of self-reliance; he'd rather suffer Job-like than ask for help. (And whom does one call for such a job anyway? The police?) "I can take care of myself so far," he says. "God gives me help."

The light bulbs are exactly the sort of daily problem that bedevils older people who try to live at home. As much as ill-health, the accumulation of these can drive people into nursing homes. Fine keeps watch over the little things. When Goldwasser had a roach problem, he fitted him out with roach motels. Fine got him on Medicaid. And he tries to provide little treats, such as an ice cream cone, Goldwasser's first in 20 years. Today he's concerned about Goldwasser's eyes.

Goldwasser has a cataract problem, but he doesn't want to go to the doctor. "The doctors now, they only know what they learned from the books," he says. Probably, he just doesn't want to submit himself to a doctor, period. Or maybe he just wants a little attention. Fine understands, and gently urges Goldwasser along.

FINE: "I'm going to make an appointment for you, for the eyes."

GOLDWASSER: "You know what they told me to do to cure the eyes? They told me to use Johnson's baby shampoo. I ask you, is that for the hair or for the eyes?"

Goldwasser shakes his finger like a rabbi making a point of Torah. But Fine persists with a light, good-humored touch. "All right, all right, it can't hurt," Goldwasser says at last. It is hard to imagine a younger person, a social worker, achieving this kind of rapport.

The two talk about Torah, talk about the old days. Fine is old enough to remember, but still young enough to help. "I have a friend better than a brother," Goldwasser says. "A brother, a sister, they wouldn't do what Mr. Fine does for me. He encourages me to live, for life. And, of course, God in heaven helps, too."

And Fine, who also lives alone, can understand the little daily needs. The thermos, for example. Talmudic law prohibits the lighting of fires on the Sabbath, which includes the lighting of stoves. Younger adherents finesse the situation by putting a pot of water on a burner before the Sabbath, and keeping it over a very low flame. This is not a good idea for people in their nineties, however, so Goldwasser passes the holy day without soup or anything warm to drink. He bought a thermos a while back, but it wasn't a good one, and he became frustrated and gave up.

Fine has been aware of the problem for months. But it's not easy getting Goldwasser to accept help. Finally, Fine resorted to a little fib. He told Goldwasser that he had bought a thermos for himself to take to work, but has no use for it since he retired. "I'll have to throw it out," he said. "So do me a favor and use it."

Today, Fine has brought the thermos. It has a carrying case and a nice wide mouth, to make pouring easy for a shaky hand (another concern that older people understand). After a few passes, Goldwasser grasps how the lid fits onto the mouth. "For me?" he asks, his voice high-pitched like a child's. "This is for me?" His eyes start to water, but Fine rises quickly to the occasion. "No tears now," he says, just a bit gruffly. "I'm just a friend."

5

But Is It Really Volunteering?

As the city council of Washington, D.C., was considering a bill to launch Time Dollar programs, some people expressed serious reservations. A number of the clergy worried that the proposal might compromise the ideal of voluntary helping. Was a deed really done in the spirit of charity, they asked, if a credit was offered in return?

Then somebody pointed out that service credits can be given as well as received. Those who earn them can turn around and put them into the collection plate, literally, for the benefit of congregation members in need. This insight spawned a new slogan: "With 1 hour you give twice: first to a needy person, then to God."

Are Time Dollar workers really volunteers? No question is raised more often regarding these programs. At first glance, the question is understandable. Time Dollar workers do appear to get a reward. The programs are indeed very different from the typical volunteer programs. Yet these differences turn out to be their strengths. And the reward turns out to be different from what it seems.

No one raises the objection more than established volunteer organizations. They paint a picture of greedy oldsters lining their pockets with this new form of currency. "We feel that one of the basic tenets of volunteer service is not receiving a quid pro quo," an official of the American Red Cross said at congressional hearings in the mid-1980s.

The Red Cross official's pronouncement begs a number of questions. Is it really so bad to draw hundreds of people into helping work who weren't engaged in it before? What's wrong with assuring those volunteers that they will get help, too, if they need it somewhere down the line? Is it truly terrible to give women, who do most of the volunteer work in America, the token of value that they have so long deserved?

Perhaps most important of all, is it really so unthinkable to design a helping program that functions like a community, rather than like charity? Time Dollars may *appear* to compromise the spirit of volunteerism, but that is mainly because we have drifted so far from a sense of real community. In practice, Time Dollars strengthen the volunteer spirit by providing a context of reciprocity that turns service into a real force, rather than just a political bromide to avoid facing social needs.

Volunteerism remains a spotty and undeveloped resource, even after a decade of uplifting national oratory—including the "Thousand Points of Light" motif that a speech-writer phrased for President George Bush. This says something about the limits of worthy sentiments, without the kind of organizing dynamic that Time Dollars provide. "A million points of light, or whatever he's talking about—there's nothing *practical* about it," says Rebecca Peters, a member of the Elderplan program in Brooklyn. "With this [Time Dollars], people might actually be able to do what he's talking about."

"People need an incentive even if they are inclined to do this sort of thing," she adds, "to stick to it and take it seriously."

MUTUAL ASSISTANCE TRANSCENDS MONETARY REWARD

Time Dollars embody the concept of reciprocal exchange: You help me and I'll help you. This is very different from a monetary reward. It is how healthy communities used to operate, before the money-driven market separated the realm of work from that of community.

In the early settlements, neighbors had to help one another because there was no other way to survive. The barn raising, the harvesting of neighbors' fields, the quilting bees, and "breaking out" bees to open snow-blocked roads—these were not just nostalgic Currier and Ives conceits. They were daily necessities of frontier life. "Farmers often swapped work and there was free exchange of equipment," reports a chronicle of farming in Pennsylvania. The term *logrolling*, which today refers to legislative favor-mongering, derives from the custom by which neighbors helped one another clear land.

Communities like that are not likely to reappear on a significant scale. Too much has changed. But Time Dollars can replicate the best functions of these communities in a way that is practical for modern life. Partly, they do this by opening up channels of contact among neighbors who don't know one another. Life provides fewer occasions today for informal, neighborly interaction: We watch TV instead of sitting on the side porch, hire electricians and plumbers instead of exchanging work with neighbors. "Society is not set up so we can walk up to someone and say, 'I want to help you,'" says Eric Berry, Director of Senior Resources in the Michigan Office of Aging, who initiated the Time Dollars program there. Time Dollars, Berry says, provide an "etiquette of introduction," a social context in which it is okay to enter another person's life.

Then, Time Dollar networks provide a dynamic that enables those contacts to take root and grow. Time Dollars are not money, as that term is normally understood. You can't stick them in your pocket and spend them on, say, a weekend in Las Vegas, any more than settlers on the frontier could take their work done for a neighbor and use it to demand a ticket on the railroad. Time Dollars only have value among the participants in a program; therefore, they tend to reinforce the bonds between those members.

On the frontier, newcomers and newlyweds were initiated into a community when neighbors appeared to help build their houses. After the new family was settled in, it naturally was bound to reciprocate with a housewarming for the neighbors who had helped. People became part of the community, in other words, by undertaking an obligation that they had to repay. Similarly, Time Dollar networks implicate members into webs of reciprocal exchange. They are like shares in a local blood bank, the blood in this case being community spirit.

One program even calls the currency Care Shares. If the original function of money was to ease dealings between strangers, then the Time Dollar concept helps to make those strangers neighbors again.

DIGNITY AND SECURITY VS. CHARITY

The conventional volunteer program, by contrast, comes from a very different tradition. The attitude of the American Red Cross is a remnant of a day when volunteers were society folks who tutored immigrants in settlement houses. Such programs are built on a status ladder: paid professional staff at the top, volunteers in the middle, and needy recipients at the bottom. This divides the world into the able and disabled, givers and takers, haves and have-nots. The model is charity, rather than community. And the volunteer becomes second-class and dispensable.

Charity is wonderful, but most people don't want it. "Many people won't accept help if it is welfare," says Berry. "But if we can point out that the person coming to help you is getting paid, the door is open." Not only that, when people sign up for help, they are undertaking an obligation to help someone else if they can—to be part of a community. The stigma of charity is totally removed.

"You don't feel like you're infringing on anybody," Herbert Kilby, a 65-year old participant in the Washington, D.C., program, told the *Washington Post*. Kilby had earned credits by driving another senior to the airport. When he had to undergo heart surgery, he got a ride to the hospital from another member of the program. "I've been on both sides of the fence," he says. "You help somebody; they help you."

This offers dignity, and the obligation is real. Even those society calls disabled find ways to be of help. Luz Cancino, for example, is a member of the VIP program at Pacific Presbyterian Medical Center in San Francisco. Cancino was born in Nicaragua and came to the United States in 1945 to flee the Samosa regime. Now in her late seventies, she says she's wanted to help others ever since she was a child. When she heard of VIP she thought, "I want to be in this." She has a pacemaker and can't get around much. So she does most of her helping work on the telephone, calling fellow VIP members when they are sick or have a birthday. "I'm a sunshine lady," she says with a big smile. In return, other VIP members accompany her when she goes shopping or to the doctor.

So in practice, the credits help the recipients of service as well as the givers. The one gets dignity, the other gets security for the future, plus more opportunities to be helpful, because more people are coming forward for help. "It is protecting the volunteers' right to give," Berry says.

People at VIP and other Time Dollar programs make a point of calling participants members rather than volunteers. "It's not really a volunteer program," explains Jeanine Randolph, Director of Senior Services at the Pacific Presbyterian Medical Center. "It's an *empowering* program. It's a self-help program. And that's why it works, because it doesn't make the [recipient] feel beholden. It's wonderful to be the volunteer, the lady who goes down to the ghetto and delivers the food packages. [But] it's a whole different feeling if you're delivering the food knowing that you're going to get something back, that you *need* something."

A HUMILIATING PERCEPTION OF VOLUNTEERS

For all the touting of volunteers, service agencies don't always take them seriously. Staffs worry that volunteers won't be accountable. Since they aren't paid, they aren't subject to the chain of discipline and control. Maybe they won't even show up. Often, paid staff regard volunteers as a nuisance, so they shunt them off to marginal duties where they can't do any damage.

It can also downgrade the work of the volunteer. "I volunteered to feed patients and do whatever I could at D.C. General Hospital," one clergy member in Washington recalls. "But the nurses resented the fact that I was there. They couldn't find anything for me to do. But then you go to visit and you see people where food hasn't been given to them, and they can't give it to themselves. It's so sad."

Time Dollar workers are different. They're on the payroll, in a sense, and built into the regular flow of work. This evokes a depth of commitment on both sides. "They become part of a real structure," said Carolee DeVito, who teaches community health at the University of Miami School of Medicine and oversees the Time Dollar program at South Shore Hospital. "What's different is not the 'pay,' but becoming part of a formal structure. The hospital likes this idea better. They couldn't count on volunteers because they think volunteers are 'extra.' These people don't perceive themselves as 'extra.' They are counted on to come through." This is one of the reasons that the drop-out rate for Time Dollar programs has been in the vicinity of 3 percent, as opposed to the roughly 40 percent drop-out rate for conventional volunteer programs.

This aspect of Time Dollars has special implications for women. To put real value on volunteer work is to give women their due. "Most volunteers are women, and it is sexist to trivialize all this work by calling it volunteer," DeVito exclaimed in exasperation when the question arose at an assembly of the American Public Health Association. "Service credits legitimize the worth of that time."

This sexism is deeply embedded in economic thought. Looking only at the realm of monetary transactions, economists define work as work done for money. They leave out the whole nonmonetary economy of helping and caring, which comprises over half the work in society, by most reckonings. (In less-developed—i.e., less-money-centered—countries, the realm of household production, from garden plots and the like, comprises even more.)

In effect, male economists define the work males traditionally do as inherently important, while the work that has fallen to women isn't even considered work. Writing ad copy for Marlboros or Twinkies is a matter of grave importance; raising children or caring for the older folks doesn't count. By extension, volunteerism doesn't count either. If it did, economists would count it as carefully as they monitor the gross national product.

This may be one reason that many women take hold of Time Dollar programs with a passion. Suddenly, the things they care about count in a tangible way. Cassie Mae Brown, a Miami Time Dollar worker, earned low wages her whole life as a nurse's aide. Now she's in an economy that values her just as much as it does the doctor. During a typical day, Brown rose before dawn to drive a man to a dialysis appointment, then visited another woman who needed companionship. The final stop was to see a third person in the hospital. Brown won Miami's Service Credit Volunteer of the Year award for racking up 570 hours. The credits, she says, "make me feel like I'm somebody."

I'M NEEDED AND (FINALLY) VALUED

Feminists have endeavored to break down the sexism of the money-centered workplace. They have done less to challenge the sexism of underlying definitions of work, which demeaned the home and helping realms in the first place. Time Dollars mount that challenge. They expand the idea of work to include the work of which society needs more. And this is done not just by valuing work that women traditionally have done, but also by making that work more attractive to men.

Leaders of conventional programs worry that Time Dollars will siphon off their pool of volunteers. But, in fact, it has expanded the pool by attracting people who never volunteered before. This includes many women, of course. But it also includes men.

Women joke about why men don't volunteer more. The only way to get them involved is to say, "You're going to eat," quipped one Time Dollar worker at the Covenant Palms housing complex in Miami. On a more serious note, the women say that, for their generation at least, men don't feel comfortable outside a work setting. "He doesn't mingle," another Miami member says of her ex-husband, who was a laborer. "They don't know *how* to mingle. All they know how to do is work. They would (volunteer) if they knew how."

The reasons men don't volunteer more vary in different cases and ethnic cultures. But the sense that volunteering isn't "work"—and therefore is not a male role—probably figures large. "Men think it's a sissy thing to do," says Marie Tofoya, a member of the VIP program in San Francisco. "They still have that thing in their head—that it's not manly."

Time Dollar programs have a work culture. Hours are recorded. The system keeps score. It is a way of saying "Your work really counts" that is separate from any thought of material reward and separate even from the scoreboard. The system also has a fluid quality that enables participants to set their own hours, make their own arrangements, be their own bosses.

Jesse Gilbeaux ran a dry cleaning business for 20 years in San Francisco. He didn't have time for volunteer work. But he retired four years ago, and now he's working with the VIP program. He cleans, shops, and does odd jobs for homebound seniors as well as driving them to doctors' appointments. "I'm a workaholic," he told a local paper.

WHAT DOES "REWARD" MEAN?

But what about those credits? When all is said and done, don't they give rewards for things that people should do for free?

That depends what you mean by "reward." The word "volunteer" means to do something from the heart, for its own sake. It doesn't exclude reward, nor could it. Most volunteers get something, if only the good feeling of helping another person. Even the Red Cross doesn't hold that volunteers must detest their work to be sufficiently pure of heart.

If some participants do look at Time Dollars as a kind of insurance they purchase by helping a neighbor, is that really unseemly? Especially when the terrible quid pro quo means another neighbor will return the help? Few would suggest that the Peace Corps corrupts the ideal of volunteerism by paying a living stipend—and that's money. Who would argue that RSVP, the federal volunteer program for seniors, is illicit because it provides reimbursement for the volunteers' transportation expenses? That's money, too. Does anyone believe that certificates and plaques, staples in ordinary volunteer programs, represent a tawdry quid pro quo?

The society-lady volunteers of yore were well provided for. But today, many who want to help have needs of their own. Tofoya of the VIP program suffers from severe arthritis, for example, and must do most of her helping work over the telephone. But she is so enthused about the program that she approaches older women on the bus carrying heavy shopping bags. "You don't have to do that," she says. "We can help you."

Tofoya has not used any service credits yet, but she does think about them. "With this arthritis, I never know when I might need help, with my laundry or with the vacuuming," she says. Is anyone going to admonish a Marie Tofoya that her efforts are tainted because, somewhere down the line, someone might return the favor? Wouldn't that be a little like saying a dinner invitation is tainted, because the friend will feel obligated to return the favor? This "taint" is really the glue that holds society together.

As it happens, however, the purchasing power of Time Dollars is not the primary lure. Gilbeaux, for example, doesn't think much about the Time Dollars he's earning. He has been "blessed" in his life, he said, and he simply wants to help others. "I don't expect to be rewarded."

BEING BACK IN THE FLOW

This is a general feeling among members of Time Dollar programs. They appreciate the security of knowing help will be there if they need it. (Perhaps as they grow older they will appreciate this security even more.) But to most, the credits, as such, don't loom large. "It's good to have the credits but that wasn't part of my reason for volunteering," says Dorothy Gochal of the Elderplan program. "I just wanted to start something. I enjoy myself now."

Many Time Dollar members don't even report all their hours. And many refuse any reimbursement for their traveling expenses. "Where I was brought up, you were taught to do good by stealth," explained one member in Boston, in a rich Irish brogue.

This is an unfathomed dimension of Time Dollars. The credits do make a difference. People volunteer who never did so before. They continue in much greater proportions than in conventional volunteer programs. They become committed in a very personal way. Yet the credits don't operate as a material reward, at least as economists understand the term.

The question ventures into a region of incentive and reward that mainstream economists treat as an afterthought. The credits draw primarily from a spectrum of value that the monetary economy either ignores or excludes. To economists, this is the realm of "psychic reward," a low-voltage supplement to the main current of acquisitive urge. Time Dollar programs suggest it can be much more powerful than commonly assumed.

At one level, the credits are simply a pat on the back, a way to amplify the good feeling that comes from helping others. For seniors in particular, the credits are a token of being back in the flow of life. "It is that sense of belonging, of security, of feeling useful in society," says Anna Miyares, who coordinates the Miami program. "They went from being productive taxpayers to being nonpersons, invisible, in a corner. One of our goals is to pull them out, to say, 'Society needs you. You have a wealth of knowledge, experience that you can offer.'"

Also, Time Dollars resurrect the kind of social accounting that used to occur naturally in small town settings, when good deeds were remembered and reciprocated sooner or later. In a mobile society such as America, good deeds often waft into space; neighbors in our apartment buildings or suburbs have no idea what we did five years ago someplace else. And so, our sense of security and reciprocity gets transferred increasingly to impersonal entities such as insurance companies, which operate through money. Time Dollars serve almost as a social memory, a way to reestablish the connection between what we do today and what others do for us tomorrow.

Time Dollars reinforce this sense of connection by providing functional reasons for people to get together. In traditional communities, work and socializing were not separate things, but aspects of the same thing. Barn raisings and the like became gala events, the social and the economic combined. "The neighbors met at dark," begins one contemporary account of a Pennsylvania corn husking bee. "The whiskey bottle goes around, the story, the laugh, and rude songs. Three or four hundred bushels are husked by nine or ten o'clock."

This is much the way Time Dollar programs operate. For seniors in particular, they are something *happening*, something new and dynamic in the midst of gray, formless days. Training sessions become a form of continuing education. At seniors buildings, the helping work naturally gives rise to parties and outings and the like. "It gives you a chance to meet people," says Daisy Alexander, a member of the program at Covenant Palms in Miami. "We have all kinds of activities. We go places and I love it."

If it weren't for the Time Dollars, Alexander says, people there "wouldn't have nothing to look forward to."

The San Francisco program has gone a step further and woven social events into the Time Dollar web. Participants get credits for planning and running a party, say, while others spend credits to attend.

This may seem like nit-picking. But it makes these activities less like charity and more like a circle of friends in which dinner invitations are reciprocated back and forth.

"AN ARMY OF LOVE AND FRIENDSHIP AND CARE"

The net effect of all this is that people get excited about Time Dollar programs, in a way that doesn't often happen in conventional volunteer efforts. That includes the people who run the programs.

The last decade or so has been hard on people in social service work. Time Dollars appeared as a way through the depressing wall of money shortages. They offer a channel for social idealism that has the growth dynamic of enterprise rather than the dead end of bureaucratized social service. "Once people get it they get very turned on by it," says Randolph of the Pacific Presbyterian Medical Center.

Nobody represents this better than Anna Miyares, who left a lucrative job as an international banker to become a banker in good works. Miyares is an intense and eloquent woman, who combines the love of freedom and enterprise of Miami's Cuban expatriate community, with a lyric social idealism. She runs the Miami Time Dollar program out of a cubbyhole office at the Little Havana Activities and Nutrition Center in Miami's old Cuban enclave. She has no secretary, no staff beyond a handful of Vista workers, and a commitment to the program—which she calls "an army of love and friendship and care"— that approaches a passion.

Miyares came naturally to banking, her father and grandfather having been bankers in Cuba. She rose quickly through the ranks; given a new branch in a Latino neighborhood in Elizabeth, New Jersey, she took a crash course in Portuguese and quickly pulled $15 million "out of mattresses," five times what her superiors expected. "I was used to suits and plush offices and all that," she says. "I was always a go-getter. But banking was not what I wanted to do." She studied psychology at night, thought of becoming a public defender, then decided she wanted to be a social worker. But she couldn't see taking time off for another degree.

Meanwhile, she had moved to Miami where her daughter was at the University of Miami. Between tuition and house payments and her daughter's new car, she had to continue at the bank.

That's where matters stood when, two months before her daughter's wedding, Miyares heard that Josefina Carbonell of Little Havana was looking for someone to run the Time Dollar program. She got a big pay cut, but a big boost in satisfaction. "I used to be a happy person," she says. "Then, as a banker I became a different person. So basically, I'm doing this because it gave me the opportunity to be myself, to do what I always wanted to do, with a program that has the potential of service credits.

"The money used to come and go for me. Now I have more friends than I had before. I used to wonder if people were friends just because they wanted me to arrange a loan."

THE ONE BIG NEED

Miyares started where any good banker would start—with market research. She read books on aging, interviewed a large number of participants. She found that retirees had many needs, but one big need: to feel included, to be part of something. To build this sense, she has organized the Time Dollar program so that each neighborhood or building is a self-contained unit, with its own leader.

"This Cuban is going to use a Communist word: nucleus. That's what they call in Cuba the neighborhood nucleus. We don't only care about the recipient; we have to take care of the service credit volunteers as well. We want to keep them together, keep them as a family. That's going back to the roots, where neighbor used to help neighbor, where neighbors used to trust neighbors, where your problem was shared with neighbors. That's what we try to maintain."

Miyares sees the new service credit economy blending with the larger economy, so as to reconcile the realms of community and work. Banks could underwrite and help manage these programs, for example, so people could bank their time and their money at the same place. Businesses could include service credits in employee benefits packages, providing not just security, but also a family feeling and an opportunity to serve. "There are so many ways, thousands and thousands of ways to make money for service credits. But I'm just one person."

There was a tense period a few years ago when a state grant ran out, and it was uncertain how the program would go on. "We decided that we were willing to continue the program if we had to work out of our homes. I was going to get a job at night. I was not afraid. We put too much heart into this. We have a commitment to the community. Service credits are going to continue, government or no government. It doesn't belong to the government. It belongs to the volunteers."

Miyares considers herself a Democrat, because Democrats traditionally try to make things easier for those at the bottom. But the Democrats also create bureaucracies, and Miyares is ardently anti-bureaucratic. "The money doesn't go to help people. It goes to pay huge salaries to create long waiting lines. If I have an agency and don't have a waiting list of three years, my funding may be cut." Time Dollars cut through such games. It is both an enterprise and a mission. "The day it becomes a regular social services agency, I will go back to being a banker, or homeless.

"Service credits are like a virus. They get into you and grow in you. I have become a human being again, recovered my identity. Why should I not work 80 hours a week? To me, this is not working. It is my extended family."

6
Why the Taxman Didn't Come

In 1830, John Marshall, then Chief Justice of the United States, decided that it was time, once and for all, to put Missouri out of the business of creating new kinds of money.

The case concerned a rather ingenious scheme that the state had dreamed up to meet its fiscal needs. Missouri had issued "salt certificates" in amounts ranging from 50 cents to $10, based on expected revenues from a state-owned salt springs. The state tried to characterize these as mere "salt coupons," like the ones people clip out of the Sunday papers today. After all, they were ultimately redeemable only in salt. In reality, however, the certificates circulated as money. And the governor was authorized to pledge the state's assets to acquire "a loan of silver or gold" in order to redeem these certificates.

This was not the first time that Missouri had engaged in a monetary experiment. Early in its history, the state had issued "wolf-scalp certificates" and "crow certificates" as rewards for killing wolves and crows in order to protect cattle herds and crops. The wolf-scalp and crow certificates were legal tender in Missouri for purposes of paying taxes.

Wolf scalps had escaped judicial scrutiny. But these salt certificates were more than Chief Justice Marshall, the great Federalist, could swallow. Marshall had authored the landmark decision of *Marbury vs. Madison*, declaring the Constitution, as interpreted by the Supreme Court, to be the final law of the land. He had reiterated that declaration in a series of other decisions. Having presided over the magnificent

75

edifice of federal supremacy, he was not about to let a puny state mock it with salt certificates.

The question of money was a touchy one to begin with in the early days of the Republic. The Continental Congress that drafted the old Articles of Confederation was run out of Philadelphia by soldiers who had fought under George Washington only to be paid by state governments in worthless IOUs. A major economic depression had resulted from precipitate drops in the value of money that state-chartered banks had issued. The Founding Fathers were understandably leery of paper money, especially when issued by states.

And so, speaking for the court, Marshall reminded the state of Missouri that Article I, Section 8 of the Constitution of the United States gives the Congress exclusive power "to coin money [and] regulate the value thereof."

MISSOURI LEADS THE WAY

One hundred and thirty-five years later, Missouri is at it again. In the mid-1980s, the state enacted a law to use Time Dollars to provide relief for people who take care of elderly family members at home. In a sense, Time Dollars are simply updated wolf-scalp or crow certificates—a way of paying citizens for performing a public service. So far, Missouri is the only state to commit its "full faith and credit" to the Time Dollar: if no Time Dollar participant is available to help a person who has earned this currency, the state will provide this help at its own expense.

This time, Missouri went even further. The passage of time has mooted Marshall's early decision: credit cards, state revenue bonds, any number of other devices, have rendered antique the notion that only the federal government can create money. That still leaves the Internal Revenue Service, however. In 1985, Missouri had the temerity to ask the agency to declare this money exempt from the federal income tax.

The IRS is not generally known for generosity where federal revenues are concerned. It is especially wary of basing exemptions on broad conceptual grounds, as opposed to narrow interpretations of the statute. Yet, the IRS has concluded that credits earned under the Missouri law will not be treated as taxable income. It did so not once but twice—first in a ruling by the regional office on a request from the state of

Missouri, the second time, in a "private ruling" by the national office in response to a request from a settlement house in St. Louis.

These rulings apply only to the particular cases involved and might not hold in different circumstances. But they are highly significant nevertheless. At a practical level, they help people designing Time Dollar programs to avoid entanglements with the IRS. (This has been a concern in some social service quarters.)

The reasoning behind the exemption is even more important. Examining Time Dollars through the exacting lens of federal tax law, the IRS lawyers saw some crucial differences between these and ordinary money that might elude the more casual mind. These differences, in turn, illuminate as well as anything that has come along the nature of the social bonds that the Time Dollar movement is seeking to rebuild.

The IRS rulings are all the more remarkable if we recall the economic climate of the early 1980s and the hostility of the IRS toward barter. Unemployment *and* inflation had both reached double digits. The economy was so low that some economists were calling it a depression. The Federal Reserve had moved to curb inflation by restricting the supply of money, thereby stifling the economy further. Federal spending on domestic programs was being slashed by a new president, Ronald Reagan. And the United States government was operating on a deficit of a mere $50 billion to $70 billion.

Back in the 1930s, when jobs and money were in short supply, many discovered barter to meet their needs. In the early 1980s, the middle class did the same. Paperbacks proliferated on drugstore counters carrying titles like *The Barter Way to Beat Inflation* and *How to Get on the Barter Bandwagon where CASH Is a Four-Letter Word*. Barter clubs arose in which members bought and sold services and wares through computerized exchange pools. Several national barter franchises prepared public offerings; Sears, Roebuck and Company created Sears World Trade specializing among other things in barter and countertrade. Magazine articles noted that nearly one-third of international trade was done using barter rather than currency.

THEN THE IRS WOKE UP

Much of this happened because the IRS was asleep to the issue. Then the agency woke up and spoiled the fun. New regulations expanded the definition of barter and required full disclosure of all such exchanges on one's annual tax return. Even worse, credits received through a barter network were determined to be taxable income *when received* rather than when spent. That is, if someone paid you 2,000 barter credits in exchange for your used car, you were taxed when the credits were added to your account, even if you had not spent them. That made good sense from an accounting standpoint. But it was terrible news to anyone who held nothing except some credits in a soon-to-be-defunct barter club.

Yet, despite its *jihad* against barter-based tax avoidance, the IRS made an exception for Time Dollars. In March 1985, the regional IRS office in St. Louis ruled that volunteers in the state program who qualified for hours of service by earning service credits would not be taxed on the value of those services. The ruling focused primarily on the charitable nature of the transaction and the public purpose it embodies. People who received these services from Time Dollar workers would have received them free from the state, anyway. This made the transaction fundamentally different from commercial barter, which is simply another form of a market transaction that might have occurred for cash.

Then in June 1985, the national office of IRS issued a "private letter" ruling regarding the Time Dollar program in St. Louis, which had been operating for several years. Grace Hill, a local settlement house, had been using Time Dollars to provide housekeeping and babysitting to residents of the community and also to provide more skilled services such as house painting. The computerized bookkeeping operated in the usual way. "When a volunteer performs a service," the ruling noted, the "taxpayer [Grace Hill] credits the hours spent to the volunteer's account and debits the hours to the service recipient's account."

Despite the obvious value of the services and the extensive record keeping involved, the IRS nonetheless concluded that these credits "have no monetary value," and service recipients do not incur a "contractual liability." The agency saw that these Time Dollars are fundamentally different from money. They provide recognition and a form of bonding, rather than a cash reward. "Credits posted to the volunteers' accounts serve merely as a means to motivate the volunteers," the IRS said. "The continued effectiveness of this taxpayers' program depends on the volunteers perceiving the value of their efforts to the community. Taxpayer hopes that knowledge of the hours they provide . . . will instill pride in the volunteers."

WHY TIME DOLLARS WEREN'T TAXED

The Time Dollar networks are different from commercial barter, the ruling said. They are simply a different form of the things neighbors do for one another. Commercial barter, by contrast, "does not include arrangements that provide solely for the informal exchange of similar services on a noncommercial basis." In commercial barter, the parties are bound by contract, and credits in a barter network are a "cash substitute." Here, by contrast, people who receive a service have no contractual—i.e., legal—obligation to repay. And people who give service get no contractual right to compensation: "The credits merely serve as a means to motivate the volunteers to continue their community service."

This ruling cut through a lot of academic fog that has grown up around the issue. A tax professor who authored one of the leading casebooks on federal taxation, for example, could not fathom how the IRS could deem Time Dollars not taxable. After all, he said, "benefit is benefit."

But the IRS did, and the practical importance of the ruling cannot be overstated. It is hard to imagine people lining up to volunteer, knowing that come April 15th, Uncle Sam was going to tax the Time Dollars they earned—even though they had gotten no money with which to pay those taxes. Even if the IRS valued the credits at only $5.00 per hour, a volunteer could easily owe several hundred dollars in taxes.

The conceptual basis of the rulings is even more important. The IRS went right to the heart of the difference between Time Dollars and money. The ruling that declared that these exchanges were not commercial barter implicitly recognized a distinction between the market and the nonmarket economy, with the important corollary that exchanges in the nonmarket economy are beyond the scope of the federal income tax laws. Not all exchanges among family members and neighbors are exempt, of course; certain trust arrangements between parents and children, for example, are blatant tax avoidance devices.

But the IRS did not see evidence of this in Missouri's Time Dollar program. It pointed out that, to the contrary, the care in question was charitable in motive and was openly reported to the state of Missouri. There was little danger that respite care syndicates would sweep the nation as a hot new form of tax avoidance.

TRUST RULES ALL EXPECTATIONS

The St. Louis ruling is even more impressive because it fleshes out a distinction that seems to elude most tax lawyers. The ruling noted that participants earning credits had no *contractual* rights to anything in exchange for their efforts. (The St. Louis program was not backed by the state.) Any expectations or increased sense of security people feel rests on their trust in the program, and particularly in their fellow members. They can't go to court to demand service from anyone, no matter how many Time Dollars they hold, because trust is all there is.

This goes to a fundamental difference between contractual obligations and dealings between friends and family. With the latter, legal rights are of limited use. You have to choose between asserting them and maintaining the underlying relationship. Resorting to the courts means you are asserting the rights of a stranger against strangers, and often, that you are operating in a context of monetary values rather than ones of trust.

Shimone Bergman, regarded as the "father" of gerontology in Israel, responded with a glimmer of recognition when he heard a description of Time Dollars. Perhaps one of the earliest precedents, he said, is found in the scriptural commandment: "Honor thy father and thy mother that thy days may be long upon the land which the Lord thy God giveth thee." Considering that Moses's followers would wander 40 years in the desert before being permitted to enter that land, the promised exchange was at best somewhat speculative in nature. A court would have thrown it out for want of mutuality or on any number of other grounds as altogether lacking in the requisite specificity.

Families and communities operate on a standard of reciprocity. That is a moral norm, not a legal one; the mechanism of enforcement is not the courts, but the sanctions that operate naturally between people. The person who takes and takes and takes becomes, at some point, like the child who cried "wolf" once too often. Anthropologists tell us that the ostracism practiced by "primitive" legal systems may be more powerful than the forms of punishment to which "civilized" society resorts when it puts miscreants in prison and turns them into polished criminals.

THE GUARANTEE: GOOD FAITH AND BEST EFFORT

Time Dollars draw from an ethical tradition, rather than the legal and commercial tradition that lies behind the Internal Revenue Code. The ethical norm was succinctly summed up centuries ago by Rabbi Ben Azzai, who said, "The reward of a good deed is a good deed." The only real guarantee is the good faith and best effort of the individuals and the organizations involved.

Indeed, there can be no "contractual remedy" that substitutes for membership in family and community. These provide a kind of all-purpose insurance and all-purpose safety net that no commercial company would underwrite and no government could afford. That is the measure of security we have lost; that is the measure of genuine security that Time Dollars seek to reestablish.

Income, said the IRS, belongs in the world of the market; altruism, empathy, and reciprocity belong to another world, which by and large is off-limits to the IRS. To be sure, IRS lawyers would warn that these regional rulings are not binding precedent. The possibility remains that as Time Dollar systems expand, and as the IRS feels continuing pressure to increase federal revenues to avert the need to raise tax rates, the agency could have a change of heart.

If the IRS really wants to decree that retirees will be taxed for driving their neighbors to the doctor, one is tempted to respond cheerily, "See you on Capitol Hill." But Congress wouldn't even have to act. This do-it-yourself currency even includes a do-it-yourself defense against the IRS.

People earning Time Dollars could simply give them to the tax-exempt membership organization sponsoring the program. They would, in effect be saying, we trust the norm of reciprocity more than the world of contract. Should we ever be in need, we would rather place our trust in each other.

If you, the IRS, insist on distorting what we are doing by perverting Time Dollars into a taxable quid pro quo transaction, then we willingly surrender any "contractual right" valued by the market mentality. That part we give of ourselves is not for sale. We have an inalienable right to the private world of family, of extended family, of community. We will render under Caesar, that which is Caesar's. But no more. There is another domain you may not touch.

7

The Health of Helping

It was a gamble for the producers of the "Phil Donahue Show," when they invited Ted Lawrence to appear on a program devoted to Time Dollars.

Lawrence is an 80-year-old man from rural central Michigan. Just seven months earlier, he had suffered the most devastating of a series of strokes. Now, with millions of Americans watching, Ted was fumbling to free himself from the brace that supported his chin and neck, while his daughter sat by his side and helped. (TV producers dread this kind of awkward silence.) Donahue leaned over in a kindly manner, trying to move the show along without putting undue pressure on his guest.

The audience held its collective breath. They were hanging on Ted's every grimace, hoping against hope that he would get through this with dignity. They strained to understand words that required great effort for Ted to get out. Somehow, through Ted's persistence and the help of his daughter, Jean, he managed to tell his story.

It was a heartwarming story, but it was also a great deal more. Ted Lawrence had come back this far from almost total incapacity, not just because of the care of others, but, just as important, because of his own desire to do something in return. A service program that stressed give and take—the need to be needed as well as the need for care—had created a condition of health.

Lawrence had been a librarian for Kirtland Community College in

Roscommon, Michigan. After retiring the previous year, he suffered the strokes and his life began collapsing on virtually every front. His wife was diagnosed as having bone cancer and died just over a year later, only weeks after Ted's worst stroke. He was alone. Ted's three children lived away from home: two sons in other parts of Michigan, and daughter, Jean, in New York, working in a courier business while she carried two other jobs part-time.

The last stroke had paralyzed Ted and left his speech severely impaired. Even now, after months of therapy, it was obvious that every word was a struggle. But the sheer intensity of Ted's desire to say his piece held Donahue riveted as the story continued.

A HEALTHY SIGN: SETTING A GOAL

Ted's daughter had returned to Michigan to stay with her father, and one day she noticed a story on the Time Dollar program in the local newspaper. She called to inquire, and not long afterward, the director, Carolyn Boone, came to the house. She asked Ted what he wanted most, having lost his wife, his mobility, and his speech. A single word came back: bridge.

Bridge is not a casual pastime to its devotees, but some groups gather regularly to play social bridge. Carolyn located such a group, which was willing to see if Ted could play.

The game does require some speech: Partners have to bid, declaring how many "tricks" they think they can make and what suit they designate as "trump." Mental agility is also required, of course.

Over and over, for days before his first games, Ted practiced the words he would need to bid and respond. When he actually succeeded, making the bids and then playing out each hand, it became a triumph. He played regularly. Meanwhile, helpers from the Time Dollar program came to visit, gave him rides to the bridge club, and spelled his daughter, who cared for him by day and worked nights at a local bakery.

Like most people who care for a disabled family member at home, Jean's life was not easy. She was struggling with a task for which there is no real preparation. "Nobody tells you anything," she said after the Donahue show. "You go to a class and they show you how to hold a wheelchair and they teach the patient how to get up after a fall. But what about when Daddy falls, and it isn't on a mat? And suppose he ends up in a crazy position that he can't get out of or he hits his head against a chair and blood starts spurting out. They don't tell you what to do about that!"

HOW CAN YOU REPAY KINDNESSES?

Neighbors were extremely helpful, Jean said. They would come and clear snow from the driveway or help out around the house. But the Lawrences couldn't impose on a regular basis. That is why the Time Dollar workers were so valuable. "You don't understand until you are overwhelmed," Jean said. "There is so much hard work to be done. How are you going to pay back your neighbors? It's an impossible situation."

The workers were Richard and Barbara Sweers, who were known as newcomers to the area—they had lived there only 16 years. (They said they joined the program because it was a way to get to know people.) The Sweers would take Ted into town—a big event—share music with him in the house, help him work on his conversation, or take him to the foot clinic.

At first they were volunteers for Hospice, an organization that helps cancer patients. When Mrs. Lawrence died, they learned they could switch over to the Time Dollar program and get credits for the hours they gave.

They might have been thinking of their own needs somewhere down the line. Mrs. Sweers was now unable to drive, and Mr. Sweers's memory was beginning to fail. He would go into the local drugstore to get a hot dog, and come out again, having forgotten what his companion wanted on it, or what he was supposed to get in the first place. By helping Ted Lawrence, they were also building up security for themselves.

"One good deed begets another," Rabbi Azzai observed. This is the growth dynamic of Time Dollar programs; and Ted Lawrence showed that the *desire* to reciprocate can be a powerful motive for recovery. He was determined to do something in return for the help he received toward physical improvement. So he went back to the Kirtland Community College library where he used to work and organized an entire resource center for caregivers. He catalogued the books and other materials; he set up a statewide lending exchange with other libraries; he even organized an 800-number call-in service available to any caregiver in the state.

The Connie Binsfeld Resource Center was named for the state senator who had sponsored the Michigan Time Dollar legislation and was subsequently elected Lieutenant Governor. On the day of the dedication ceremonies, Ted Lawrence got out of his wheelchair, walked haltingly to the podium and, thanks to hours of practice and rehearsal, presented the dedication to the senator in person—in his own words.

That was perhaps the proudest day of his life. At least until that January day when Phil Donahue listened in absolute amazement while Ted told his story to 20 million people. When he was through, Donahue had a question. "When this all happened, did you think, did you ever think that you would be here appearing on . . . "—pause, while Donahue realized what he was about to say—". . . appearing on—of all things—a national *talk* show?"

The camera focused in on Ted as he turned awkwardly toward his daughter. His eyes were moist, his mouth cracked upward in delight. Not a sound came out, just a beatific grin that spread slowly over his face. It was a moment of moments.

GIVING IS RECEIVING

Ted Lawrence's progress from invalid to inspiration illustrates a fundamental shift in thinking about disease and health. In contradiction to the old medical view that the body is a mechanism, essentially separate from a person's inner life, new evidence strongly suggests that the body is deeply influenced by the mind and the emotions. That means people participate in their own healing in ways not appreciated before. One of those ways is by being involved in relationships of trust and care.

Giving unto others is, literally, giving unto yourself *and* others. A team from the University of Michigan Survey Research Center documented this in a ten-year study of 2,700 people in Tecumseh, Michigan, a town of 7,000 in the southeastern portion of the state. The study showed that people who volunteer live longer than others, and that is especially true of men. Numerous other studies have reached a similar conclusion.

Such results mesh with a centuries-old tradition holding that one way out of illness lies in thinking less about yourself. At Lourdes, a place of religious pilgrimage and healing in France, the emphasis is on self-forgetfulness and devotion to the welfare of others. The pilgrims pray for the sick and for each other, not themselves. Members of a certain Japanese religious group "stand facing each other and pray that one another's unhappiness will diminish."

Many of today's most respected medical experts make use of similar measures in their therapy. For example, Dean Ornish, M.D., an internist at the University of California, San Francisco School of Medicine, teaches heart patients to deal with their hostility as part of their treatment. He once had two patients who disliked one another do each other's laundry. In other words, to help a bad heart, do something that reflects a good heart. Ornish reports that such endeavors help reduce cholesterol levels and minimize chest pains.

No one knows exactly how, but people are actually more able to resist disease when they feel good about themselves, and in particular, when they are involved in helping others.

There is a growing medical lore of patients, like the late Norman Cousins, who overcome life-threatening diseases essentially by rejecting depression and sharing human contact and laughter. The most significant findings concern the role of social affinity in this healing effect. People do better when they act more like friends.

IS OUR ECONOMY TOXIC?

Seen in this light, an economy that turns neighbors into strangers and that dries up the channels of daily helpfulness and sharing, becomes doubly toxic. It doesn't just invite social problems like drugs and crime, it also becomes a breeding ground for disease. Building community means building health, because a community is the natural setting for thinking about others.

Research has shown that the sense of social connection can be even more important than the purely physical factors with which the nation is obsessed. In her book *Minding the Body, Mending the Mind*, Joan

Borysenko, M.D., director of the Mind/Body Clinic at the Harvard Medical School, cites the case of Roseto, a small town in Pennsylvania, noted for its remarkably low rate of heart disease. Researchers attracted there to find the source of this good health expected to find a community where people did aerobics at 6:00 A.M. and had broccoli for lunch. What they found was something totally different.

The health habits of the Rosetans, from a medical standpoint, were "terrible," Dr. Borysenko writes. "It turned out that their protective factor was actually the social fabric of the community. The extended family was alive and well. People tended to stay within Roseto, and so there was a great deal of closeness. People knew one another, their family histories, their joys and sorrows. In Roseto, there were plenty of people to listen and to lend a hand when needed."

Perhaps the most revealing finding concerned the people who moved away from Roseto: The rate of heart attack among them increased. "Social support, the great stress buffer, turned out to be more important than health habits in predicting heart disease."

It is significant that the qualities of money, discussed in chapter 3, are associated in the above passage with disease. A medium of exchange that exhalts mobility over cohesion, and that turns things people do for one another into things they buy, is literally a medium that cuts people off from the sources of their own health. The *doing* is an ingredient of the thing itself; and Time Dollar programs, by countering the isolating pathologies of money, tend to restore the conditions of neighborly doing and therefore of health. Strangers become neighbors, and the dynamic of a Roseto, Pennsylvania, begins to take hold.

This is one reason that community-based hospitals and care programs embrace the Time Dollar program with such enthusiasm. It establishes conditions in which both givers and recipients can feel good. An example is Avis Rhodes, the member of Elderplan in Brooklyn who was introduced in chapter 4. Rhodes gave a talk to new Elderplan members in which she spoke of the rewards of her work. "It's like going out there and seeing a wounded bird," she said in her lyric Jamaican patois. "You pick it up and nurse its wounds. You see it get well and let it go and it flies. . . . Sometimes even just touching somebody, to let her know you are there, and to see the smile on her face when you take her hand and hold it—it's such a light."

Such experiences are among the reasons Elderplan lets members pay part of their premiums in Time Dollars. Much as people who give up smoking become better insurance risks, so people who help others—and become part of a community of helping—are more likely to stay healthy than people who live isolated and alone. Moreover, this form of fitness has a bonus: In helping themselves, the Time Dollar members are helping someone else as well.

WHEN LIFE LACKS PURPOSE

Many psychiatrists are moving toward a broader view of the inner life; helping and caring, far from denying our basic nature, actually respond to deep human needs. Viktor Frankl, M.D., a well-known author as well as a psychiatrist, has been a pioneer in this work. He points out that psychiatrists today deal increasingly with complaints of lack of meaning and purpose. The great need, he says, is for greater engagement with and caring for things outside the self. "What people need is not freedom from suffering," wrote Washington, D.C., writer Colman McCarthy, paraphrasing Frankl, "but something to suffer for."

Time Dollar workers tend to follow this prescription. They deal with their own problems in part by taking on those of others. "Many of our volunteers are very sick themselves," says Mashi Blech, director of the Elderplan program. "They tell me that keeping themselves busy, they feel better."

One could be Herbie Fine, walking on swollen feet to visit his friend Hyman Goldwasser to make sure the 95-year-old has what he needs (see chapter 4). Or the woman at the VIP program in San Francisco, who insists on helping to clear the tables after the seniors' lunch, even though she is so ill she can barely finish clearing one. Then, too, there's Betty Little, a member of the Washington, D.C., program, which is sponsored by the Southeast Community Hospital there.

Little is a warm and soothing woman, with a cheery manner and a voice suggestive of homey things. She spends virtually all her time in helping work. She teaches an adult literacy course for retirees. She volunteers at another D.C. hospital, finding nursing homes for elderly patients. She also writes letters for a woman who is blind.

You would never guess that Little is battling a host of diseases that forced her to retire at an early age. Or that she bustles about on an artificial leg. "I need to know I'm doing something to help," she says. "Him to whom much is given, from him much is expected."

Little grew up in a close inner-city neighborhood in Buffalo, New York, where the kids on the street were like "family." When she was 11, she recalls, her mother came home from work one day in tears. Her grandmother, whom they called Babe, had been diagnosed as having cancer. "Bring her home," her father said. So Babe moved into the girls' room; Betty and her sister slept on sofa beds.

Little speaks proudly of a daughter who "gives from sacrifice instead of from excess." She worries about the decline of the principle of giving up the bed for Babe. Government programs were part of it, she thinks. But the main villain is the thing America has most avidly pursued. "I think affluence rubs it out," she says. "It is very difficult to be affluent and be a laying-on-of-hands person. If you are a delegator in your work, you are not comfortable doing the job yourself.

"It is taxing but it is a natural tax, the tax of living," Little says. "How do you live with yourself if you don't contribute?"

LEARNING AND TEACHING AND WORKING FOR THE LORD

One of the students in Little's literacy class is Rev. Emerson Pittman, who left a job delivering bricks about ten years ago to devote full time to preaching. Pittman grew up in North Carolina, never learned to read, memorized the bible passages he preached on weekends. "Back when I was born, the white man would say, 'I want him to work,' so I went out there to work in the field," Pittman says. "I couldn't go to school." So now he's learning under Little and "paying" by providing transportation for homebound seniors.

Pittman came to Washington in 1939, at a time when people were not making a dollar a day on the farm. He got odd jobs and went into the service, after which he drove the brick truck for 38 years. By his own admission he was a "free liver"; but he went to church one Sunday and felt something different. "The Lord just called me," he recalls. "I didn't want Him, but he called. Everything I did wasn't right until I responded to His word." A few years later, Pittman was driving the truck from Virginia into Maryland, when the next thing he knew he was waking up in a hospital room with a broken shoulder and wrist. "The Lord told me to get off that truck. I said, 'I got bills to pay.' But I've been doing better ever since."

Elder Pittman, as people call him, is lean and angular, with the slightly stiff movements of a man who spent almost four decades hauling bricks. His face is unlined, except for a touch of tiredness around the eyes, and his voice has a soothing country timbre although whole sentences can disappear in quick aural glides. The New Born Church of God in the Spirit of Christ is an independent church, founded in 1959, and Pittman sees it as full-time missionary work. He drives the church van around the city, picking up homeless people, and feeding them dinner in the church kitchen, where the rear seat from an old van serves as seating.

He recounts these episodes in the rhythms of the Gospels. "One young man, he asked for money. I told him I don't have no money, I have Jesus. He said, 'I don't have no car.' I said, 'I'll pick you up.' He said, 'I don't have no clothes.' I said, 'Come as you are.' From that day up to now he done never looked back."

Pittman's church schedule would seem grueling to most people. He teaches Sunday school at 10:00 A.M., conducts the service at 11:45, then holds a fellowship that evening. He teaches bible class on Tuesday night, and holds another service on Friday night as well. "The more you go, the more you want to go," Pittman says. "It makes you feel better."

In the Time Dollar program, Pittman drives people to regular doctor visits in his big Mercury with a spongy ride. His first "customer," as he puts it, was a white man and his wife; the man had suffered a heart attack, and Pittman drove the wife to the hospital to visit. "I went over there early, and we had a prayer session before we went," he says. "He came out of it and he's doing okay now."

In return, Pittman has security for the future. Plus the reading classes, which have helped him read the Bible—he used to memorize the verses—plus he's writing checks now for the first time in his life. His current aim is to get his high school equivalency diploma. "I'm going all the way," he says.

The thing Pittman likes about Time Dollars is that people can ask for help without asking for charity. "In service credits, they call when they want help because they've been doing it for others," he says. He's thinking of starting a program in his church. And he'd like it to grow far beyond that. "I'd like it to be world wide," he says. "I'd like for it to be *known*, like the Word of God."

The other teacher in the literacy class is a woman named Ada Poole, who used to go to church with Elder Pittman at the New Born Church of God. ("We grew up in the Lord together" is how she puts it.) In 1982, Poole and her husband moved from Maryland to Anacostia, in the remote southeast section of D.C., where they decided to start a congregation. They met for a number of years in their living room, and the congregation grew slowly until they got their own building last year.

Poole is a handsome woman who projects a quiet sense of dignity and poise. She has an autistic daughter, and caring for her can be a grueling, endless job. Family members come by to help, but when the daughter has a problem at 2:00 A.M., "It's one on one," as Poole puts it. The D.C. government provides no help for autistics over 21, except to take them away from their parents and put them in special homes.

ADA KEEPS THE OLD WAY ALIVE

Ada Poole was on a special advisory committee to the D.C. mayor, and she has in mind a service credit program for parents of autistic children, in which parents would take in one another's children for a weekend, to give each other some relief. "I like the sharing," she says of the service credit idea. "Credits are a form of sharing, back and forth. You write me a letter, and I bake you a cake." That's how they did it on the farm in North Carolina where Poole, like Elder Pittman, grew up. "There was no such thing as service credits," she recalls. "You just helped one another. Somebody had a cancer, a dreaded disease, if it was a woman, the women kept house, took care of the kids, washed and ironed and did all that. You took food over, whatever was necessary."

Despite her own problems, Poole tries to keep that old way alive. She joined Betty Little in teaching the literacy class, at the urging of Elder Pittman. She never finished high school, and only has a G.E.D.

degree. But she took a special course at a community college, and now she's teaching. Like Little, she gives her service credits back to the program. "As much as I have, I can give," she says.

One Monday in December, Poole was teaching the class alone because Little was ill again. The class is supposed to start at 10:00 A.M., but it is 10:15 before the students start drifting in. There are three of them, two men and a woman, all retired. Elder Pittman came in last. He was "fellowshipping" with the older folks who pass the day in the lobby. (The class is held in a special nursing home for seniors.) Pittman was on the Peter Jennings show the night before, a segment about Time Dollars. He seems to be enjoying the celebrity status but not taking it too seriously.

Poole begins the class with easy banter. "How are you, Brother Wood?" she says, "Who preached yesterday?" She has an air of calm authority; and the students—all retirees—seem almost like third graders as they hunch over their workbooks, chewing the ends of their pencils. The lesson proceeds in methodical fashion. There is no flashy technique, just following the workbook, lesson by lesson. "In the country, they don't teach like this," Pittman says.

When the class is over, Poole has to hurry home to fix dinner for her daughter. And wash the dishes in the sink. And make the beds. But before the class breaks up, she reminds the class that Little isn't well. "We can pray for her this week," she says.

TED KEEPS CONTRIBUTING

The day after the Donahue show, a picture of Ted Lawrence and Donahue appeared in a four-column photograph in the local newspaper, under a banner headline that proclaimed: "National Talk Show Host Says 'You're My Hero.' " Lawrence has become a local celebrity, but he isn't resting on his laurels. He speaks (!!) to church and civic groups in the area, running a tape of the show and recruiting new Time Dollar workers. He's taken on more volunteer work as well. He orders books for the library, after perusing the book reviews. He also visits an 82-year-old man who was injured in an automobile crash.

There is sad news, too. Due to state and federal budget cuts, the heated pool where Lawrence took therapy is slated for closing as this is written. He will now have to drive to Traverse City, which is 1½ hours away. The Connie Binsfeld Resource Center is open; but it isn't used as much as it should be because there is no money in the budget for special staff.

But the Sweers still visit Lawrence once a week. And Jean Lawrence has joined the service credit program, too, taking care of a mentally impaired person as well as her father. One of her brothers, who lives downstate, is doing volunteer work, too; and he may be able to earn credits which he could then give to his father through the Michigan state program. It would be a kind of long-distance time share. Ted Lawrence's son would help someone else's parent in his own community, and someone in Roscommon would help Ted Lawrence in return. "That's such a right-on idea," Jean says.

Both Jean and Ted agree that Ted might be in a nursing home but for the Time Dollar program. Getting him into the bridge club was especially important. "It gave me a social acceptance," Lawrence says. "It was the first group I had been with after the stroke." Lawrence has become a celebrity there, too, but for another reason. He's gotten so good at bridge, everybody wants him as a partner.

8

Florida I: How the Bureaucracy Almost Killed Time Dollars

In 1987, the state of Florida issued an official evaluation of the Time Dollar program enacted by the legislature in 1985. It had not worked, said the state, and could not work, at least as enacted.

Florida officials offered a variety of explanations for their conclusion. Some referred to defects in the legislation, some to issues of implementation. But they boiled down to one thing: a belief that ordinary people aren't up to the task of taking care of others. "Volunteers," the report stated solemnly, "are least suited to the types of services required for [Time Dollar programs], specifically personal care, homemaker, health support, and in-home services in general."

The main evidence for this conclusion was a survey of old-line social service agencies; these insisted, not surprisingly, that only paid social workers were "suited" for such technical tasks as helping a frail person clean house. "Volunteers are best suited for indirect services and those that do not require a regular schedule," the state report concluded.

It was a curious proposition. For generations, friends and neighbors—volunteers, if you will—have been helping the elderly in their homes. They have cleaned around the house, made sure the medicine was taken and the bills were paid—tasks social workers call in-home services. The proposition was especially curious because, at the very time Florida was declaring the Time Dollar program dead, it was growing elsewhere. Two states, Missouri and Michigan, had initiated highly successful Time Dollar programs. The Robert Wood Johnson Foundation had just sunk $1.2 million in funding six demonstration programs.

On top of this, the Miami program that was the subject of the state's obituary was already springing back to life, through the combined efforts of Cuban, black, and Jewish groups. Since the state wasn't interested, these groups decided to do it themselves—even though they did not exactly have a reputation for harmonious cooperation in that racially divided city.

IT'S ALL A MATTER OF ATTITUDE

How could the experts at the Florida Office on Aging have so totally missed the boat? The real reason they concluded that service credit programs can't work is that the state Office on Aging had never *tried* the concept, had never even seen it in practice. It was supposed to have done so. The state legislature had directed the Office on Aging to conduct such an experiment. But it didn't. Instead, this agency spent an entire year dredging up one bureaucratic obstacle after another against Time Dollars. Then, it wrote a report telling the legislature why the idea wouldn't have worked, even if it had been tried.

Where others saw promise, the Office on Aging saw potential liability and risk. The agency fixated on legitimate concerns—the need to provide some form of insurance for participants, for example, and the importance of screening out unsuitable volunteers—and blew these up into insurmountable obstacles. The office became especially preoccupied with a provision in the law that required the department to do its utmost to ensure that whatever Time Dollars were earned while helping others would be honored when people went to spend them. A concern, yes, but one that could have been resolved, given a desire to do so.

There is nothing in the genetic coding of bureaucrats or professionals that makes them respond in this manner. In Michigan and Missouri, enlightened state officials saw both the potential in Time Dollars and the need to protect the program during its early phases from the stultifying forces of bureaucracy. Florida, by contrast, is a test-tube case of bureaucratized benevolence, acting as an obstacle to community building and social change.

The governmental effort in Florida offers a classic example of how even a simple concept can be derailed by a combination of bureaucratic, legal, and professional biases. The story is instructive on several levels. For one, it provides a textbook for those who desire to start Time Dollar programs, showing the obstacles they may meet from hostile public officials. This in turn offers an important lesson in why mainstream assumptions have frequently run aground over the last two decades. Since the New Deal, a central premise of political debate has been that enlightenment lies at the center, and that social progress results from programs conceived by experts there. But the Time Dollar story in Florida shows how centralized social service can become a negative force, blocking new ideas that recognize that individuals and communities can do things for themselves.

MEET THE "MIDDLE" MIAMI

There are two Miamis that sit together uneasily in America's consciousness. One is the teeming den of drug smugglers and racial tensions and anti-Castro intrigues, the city whose most famous journalist is a crime reporter. The other Miami is the retirement Shangri-la of golf carts and condos and daily calls to Merrill Lynch. Somewhere between the two is the city that most Miami residents actually dwell in. The ghetto areas are southern and outwardly peaceable; but the drug problem is so bad that seniors in some neighborhoods don't plant flowers any more for fear they'll be stolen and sold for crack.

There are wealthy retirees, but many poor ones, too. Even on Miami Beach, elderly whites live on social security, in buildings where the stucco is cracked and the air conditioners make a racket throughout the day.

Florida has the nation's largest concentration of old people and therefore a legion of problems that go along with aging. The problems are worse because so many residents have migrated from elsewhere, and, lacking close family, are highly dependent on service agencies and the state. Yet Florida ranks last in social spending, and the mere mention of a state income tax is political self-immolation.

During the Reagan years, the space on the graph between needs and resources was getting even bigger. The legislature enacted a sales tax on professional services—if the state taxes car batteries and shoes, why not advertising agency fees? But professionals went berserk, the tax was repealed, and the needs kept growing. In 1985, Florida spent over $400 million in Medicaid funds to keep elderly people in nursing homes. By 2000, that figure is expected to exceed $2 billion, and the number of people with disabling chronic illness is expected to grow by more than 200 percent. The state was emerging as a kind of test case for the nation. "By carefully watching what is happening now in Florida," John Naisbitt wrote in the popular book *Megatrends*, "we stand to learn a wealth of information about the problems and opportunities the whole nation will face in the future."

Too many seniors, not enough money. With the whole population getting older, there was no way out of the dilemma—unless one started to question the terms: that resources are defined exclusively by money, that money is the only way to activate time, and that aging people have nothing to offer, only needs to be met. One who did question those assumptions was Carrie Meek, the state's first female black senator. "When I heard of service credits, I thought, 'This is really something,'" Meek says. "I had experienced other forms of volunteerism but none of it paid back the individual."

That was especially important in Miami's minority community because there isn't an affluent class of "givers" who can spend their days in settlement houses for free. All have needs. "Many of them are so poor, and the times are so hard, the only way they can exist is by sharing. I could see this [Time Dollars] as a very good opportunity, especially for older people," Senator Meek says.

LIKE WASHINGTON'S PICTURE

The question was where to start. Money systems aren't something people launch every day, and there was no experience to draw from, no tracks in the sand. It seemed important to get the state government involved. This would diminish the play-money aura of a new currency, and would give it gravity, like George Washington's picture on a dollar bill. For seniors, the backing of the state would trigger associations with World War II, when civilians got recognition for volunteer work. And shouldn't the state embrace with open arms an idea that would cost so little and could eventually save the taxpayers so much?

Supporters drafted a simple bill that basically called for a one-year experiment, sponsored by the Florida Department of Health and Rehabilitation Services, or DHR. Prospects seemed good. One lead sponsor was Senator Roberta Fox, a former Legal Services attorney who represented a portion of Miami; Senator Fox chaired the appropriations subcommittee that controlled the DHR budget. Senator Meek was another prime sponsor. The bill also had the backing of Josefina Carbonell, head of Little Havana, which is a senior center in Miami's Cuban district. Popular wisdom had it that Little Havana could deliver a voting block of upwards of 20,000 elderly Cubans, plus their children and grandchildren and in-laws and acquaintances.

In the legislature, Time Dollars appealed to conservatives and liberals alike. "This is the first good idea you've had since you've been in the Senate," one conservative colleague told Senator Fox after she introduced the service credit bill. The bill passed nearly unanimously, with strong support from both parties, on May 30, 1985. Two days later, the legislators went home, as Florida law stipulates. The service credit program was now in the hands of Margaret Lynn Duggar, the head of the Florida Office on Aging.

SERVICE CREDITS AND SELF-HELP — WHAT'S NEXT?

Florida's aging population has spawned a sizable infrastructure of agencies that dispense public monies for the aging, and these have become a political force in the state. Duggar was a career public employee and a product of this expanding hierarchy. It was a measure of her political base that she was one of only two senior officials to keep their posts when Republican Bob Martinez succeeded Democrat Bob Graham as governor in 1986.

Duggar is an imposing woman in her early fifties. Her dedication to helping seniors was never at issue. But as a product of the professional service culture, her main interest lay in expanding the network that was her political base. The department's legislative pitch that year was for more *paid* services to the homebound elderly and also for more institutional care. In this context, service credits and self-help were inconvenient thoughts at best. At some unspoken level, they could be positively unsettling; if retired grandparents really could do things that public employees do, then who knows where that might lead.

Besides, the Time Dollar concept was just a nuisance. It didn't fit any of the existing bureaucratic forms or procedures. And Duggar was just a bit peeved that the legislature would foist this "crazy, off-the-wall" idea—as she once put it—on her without her expert counsel. "When I sponsored the bill, I got a real cold reception from HRS," Senator Meek recalls. "They saw this thing as another level of work."

At first, the department tried to stymie the bill with a fiscal impact statement designed to make the legislature choke. Two hundred and fifty thousand dollars for a sprawling, computerized, statewide network, they said. Senator Fox didn't buy that, however; and the department couldn't openly oppose the bill, because Senator Fox controlled its budget. But once the legislation passed on May 30, 1985, the next to last day of the 1985 session, the legislature went home, not to reconvene until the following April. Duggar then had the field to herself and the bureaucratic impediments began to issue forth.

ALL IN THE NAME OF UNIFORMITY

It was all high-minded, all by the managerial book. Needs tests, for example, are an exemplary professional concern reflecting an awareness of the importance of prudent fiscal management. One couldn't have housebound seniors getting free rides to the doctor's office if they didn't meet the official criteria of need. To prevent such potentially outrageous acts of helpfulness, anybody seeking to spend a Time Dollar would have to fill out a 10-page "standardized instrument" with over 30 pages of instructions. It was the same form used to determine eligibility for state-subsidized nursing homes.

Then there was the matter of records, the agency's home turf. In the name of uniformity, the bureaucrats required that any computerized records of credits and debits in the time banks would have to be part of the state's massive Medicaid/Medicare Management Information System. That system was known as the great black hole of data. And obviously, if the time banks developed their own computer programs, they would have to run on the department's quirky computer system.

Other offices within the department inadvertently joined the cause. The state office of volunteer services, for example. How could it tolerate a new volunteer program not under its own jurisdiction? It was a question of principle, of appropriate jurisdiction, even if barely $50,000 was at stake. Having lost a fight to administer the program, the office attacked it. First, it questioned characterization of the program as a volunteer program since the participants were "paid." Next, it insisted that since this was a volunteer program, all regulations and procedures applicable to volunteers at state agencies must be applied to Time Dollar volunteers—even if the volunteer worked with a grass-roots community organization.

That sounds innocuous enough—until you get down to details. All volunteers to state agencies have to be covered by workmen's compensation; mere volunteer insurance, which is standard in private charities, was not enough. The state could readily secure workmen's comp coverage from its own insurers. But the small grass-roots agency in Miami designated to run the first pilot program could not. In insurance parlance, there was no "experience rating" for Time Dollar volunteers. That is, since there had never been Time Dollar volunteers before, private insurance companies had no statistics from which to calculate the risks of, say, helping a blind woman read letters from her children.

Not to mention the risk to the blind woman. What if the retiree reading the letters turned out to be a sexual pervert? Suppose a reader began sticking silverware into her pocketbook on the way out? Professional advocates for seniors had fought for years to protect the elderly from abuse in nursing homes. The legislature had just wrestled with the problem of child abuse in a notorious child care program. In this atmosphere, the specter of frail old folks falling prey to criminal elements among their peers was enough to spook the well-intentioned advocates. The "responsible" answer for any true professional was clear: require a full criminal reference check for volunteers.

The paperwork was growing. Had the department been assigned to invent the family, the procedures would have exceeded the entire Code of Federal Regulations, with further studies pending.

PROTECTING AGAINST A RUN ON THE BANK

There was still the thorny question of the credits themselves, and what they represented. To the bureaucracy, the credits building up in Time Dollar accounts were claims against the state, not unlike the claim that holders of dollar bills have against the Federal Treasury. Another specter loomed: a run on the bank, with angry seniors storming the capitol in Tallahassee to demand rides to the supermarket in payment of their Time Dollar accounts.

This was a valid concern, but one the bureaucratic mind can inflate to bizarre proportions. Leave aside the moment of truth that would occur if every holder of a dollar bill were to demand payment from the Treasury. The vast majority of service credit volunteers think about Time Dollars differently than they think about regular money; the new currency is closer to the relations involved in family and community, than to those of money and contract. Participants see the time bank as a vehicle for the kind of natural reciprocity one expects when doing a favor for a friend, rather than something legally owed. They think more about the good feelings they get from working in the program than what they might get out of it.

There are a variety of ways the state could have protected itself against the hypothetical run on the bank, especially during a one-year trial. In Miami, for example, one private company that provides home care agreed to donate free time to the time bank, as a goodwill gesture. In Missouri, the legislature had decided that the problem was minor, considering the money the state would save by enlisting volunteers to do this important work.

But the Florida department seemed more interested in consigning the proposal to the legislative purgatory called Can of Worms. Its solution came straight from the chapter in the bureaucratic warfare text called You want it, you'll get it. In order to "honor" the guarantee, service credit volunteers would be empowered to "bump" seniors who had been on waiting lists for services for months or even years. The arthritic widower, confined to a wheelchair, who had been waiting patiently for a half-day of housekeeping help for over a year, would have to step back in line while a 65-year-old marathon runner and service credit volunteer got the housekeeping help instead. It probably would never happen. But the mere specter was enough.

Problems like these require much study and deliberation, of course. The law was supposed to take effect five months after enactment, on October 30th. But a director wasn't hired until December, and even then it was an old friend of Duggar's, with no experience in normal bureaucratic thickets, let alone the ones that sprung up around this program.

Then, in February, Duggar established an advisory committee, composed primarily of HRS employees and others presumably cold to Time Dollars. Duggar's objective was to get this group to give its blessings to the regulations and procedures that would ultimately do the program in, thereby spreading the blame for the program's hoped-for demise. But at the very first meeting, things began drifting in an unexpected direction. Even HRS employees were interested in the idea, wondering aloud why there had to be so much red tape. Was it really necessary to have a ten-page needs assessment? Should they really use the clunky state computer system? Before the first session was over, Duggar announced that the group would not meet again. Something to do with state regulations authorizing advisory groups.

By now the legislature was about to come back in session, and a show of movement was important. Duggar decided her best bet was to bestow some money and the whole troublesome issue on Little Havana, a critical constituency of Senator Fox, the legislator she most needed to appease. But Duggar hadn't reckoned on Josefina Carbonell, the executive director of Little Havana.

Carbonell is an exceptional individual, a female authority figure in a macho culture who has survived Miami's ethnic turf wars with a seasoned idealism and a vision that extends beyond getting a bigger share of the budgetary pie. Carbonell had been using volunteers to help run her hot meals program for seniors, and the state bureaucracy was giving her a hard time. Her per-unit cost was much lower than that of other groups, and she wasn't spending all the money allotted. This caused the bureaucracy to balk. "The tradition has been with government-funded programs to ask for more than you really need, and then to try to spend every damn cent," she observed. "If you send money back, it's a no-no. You just don't get rewarded for being efficient."

SHE REFUSED TO PLAY THE GAME

Carbonell had seized upon the idea of service credits as a way to encourage more volunteering and replicate the traditional extended family culture of Latin communities. "Everyone kept saying it was not going to work, when I was so confident from day one," she recalled. "This is part of our culture, the one-to-one helping." Carbonell had visions of bringing schools, churches— the whole community—into a service web. She wanted to bridge the destructive gulf between Hispanics, blacks, and Jews; she was tired of the bureaucracy's attitude toward volunteers, and she wasn't about to be a pawn in two-bit power games. "All of us were committed to make [service credits] work in a tri-ethnic community," she said.

Rather than tolerate the ethnic war that Duggar's favoritism would have predictably triggered, Carbonell had helped form an alliance that presented itself as a single applicant. Duggar ignored the request and bestowed the grant on Little Havana anyway, with as much fanfare as possible for a low-visibility issue.

Then Carbonell did something one just doesn't do in Florida politics, or anywhere else for that matter. She flew to Tallahassee and told Duggar, to her face, that she wouldn't take the money. The alliance had designated one of its members, a group called the North Miami Foundation, which served white blue-collar retirees, as the lead agency to initiate the program, and the money should go to them directly—if it could not go to the entire consortium. If Duggar didn't like it, moreover, then Carbonell would take up the matter with Senator Fox, whose office was a short walk away. Moreover, the North Miami Foundation just happened to be in the district of Representative Elaine Gordon, acting Speaker of the House. Representative Gordon would hear about the matter, too.

MORE HURDLES TO JUMP

Duggar backed down, and the foundation was designated to get the money. But not right away. First came the regulations—the criminal record check, for example. The North Miami Foundation ran a program in which youths charged with minor offenses served alternative sentences through community service. They cleaned yards, painted dilapidated houses and the like; the department's insistence on police investigations would have stigmatized these volunteers. North Miami said it would make its own judgments, and the state backed down. But more time had been lost.

Then came a battle over use of the state's computer system. Not only was it a loser, but the department wanted to put service credit volunteers into the state's Medicaid tracking system, with full disclosure of assets and the like. North Miami countered that this would violate the privacy of service credit participants and why should it use a computer system from which it was almost impossible to retrieve useful data. The state backed down again—but the clock was still ticking.

Workmen's compensation insurance proved more difficult. Clearly, the service credit volunteers weren't state employees. But the department's General Counsel ruled that an obscure cross-reference in the service credit law meant that workmen's compensation coverage would be required. Private insurance was too expensive, for reasons already mentioned. With no way around that requirement, the North Miami Foundation had to end a long relationship with its own insurance agent to get into the state plan.

This caused great pain and turmoil within the organization. But the foundation doggedly kept trying to play by the rules. Finally, in late May, a year after the law had been enacted, the North Miami Foundation got official notice that it had been approved as a site under the service credit law. A check for the grand total of $3,000 would soon be forthcoming (out of an appropriation of $50,000, most of which went to producing red tape). The North Miami Foundation itself had spent some $20,000 out of its own pocket already.

Oh. One more thing. The fiscal year would be over in five weeks, on June 30, 1986. Within that time, the foundation would have to run the program and file an interim report and a final report. The state wouldn't carry over any credits earned past June 30, when the initial budget appropriation ended; Duggar wouldn't even recognize the foundation as a pilot project after that date.

The foundation didn't want more money. It just wanted the official designation, for the sake of the credibility of the program. The legislature had given the department a nice increase in budget and staff positions for the coming year. All the personnel who had so inventively frustrated the service credit effort were still on board. But Duggar was going by the book again. The agency had no specific authority from the legislature to continue to monitor the program. So sorry.

In September, at last, the department issued final regulations for the Time Dollar program. It had even found an answer to the run-on-the-bank problem: The state would stand behind the service credits by recruiting younger volunteers to provide those services earned and needed if Time Dollar workers were not available. It was a nice idea. The only problem, of course, was that the program no longer existed.

RULE ONE: NEVER GIVE MONEY BACK

That was the end of service credits in Florida, round one at least. Except for one last thing. The agency still hadn't spent the entire $50,000 appropriated in the previous year. The first rule of bureaucratic management is never give money back. This raises suspicions among legislators that they are giving you too much to begin with.

So Duggar went to the second rule, which is, "Don't do—study and evaluate." Nothing gets the juices going among social work professionals like the opportunity to study and evaluate. It is the chance to put their professional training on stage—to show their powers to discern problems requiring further study, issues that cannot be decided given the existing data. From the department's standpoint, it was a chance to expose every last worm in the can. And also, to spend the money.

That the program had never happened posed only a minor problem. The department would take a leaf from economists, who simply assume the situation they then seek to explain. What *would* have happened had the department done what it was supposed to do (i.e., try the concept), but didn't? So they hired a consultant who proceeded to ascertain how local service agencies thought the program would have worked if it had been tried.

The agencies surveyed received state funds from Duggar's office to provide paid homemaker services to persons on public assistance. If they used volunteers, it was primarily as help around the office. Not surprisingly, the possibility that these underused volunteers could do some of the same things the agencies pay their staffs or commercial concerns to do, was not greeted with uniform approval. Seventy percent said they wouldn't have participated in the program anyway. Under the circumstances, it's remarkable that nearly a third actually expressed interest in the idea at all.

The report noted, without irony, that it couldn't say whether a statewide service credit program was feasible, because "the brief pilot effort was not able to provide adequate information." Note the curious construction: the pilot effort, not those in charge of it, was to blame. The report then proceeded, with obvious relish, to launch into a host of troublesome points, such as the problem of guaranteeing credits, and the problem of writing job descriptions for volunteers.

Virtually every item was an insuperable obstacle only to the bureaucratic mind; people like Dolores Galloway in Washington, who had started real programs from the ground up, hadn't given them a thought. At one point, the report acknowledged that heavy-handed bureaucracy was at least partly to blame. "Although the original concept . . . is basically simple," the report said, "the necessity to create a uniform program that meshes with existing state-administered services resulted in a relatively complex program."

But again, that "necessity" was one that existed only in the bureaucratic mind. The real threat came out at a different point. "There is an underlying assumption that volunteer services can be equated with professional services," the report said with disapproval, "to the extent that volunteers can be used to address the unmet need for state-provided services such as respite, homemaker, and related services."

Exactly right.

9

Florida II: How Grass-Roots Groups Built the New Currency on Their Own

When Esterlene Colbrook retired about five years ago, she set out to find an apartment in a senior citizens building in her native Miami, so she wouldn't be a burden to her daughter. She quickly discovered it was no easy task. Where to go? How to get help? There were long lines wherever she went. "If I do nothing else," she said to herself, "I'd like to see that seniors know where to go to get different things."

Colbrook is a perky and attractive woman with an easy Southern manner and just a touch of Nina Simone, the singer, in her voice. Her father was a minister who lived to be 120. Her grandfather was a slave. She is a former special duty nurse, with 11 children and a pack of grandchildren as well.

She was tired of sitting around the house, anyway. So she started to volunteer at seniors organizations and at a local hospital so she could use her nursing skills. Eventually, she heard about a new program that was then based at South Shore Hospital in Miami. Something about seniors helping other seniors, and people looking out for one another.

That sounded a lot like the Miami neighborhood she grew up in. "We knew everybody on our street, and everybody looked out for each other," she recalls. When a neighbor was ill, one of the older ladies on the street—grandmothers they were called—would cook a pot of soup and take it over. "If you had to go to the store, you didn't have to worry about baby-sitters. You just called across the street and said,

'Watch out for the children.' That was my raising. That's what I was used to. Everybody on that street was kin to each other."

She signed on, and soon her trunk was stuffed with file boxes, forms, brochures of various kinds. Colbrook has become a coordinator in the program, and the woman the director leans on for guidance and counsel. This "retiree" works every day visiting with volunteers, trying to recruit more and line up new sites. "I'm excited for this program," she says. "I'm really excited for this program."

The reason is contained in the files in her trunk, which contain weekly records of credits earned and spent—a growing bank of good deeds. They are also a daily refutation of the bureaucrats in Tallahassee, who said mere volunteers are "not suited" for the rigors of helping frail people in their homes.

"I KNOW, I'VE BEEN THROUGH IT"

The consultant who wrote that report apparently had never met Millie Hurley, for example. Hurley takes care of a woman who is almost blind. The woman had spent years caring for her husband, who had Parkinson's disease, and when he died, she felt helpless and alone. "I know," Hurley says. "I've been through it."

Hurley has been through a good deal. She was born and raised in Shanghai, and as a teenager became a nanny to the children of a tea merchant. She raised three kids in New York City, making ends meet as a building superintendent. Then she raised a fourth in Miami. She wasn't exactly an ingenue—as the state bureaucrats seemed to assume—when it came to helping a service credit friend get her life together.

Hurley arranged for a special transit program for seniors to take the woman to the supermarket, where a clerk helps her shop. (The woman likes to be independent, so this is important.) Hurley got her involved at the Lighthouse for the Blind, where she is sewing and knitting. Hurley even found a state program that will provide home-care services. (The state aging officialdom doesn't always know about the people it says others aren't "suited" to help.) "I call her two or three times a day," Hurley says. "I ask, 'Are you Mrs. Touchy or Mrs. Smiley today?'"

Some of the people in Colbrook's file box are confined to their homes, but they help, too. One is Jack Dreitzer, a widower in his late seventies. Dreitzer started out as a counterboy at Nathan's hot dog stand at Coney Island, and worked his way up to financial controller for the company. He has the robust, pastrami-on-rye voice of a tanned New York retiree who spends his days on the golf course. But Dreitzer has a bad case of arthritis and can't get out much. So he puts his gift of schmooze to use calling homebound people in their nineties and keeping them company on the phone. He scolds them when they sound morbid ("Look, I don't want to hear you talking like that.") and generally tries to cheer them up. One woman, who is 98 years old, has become like a long lost aunt. At the end of every call she says, "Don't forget to call me."

The official report on service credits said volunteers can't keep regular schedules. Whoever wrote that obviously had never met Consuella Gomez. Gomez is a quiet little woman of 88 who moves about a local senior center in Miami with a serene smile. She has been in the United States only ten years, speaks no English, and was very sad and depressed staying at home. "I was losing my mind," she said through an interpreter. "I used to forget everything." She was a prime candidate for professional "intervention," as the social workers put it.

Instead, Gomez signed up for the service credit program at her senior center, the Little Havana Activities and Nutrition Center, which was a founder of the Miami program. Now she comes in every day, from 8:00 to 3:00, to help in a special unit for frail seniors. She brings coffee and meals, helps them go to the bathroom, whatever is needed. The thing she most needed was the thing the bureaucracy said she couldn't keep to—a regular schedule. Gomez got her own mind back through the opportunity for helping others. Her only wish now is to work Saturday and Sunday. "I've never been happier," she says.

A MATTER OF DIPLOMACY

Gomez almost didn't get that chance. Miami's Time Dollar experiment easily could have died with the state's obituary. But then two things happened. A couple of foundations, the Florence Burden Foundation and the Robert Wood Johnson Foundation, stepped in to supply what the state hadn't by way of nurturing support.

More important, State Senator Carrie Meek, a pillar of Miami's black community, almost singlehandedly brought Miami's divergent ethnic factions together around the program. So doing, Meek demonstrated the power of a new concept of money to shift the political calculus from combat to cooperation.

Miami's black community was feeling beleaguered and defensive in the spring and summer of 1986. The Honorable Alcee Hastings, a black federal judge who had recently been acquitted on bribery charges, was now the target of a federal impeachment proceeding. The acquittal of a Cuban policeman accused of killing a black youth had inflamed community sentiment. And more generally, blacks were feeling particularly powerless as Haitian and Hispanic immigrants moved past a dispirited Southern black populace that appeared mired in poverty and in the past.

In this setting, it seemed especially daunting when black organizations lost interest in the Time Dollar coalition, in the face of the state's obstruction. The remaining cohort was largely Anglo and Hispanic, with some university types thrown in. In Miami, that had ethnic ownership implications that would make blacks feel unwelcome for the foreseeable future. T. Willard Fair, the militant director of the Urban League, was blunt: "I like the idea but I want the whole Miami 'franchise' or I won't play. I'm tired of having things we do taken over by others once we make them work." Fair was more gracious than his inflammatory public image, but the "franchise" was the bottom line.

The local community action agency, which blacks had captured early in the war on poverty, had a different answer. "The black community does not volunteer," a representative said. "We're tired of that stuff." She would only be interested, she said, if the program carried a stipend for volunteers—like the Foster Grandparents Program or the Senior Companion Program. What about the black churches, some wondered. Hadn't they galvanized the civil rights movement on a volunteer basis? Didn't every congregation have its core of dedicated volunteers? But in Miami, the churches didn't have the cohesion, the following, or the resources common in other communities. And there was no single black minister who seemed likely to take a lead in pulling a coalition together.

RECLAIMING LOST SOCIAL TERRITORY

Then Senator Meek entered the picture. Senator Meek is a respected presence in Miami politics. She is gutsy, outspoken, and a tower of rectitude. When she speaks, other black leaders listen. And when Senator Meek issues an invitation, black community leaders view it as a summons.

Senator Meek had been one of the two primary sponsors of the service credit legislation, and she bore the state's Office on Aging no great love. In her view, it had ignored the black elderly; it was now proposing to reduce the funding for senior citizen programs in Miami by several million dollars. To Meek, the killing of the service credit program was part of this same pattern.

Senator Meek saw that service credits were more than a sweet, harmless program for volunteers. The concept triggered her memories of the world she grew up in. "It was a very giving and caring environment," she recalls, in words that echo Esterlene Colbrook's. "Some were old and infirm, but everybody looked after them. We were all very, very, poor, but of course we didn't know it. Everyone was giving. Whatever they had, you could share. My mother used to say that if you keep your hand closed, nothing can come in. But if you open it, things can flow in and out. Everyone in the neighborhood was like that."

Somehow, Time Dollars seemed to offer a way to reclaim some of that lost social territory. And like many minority politicians, Senator Meek realized that this was more than an exercise in nostalgia—that it had implications for empowerment. There were not enough jobs for her constituents. The Time Dollar program gave rise to a guaranteed job market for every human being, so long as another human being was in need. Her instincts told her that a currency that could convert underused personal time into both neighborly helping and real purchasing power could mean the power to rebuild community. She was determined that blacks would not miss out on one more opportunity.

So Senator Meek arranged a luncheon, called every invitee personally, and made clear that those invited had better show. She knew she could count on a core of hand-picked protégées who owed much of their present prominence to her. But the attendance was more than double what even she anticipated.

Meek went into her Bible thumping, Baptist revival mode. "Brothers and Sisters," she began, "we missed out on urban renewal. We missed out on the War on Poverty. We missed out on the money to rebuild Liberty City after the riots. And we are *not* going to miss out on this opportunity." Her plan was to appoint a group of "volunteers" to constitute a steering committee. They would get their act together, and then meet with the broader Miami coalition, which was called the Greater Miami Service Credit Consortium.

Meek stood behind Eddie Pearson, an assistant superintendent of schools, and gave him an affectionate embrace that looked suspiciously like a choke hold around his neck; then she thanked him for accepting the chairmanship of the group. She was even more enthusiastic as she informed the audience that Pearson had volunteered to provide full logistical support, including a meeting place, a secretary to transcribe minutes, parking, and even refreshments.

Meek then volunteered other members of the audience and promised that she would attend the first meeting herself.

"A NEW FORM OF GETTING BACK"

For the next three months, Meek's volunteers met almost weekly, trying to reinvent the linkages by which people in their community could help one another. Promising alliances evolved. Many senior citizens are not able to break up the hard ground to plant vegetable or flower gardens, for example. But students at Florida Memorial, a historic black college, could help. They could even build boxes on legs so that seniors could garden without bending over.

At the same time, the college needed dorm monitors, and day care for faculty kids. Students needed a home away from home. Soon, the planning committee held a test run that yielded vegetable gardens for the elderly and a Thanksgiving day turkey dinner for out-of-state college students.

Using that approach, each group on the Steering Committee—the Urban League, Miami Dade Community College, and others—developed its own program model, linking it to other groups in order to match needs and resources. Before they could meet formally with the coalition, however, they had to make one critical decision: If only one program could be funded, which would it be? So committed had the group become, that they passed this potential mine field with barely a ruffle. The group selected was the Urban League's senior housing project—and this time, T. Willard Fair did not demand an exclusive franchise for all of Miami.

It was time to approach the larger Time Dollar coalition. The meeting started awkwardly. There was no clear agenda, and Senator Meek simply took over and chaired. Each group described its program and circulated hand-outs. After 2 hours of preliminaries, it was suddenly five to five. Soon everyone would have to go. And they still had to address the real issue: Who would get the money the Robert Wood Johnson Foundation had committed to the coalition?

In Miami, it is customary for racial and ethnic leaders to fight over every penny. Yet this decision took less than 5 minutes. Each bloc in the consortium—black, Hispanic, Anglo/blue collar, and Jewish— would get funding for its strongest program. There were no arguments and, because of the novel dynamics of Time Dollars, no losers. If the program succeeded, it would move out in waves, from 4 components to 8 to 16 to 32. Everyone could be a winner, and each bloc's success was linked to the success of others.

While the coalition was courting the Robert Wood Johnson Foundation, Little Havana Activities and Nutrition Center was using its pull with Republicans in Washington to deliver 12 VISTA workers (Volunteers in Service to America) who would be paid a stipend of $100 per week. These were essential if the program was to meet its ambitious goals: take root simultaneously in the black, Hispanic, and Anglo communities, while developing day care centers for both seniors and children, along with numerous other initiatives.

Miami was the only community where the Time Dollar concept was undertaken by an alliance of programs. It is testimony to the power of the concept, that it could grow to its present scope under such difficult political circumstances. Much of that power lies in the way the concept touches people at an intuitive and personal level, offering a connection between a life people remember and a life they can build.

"It's not new to the people I'm talking to—the seniors," Colbrook says. "Years ago we did that—we took care of our neighbors. I tell them, 'We have to get back to that, and this is a new form of getting back.'"

A TV SHOWCASE FOR TIME DOLLARS

About two years after Senator Meek helped pull these groups together, the producers of "Inside Edition," the well-known TV news magazine, were looking for a locale in which to see Time Dollars in action.

They asked Ralph Nader, who does commentary for the show, and he immediately suggested Miami. The program there had grown to the point where it had the greatest number of volunteers, the greatest ethnic diversity, the most credits being earned—some 8,000 per month, through 28 different programs spread throughout the sprawling Dade County area. And the program was spanning generations: Retirees were helping at day care centers, for example, and getting credits they could use when they needed help themselves.

The producers took Nader's advice. The result was a 10-minute segment that prompted some 2,500 letters to Nader's office in Washington, asking for more information. The segment provided a moving glimpse of the power of this concept to empower neighbors to act as neighbors. The days of filming, moreover, comprised an A-to-Z tour of a Time Dollar program in operation.

Andrea Fleischer, the "Inside Edition" producer, went first to South Shore Hospital, which functioned as administrative hub of the program. There she met Anna Miyares, who had left a lucrative career in international banking to become manager of this new bank of good works. The nuts and bolts were easy enough to explain. New volunteers fill out forms indicating both their skills and needs, and this information goes into a computer. When requests for help come in, they go into the computer, too. Miyares then calls up a list of names of people who might be available; but the actual matching requires a sense of the personalities, so she makes the assignments herself.

The computer functions as a kind of time bank; when one member provides service to another, a credit—or Time Dollar—is transferred from the account of the latter to the former, one for each hour served. Miyares also uses the computer matching system to spread assignments around, so she doesn't burn out her best volunteers or lose the ones she doesn't know well. Showing the business savvy she learned running branch banks in poor communities, Miyares tries to assign new members to a person in need within 48 hours, so they bond quickly to the program.

Miyares had a staff of 12 VISTA volunteers, all retirees like Colbrook, who act as field agents and site managers. They gather service reports for their areas, monitor the work of volunteers, and recruit new volunteers through talks at civic groups and the like. Since she was hired, Miyares has stripped away bureaucracy and made the program more free flowing. She dropped a training program for new volunteers, for example, because she thought it insulting; now she uses the mentor system, sending an experienced volunteer or a VISTA along with a new volunteer on each first assignment.

Similarly, the paperwork at first reflected a business auditor's mentality. A worker who drove an elderly patient to the doctor, for example, would have to get the patient to sign a slip attesting to the hours. Now, Miyares simply takes Time Dollar workers at their word.

NAVIGATING THE POLITICAL SHOALS

Covenant Palms is a low-income senior housing development in the Little River section of Miami, owned and operated by the local Urban League. The project is about 85 percent black and 10 percent Hispanic, with a smattering of whites making up the difference. The low-rise bungalows seem reasonably well-kept. But the project has been a virtual Siberia in terms of gathering financial support for senior programs because T. Willard Fair, the head of the Urban League, has antagonized the political establishment—blacks included.

Covenant Palms couldn't even get funding for a hot meals program until Little Havana, the Cuban settlement house, applied for a grant on its behalf. But then, the money had to be funneled through another black agency, in accordance with ethnic turf prerogatives. Such are the politics around which the Miami Time Dollar program has had to navigate.

The program has been the catalyst for a burst of new activity at Covenant Palms, including a food bank and a shopping group. Participants are enthused not just at the opportunity for helping, but also the social activities that the sense of community has produced. One of the most enthused is Daisy Alexander, a retiree from Montclair, New Jersey, who has a big heart and a rambunctious wit. "It gives you a chance to meet people," she says of the Time Dollar program. "We have all kinds of activities. We go places and I love it."

Daisy is also big on the mutual helping, and she was one of the first involved. She had taken on the job of tutoring at the elementary school across the street. Originally, several Covenant Palms seniors wanted to start a program where they tutored the children in their homes after school. But management didn't want the kids on the premises; they don't even want grandkids around. So Daisy went across the street and offered her services to the school, where she has been helping ever since. Time Dollars encourage this kind of entrepreneurial spirit; as a currency, they can flow wherever people seek to serve.

The "Inside Edition" cameras got a scene they probably were looking for: children huddled around Daisy in rapt attention, as she taught them the alphabet and recognition of animals. "This is a GOAT," she is saying, with grandmotherly patience. "Say 'GOAT.' " The affection going back and forth is palpable. Then, the edited version jumps to Daisy writing down her hours on a Time Dollar form, and then to an energetic man with white hair knocking on the door of her small bungalow: "Daisy, this is Pepe."

Pepe is another Time Dollar worker, who has come to take Daisy to the store. Gallantly, he helps her to his car; she is an amputee with an artificial leg and a cane. Then he explains that his English is no good and lapses back into his native Spanish. Daisy says she doesn't know what she would do without Pepe. (Frequently, seniors have to pay people in the neighborhood for rides to the supermarket and the like.) "He is a good amigo," she says, while the camera shows them putting groceries into the car. This kind of friendship may be the most remarkable thing about Time Dollars in this "racially divided city," the voiceover notes.

The scene shifts to the senior center at Covenant Palms, where preparations are underway for a Thanksgiving party. Pepe's wife, Thelma, is talking about the Time Dollar program. "Before, I don't know what I could do," she says. "I was i-so-la-ted—staying at home, just watching TV with Pepe." Now she has a great deal to do, helping senior citizens in a predominantly black housing project where ethnicity and language have ceased to be a barrier. It was revealing that the "Inside Edition" camera crew—native Miamians, but Anglos—didn't have the slightest idea how to get to Time Dollar sites such as Covenant Palms. Their distance from the world of blacks and Cubans in the city stood in marked contrast to the racial bridges that were forming in the Time Dollar program.

The next day, the film crew went to a day care center operated by the Little Havana Activities and Nutrition Center in the heart of Miami's Cuban district. The concept behind the day care center is to tap the time and experience of those retirees to help care for the next generation. Time Dollars form a link between the retirees and working parents. Seniors get these for their service at the center, and they can spend them on services offered by Time Dollar volunteers. The goal is to foster exchanges between the volunteers and the parents: A father could help a retiree wash her windows on a Saturday, for example, in exchange for the retiree's help at the day care center during the week.

On this day, the camera caught the seniors dancing with 4- and 5-year olds, in a scene of disarming gaiety. Then a mother of one of the children explains that she'd have to go on welfare without this day care help.

The segment ended with a celebration at Miami Dade Community College. Blacks, whites, and Cubans were all dancing together—heart-warming, but with a telling point. In ordinary volunteer programs, the narrator noted, drop-out rates are in the 40-to-60-percent range. The Miami Time Dollar program, by contrast, boasts a drop-out rate of only 3 percent. This celebration may be around for a while.

PRIME THE PUMP

But where did this money come from, Fleischman wanted to know? When you start a program, how can people buy services with credits they never earned? Miyares tried to take it from the top. You couldn't possibly start a program without first priming the pump, she said. So the first group of needy recipients in effect get their help for free. Does anyone object to homebound retirees getting a ride to the store, even though they haven't "earned" it?

Fine. But this was three years into the program, and participants were earning these at a rate of 8,000 a month. That meant 8,000 Time Dollars piling up in computer accounts. How many got spent? "I would be surprised if it amounted to 10 percent," Miyares answered matter-of-factly. "But how can you just keep giving away service?" Fleischman replied. Miyares had to smile to herself, because that very question bothered her boss at South Shore Hospital. Didn't this represent in effect a "deficit" of nearly 100,000 Time Dollars a year that the hospital would have to make good on? And all Miyares could say was, "This is going to continue for at least ten years, and maybe longer."

This hard-nosed banker hadn't lost her senses. She had two very solid reasons for her seeming nonchalance. Much of the deficit was simply a function of age. Younger retirees tend to be the givers in Time Dollar programs; the average age of people earning credits in Miami is 63. People receiving those services, by contrast, average 20 years older. So in 20 years, the current givers will be spending their credits on services, and the next generation coming along will be earning. Prime the pump with one generation, and the system begins to sustain itself. And by that time, if things go as planned, there will be a broader range of services for the younger participants to buy: yard work from high schoolers, for example. There could even be link-ups with the cash economy, such as discounts at supermarkets and pharmacies or credits against their taxes.

Miyares has another reason for her confidence, however. As a banker, she understands that any currency ultimately is based on trust. Prudently or not, most people trust the federal government to stand behind the dollar, even though it is more than a trillion dollars in the red. Time Dollars are building trust among people that can be no less solid. "This program isn't about earning money to spend," Miyares said. "People like the numbers. It means a lot to them to know they have the extra cushion. They may never spend them. But if they do, don't worry. We won't have any problem honoring them."

Asked later to amplify, she said, "How are the credits guaranteed? We will guarantee the credits. I feel so proud because what we have here is a family."

10

"Disabling Professions": A Way to Take Back the Right to Help and Care

A number of years ago, the city of London did a study of what professional home-care providers actually do during the day. The results showed that these trained city workers don't do what people think they do. They don't spend most of their time on difficult tasks— such as bathing frail seniors—for which training and a certificate are required. Instead, about 40 percent of their time goes to such chores as shopping and going to the post office to pick up welfare checks for their clients.

That is not the best use of hard-to-get trained personnel. The home-care workers could only spend a little over 2 hours a day with each person, under the Thatcher government's budget cuts. So after the errands were done, there wasn't a great deal of time for anything else. This was a little like paying surgeons to stock the shelves in the hospital supply room.

Yet the supervisor of this agency didn't dare take this work away from the professionals. "That's what they enjoy doing," he said, speaking of the shopping and errands. "If we took that away, I couldn't fill the jobs."

WHY TAXPAYERS PAY—AND PAY

It is understandable that a home-care worker might enjoy a stroll to the market, as relief from bathing old people or cleaning up after incontinents. But such indulgence is not a luxury the public can afford. If Time Dollar workers ran the errands, for example, then more needy recipients could get the care they need, with less stigma of charity. The taxpayers would get more for their money. Plus, the licensed workers would enjoy more stature, because they'd be doing the work for which they were trained.

Regrettably, however, in many lines of helping work, artificial barriers stand in the way. You aren't permitted to do the job unless you have the proper certificate or degree. This can be a basic conflict in a service-oriented society. In each different line of work, those already in the job seek to increase and protect their status by making it hard for others to enter. The established professionals like lawyers and doctors did it first. Then others—such as teachers and social workers—followed in their footsteps. The desire for respect and a living wage is understandable. So is a desire to assure a minimum standard of quality. But too often the result is to put help beyond the reach of those who need it and to put helping work beyond the reach of many who want to do it.

This is not just a question of professional interest groups. Underneath is an economic theory that gives sanction to self-interest. As explained in chapter 3, economists believe that progress lies in buying more and more from the market, and doing less and less as friends and neighbors. As the economy shifts toward services, it can only grow as each individual needs more services. And this, in turn, means leaning on family and community less and less.

A CHALLENGE TO THE BUY-MORE-DO-LESS TREND

The much-vaunted service economy is just another way of saying that America has contracted out to the marketplace the things that people used to have and do for free. The Time Dollar concept poses a basic challenge to this trend, at two levels. First, and for the first time, it offers a practical way to mobilize nonprofessionals on a large and self-enlarging scale for helping work. This could force a debate over why nonprofessionals are excluded from work they can do and want to do. Does this really protect the public? Or just the group or profession in question?

Second, the Time Dollar concept raises a basic question about the doctrine of division of labor: Does life get better to the extent that we buy more and do less? It points to the possibility that often the opposite is true; that the connective tissue of family and community can only be maintained by use, and this requires doing instead of buying. Some even argue that, in a general way, the professions today serve to *disable* people by creating dependency and co-opting functions that are better provided at the family and community levels.

Of course, such assertions are too sweeping. Many professionals in America are dedicated to helping others and are possessed of needed skills. Few people want to entrust heart surgery or complex litigation to an untrained volunteer. But closer to the borderline, there is a large zone of competence that has been expropriated by the market. To say lawyers, for example, do many useful things, is not to say they are needed to do everything. Yet the dynamic of the profession is to burrow deeper and deeper into the fabric of life. America lacks a sense of boundary, a territory within which the functions of family and community should be protected. We need a standard of appropriate expertise—of self-sufficiency and coping skills—to counteract the market forces that beckon us to contract out ever larger portions of our lives.

That doesn't mean less challenge or work for professionals. It can mean more. But the more will be different: less doing things for clients or to patients, more enlisting them in the process of their own help and care.

LIMIT EXPERTISE TO REAL NEED

The stakes in these questions are becoming very high. Budget shortfalls at all levels of government—and in families as well—make it crucial that people not be forced to buy more expertise than they really need. To restore stability to families and communities, we have to reclaim the life functions that the commercial marketplace and government have taken away. What we are learning about the health of helping (see chapter 7) makes it imperative that people not be denied the opportunity to engage in helping work, and be rewarded for it—for their own well-being as well as for the people they help.

Some conventional notions of progress have to be turned upside down. In early nineteenth-century England, bands of workers attacked the new factories and machines, believing that these were responsible for their low wages and unemployment. They were called Luddites, after one Ned Ludd, who had broken up stocking frames in 1779. Ever since, the term Luddite has been a term of disparagement, for mindless opposition to progress—which was seen always as technology, sophistication, division of labor, and expertise.

The expanding knowledge about the roles of patients in their own healing, students in their own learning, communities in their own security, and so forth, throw this equation into reverse. Progress now means, at least in part, trying to replace bonds that have been broken and to restore forms of competence that have been lost. It means *reducing* reliance on certified occupations and professionals where that reliance has been disabling. To the extent professionals resist this change, and refuse to redefine their roles, they will be the new Luddites. They will be seen as striving to protect their status against a new and threatening concept of autonomy and self-sufficiency.

The role of experts in American life has grown exponentially since World War II. As people become more affluent, they tend to purchase the services they used to perform themselves; and the expertise purchased has become a major part of the U.S. economy. People consult experts concerning the most basic daily functions such as shopping, dressing, eating, getting a little exercise. Even journalistic aunties like "Dear Abby" and "Ann Landers" now advise a good proportion of their correspondents to "seek professional counseling."

This is a curious development for a nation weaned on the virtues of self-reliance, from the legacy of the frontier to Henry David Thoreau. Yet the dogma of division of labor is so widely accepted, the social status of professionals so firmly entrenched, that the issue barely exists in American public debate. By and large, the leaders of public opinion identify with professionals. They went to college with people who are now lawyers and doctors and economists and the like. They look to them for quotes and equate enlightenment with credentials and degrees.

On the fringes of respectable opinion, however, another view has been gaining. Ivan Illich, the noted author, coined the expression "disabling professions." When lawyers settle all the disputes, when teachers do all the teaching, when doctors do all the curing, Illich said, then people lose their capacity to do these things, and the result is an ever-enlarging cycle of dependency and need. The professions can even contribute to the problems they are seeking to resolve.

John Taylor Gatto, recently named Teacher of the Year in New York City, contends the schools contribute to illiteracy. It's not because their methods aren't good enough and not because they don't spend enough. Rather, it's because the premise is wrong: Schools separate children from their native interests, and thus stymie the desire to learn, which is the goad to reading. "When children are given whole lives, instead of age-graded ones in cellblocks, they learn to read, write, and do arithmetic with ease if these things make sense in the kind of life that unfolds around them," Gatto said in a speech while accepting his reward. "Experts in education have never been right; their 'solutions' are expensive [and] self-serving."

These are not the musings of a cloistered romantic. Gatto teaches in a junior high school at the edge of Harlem; he has to shove file cabinets in front of the door in his classroom to ward off disruptions from the hall. Gatto devotes substantial time and energy to designing projects for his students outside the school. On a typical day, he arises early to drive some students from Harlem out to New Jersey to spend the day with the head of a trucking company. Then he hurries back to take another group to a Manhattan hospital to follow a doctor around.

"Right now we are taking all the time from our children that they need to develop self-knowledge," Gatto said. "This has to stop."

PROFESSIONAL PROBLEM-SOLVERS CAN CREATE PROBLEMS

This observation applies across a broad range of helping work. The professional problem-solvers can become part of the problem. "Do we get more sickness from more medicine?" asked John McKnight of the Community Life Project at Northwestern University in Chicago. "Do we get more injustice and crime with more lawyers and police? Do we get more ignorance with more teachers and schools? Do we get more family collapse with more social workers?"

Law is perhaps the most obvious example. Having more lawyers in our society hasn't reduced legal problems; rather it has caused them to multiply. Also, these numerous lawyers have not increased respect for law and the legal system. John Holt, the late author and leader of the home schooling movement, noted that lawlessness as well as litigation increase to the extent law belongs to lawyers. "If the law can't be understood, if it is not accessible and reasonable," he wrote to a law professor, "people will feel very little compunction to obey it." This is because law is then no longer internal, felt as a personal experience, but merely something one buys from a lawyer.

McKnight and others have noted the same thing in other fields. In medicine, for example, disease seems to increase along with the sophistication of treatment. Doctors and drug companies are ever redefining states and stages of life as diseases to be treated. Stated another way, at their lowest, the professions operate as economic interest groups. Much as McDonald's wants to lead people to feel overwhelmed in the kitchen and depend on fast-food outlets for their meals, so lawyers tend to make people feel helpless in the face of routine life problems such as paying taxes and buying a house. The field of social work, as a whole, sometimes seems more interested in finding needs and disabilities than discovering capacities for self-help.

The vocabulary of illness has far outstripped that of health. (Addiction alone has spawned a lexicon of specialties.) "The basic function of modern professionalism," McKnight wrote, "is to (turn out) human beings whose capacity is to see their neighbors as half empty." This is not a case of bad people. Rather, the underlying dynamic, the whole economy, in fact, depends on people having more needs, and therefore consuming more services, so there can be employment and growth. "An economy in need of need," McKnight called it. "Nations have an increased need of personal deficiency."

One result, not much noted, is a breakdown of social bonds, because paid services take their place. Take the family, for example. "The history of the modern family, especially in the United States, is of systematic defunctioning," McKnight said in an interview with the publication "Growing without Schooling," founded by Holt. Health became the province of doctors, justice of lawyers, education of teachers, food of McDonald's, and so on down the line. "A family as a consumer of professional products is a family with no function except procreation, and it will fall apart, which is what is happening."

The same thing is happening to communities. It is often noted that New Yorkers are inclined to watch passively while robberies and even murders proceed before their eyes. The usual explanation is that the city's residents are frightened or hardened or whatever. But it's also possible that people trained to let experts deal with problems lose a capacity to respond on their own.

This is not just the thinking of a few intellectuals. Others feel it, too, though they express it in different ways. "When people became dependent on government and (professional) services, they could believe they would get better services outside the circle (of family and community) than inside the circle," says Betty Little, a volunteer in the D.C. Time Dollar program. "Someone who can make a nice chicken soup and give you a back rub is as good as a registered nurse. And I'm an R.N."

PROFESSIONALS AS OUTSIDERS

There is a scene in the novel *Famous All Over Town* in which a social worker visits a Chicano family in a poor neighborhood of Los Angeles. The social worker is Japanese, and he has come with some questions regarding living arrangements and the like. While he sits by politely, the family reverts to Spanish to discuss how they will finesse this touchy subject. As he leaves, the social worker offers a parting remark—in perfect Spanish.

The scene suggests the sense of inside and outside that people often have regarding social workers and professional "service providers" of other kinds. For all their commitment and good works, they are outsiders, paid for what they do. In the case of social workers, they represent the government and have the power to make trouble and take benefits away. And so, no matter how caring or sincere they seem, recipients of help often regard these professionals with suspicion.

It is not necessary to buy into the whole critique of disabling professions to see that people could do a lot more for one another, without the intervention of professionals. Often, volunteers and friends can do things professionals can't. They can cross the line that divides the realm of family from the realm of government and economics. Intimacy and trust can be as important as professional skills.

Many older people simply don't want social workers in their homes. They are worried about snooping, and the thought of welfare threatens their last shreds of dignity. "People in this building do not want them," says Dolores Galloway, who organized the Time Dollar program at the Walker House, a senior citizen's apartment building in Washington. "I've heard a lot of people say they pry, they get into your business. People around here are very protective about their business."

Sometimes, too, elderly people don't want intrusions on their life routines. They don't want to bare their infirmities and fears to social workers who could be their grandkids.

Elderly people usually don't say these things, except to one another; the reluctance is a silent barrier to communication and care. Time Dollar workers often can get past this barrier, because they operate as friends. They have time to sit in the kitchen and talk. They are there simply because they care. Because they are peers, they can understand.

Even in nursing homes, a controlled professional setting, volunteers bring a special touch that some professionals acknowledge. "The hardest thing to get is individuality," says Shifrah Nimchinsky, respite coordinator at the Parshelsky Pavilion, a nursing home near the boardwalk on Coney Island, where Elderplan members assist fellow members who are residents. "When someone comes only to see me, wants to know how I feel, then I'm not part of a caseload," says a resident.

Such attention helps the elderly person in very practical ways as well. "One of the first laws of the nursing home jungle," Nimchinsky says, "is that the person who has the visitors is the person who gets better care."

HELPERS ARE BARRED FROM HELPING

Though the issue is rarely posed in precisely these terms, attempts to restore a measure of family and community self-help can be threatening to the service industry. This may be why the Florida bureaucrats were so troubled about service credits, as described in chapter 8. There are numerous cases in recent years of certain professions blocking individuals who try to reclaim their native ability to help and care. These are instructive because they suggest the kinds of conflict that could lie ahead as Time Dollars help reestablish an ethos of helping in American life.

The most publicized case was probably that of Rosemarie Furman, a 56-year-old former legal secretary and court stenographer in Florida. Furman had set up a small business helping impoverished women fill out forms for simple legal matters such as wills, name changes, and uncontested divorces. The state bar association went after her with a fury, and ultimately she was sentenced to 120 days in jail for the "unauthorized practice of law."

There had been no complaints against Furman from her customers. They apparently were delighted at the chance to solve their routine legal problems for a modest charge of $50 to $100. The only complaints came from other lawyers, and Furman had a notion why. "Every time I make $50 in this office, some lawyer loses between $500 and $5,000," she said. As a former legal secretary, Furman knew that high-priced lawyers often give such simple cases to their secretaries to execute, then simply review the finished paperwork. So their fees are often pure gravy.

More important, the women Furman helped didn't have anywhere else to turn. The same Florida bar association that got Furman thrown into jail had found, about ten years before, a "vast unmet need for legal services." The situation had grown even worse in the intervening years. The Reagan budget cuts forced the legal services program in Miami to cut its staff by 40 percent, and another report of the state bar found that private attorneys were doing very little to fill the breach. Voluntary "pro bono" programs had "very limited participation by private attorneys," the report said.

The situation with service credits in Florida was very much the same. An enormous human need was growing larger by the year. People were ready and eager to help meet that need. A proposal had come forth to mobilize that resource on a large scale. Yet the established social work hierarchy reacted as to a threat. They couldn't put the proponents in jail, of course, but they did all within their power to kill the idea. That both episodes occurred in Florida could be a coincidence. But it could also be that, in a state with so many senior citizens, professionals are even more inclined than usual to see the public as helpless consumers of their care.

WHY HEALED PATIENTS CAN'T LEAVE THE HOSPITAL

Hospitals are a prime example. One of the last things America needs right now is to pay for hospital rooms that patients don't really need. Yet that happens every day, at a cost to taxpayers and health insurance customers of millions of dollars per year. The reason is very simple. Elderly patients and others have to stay in the hospital much longer than they should, because there is no one to take care of them at home.

"People are going home alone, and three weeks later they are back in the hospital because there is no food in the refrigerator," said Carolee DeVito, who heads the Department of Research at the South Shore Hospital. Two-thirds of the patients at the hospital live alone, and most of them are elderly. As a result, hospitals turn into nursing homes, at a cost per patient of hundreds or even thousands of dollars a day. "People are ready to go home by any hospital standard," DeVito said. "But we can't send a social worker home with every discharge."

A ripe situation for Time Dollar volunteers, in the thinking of DeVito and others. They are more reliable than ordinary volunteers, she says, and so can be entrusted with this kind of work. They are well-prepared by life experience to handle the basic functions that enable an invalid to stay at home. Time Dollars, moreover, can be a real economic link between the hospital and the volunteer. The volunteers could use Time Dollars to defer part of hospital expenses of their own; and the hospital would gain by building a client base and goodwill in the community.

Despite all this, hospitals have been unable to move ahead with the idea—even hospitals like South Shore Hospital that have *sponsored* Time Dollar programs. Bureaucracy and institutional fiefdoms are both involved. But another problem, stated in simplest terms, is that professional staffs tend to be suspicious of efforts of this kind. Either professionals don't think ordinary people can do the job. Or else, if such people *can* do the job, professionals worry that their own jobs may be on the line.

This was sadly evident in the fate of a "home visitor" program in upstate New York. As the term is used in social work, home visitors are laypersons trained to visit young mothers during pregnancy and the first years after birth, to offer advice on nutrition, child rearing, and the like. This tradition has very deep roots, especially in the South.

These programs have gotten glowing reviews as a way to reduce infant mortality and child abuse. A General Accounting Office (GAO) report issued in 1990 cited an impressive list of accomplishments. In South Carolina, for example, pregnant adolescents in rural areas had significantly fewer underweight babies after participating in a home visitor program than a similar group that didn't. The National Commission to Reduce Infant Mortality found that home visitor programs had tangible benefits to taxpayers as well, cutting hospital costs for underweight babies and reducing the number of emergency visits for routine health problems.

Yet when a grass-roots home visitor program in upstate New York was transferred to the Public Health Service, the effectiveness and *spirit* went way down. Professionals just couldn't work up the enthusiasm that the amateurs could. Predictably, the GAO report, which recommended expansion of the home visitor approach, got a very cold reception among professionals at the Department of Health and Human Services. These argued that most of the roles of home visitors could be better filled by public health nurses and by professional social workers.

BASELESS FEAR OF BEING DISPLACED

The sense of threat is revealing of the professional mind, because that's the only place it exists. Given the escalating demands for help and care, the notion that laypersons and volunteers are going to take the jobs of the nation's trained social workers approaches the absurd. In practice, Time Dollar workers are unlikely to encroach on areas that truly require professional skills. If for no other reason than to avoid lawsuits, volunteers stay away from lifting invalids and the like, and program leaders instruct them to do so. "Don't give medication," the training manual for one Time Dollar program states flatly. "Don't lift, toilet, or bathe your client under any circumstances. Remember, if you do so, you are fully liable."

The people who run Time Dollar programs have no intention of being used as excuses to cut public funding further. "We need to be careful not to substitute for services people have a right to," DeVito says. "We want to increase the service pie, not substitute for things people are entitled to or that Medicaid pays for." In fact, when communities are organized as Time Dollar networks, they can wield more political clout to gain such increases. And when they are going the last mile to help themselves, their case for government help becomes all the stronger.

11

A Money Supply for Entrepreneurs Who Build Community

Josefina Carbonell heads the Little Havana Nutrition and Activities Center in Miami's old Cuban district. She has the competent air of an executive—though with a soft, feminine touch—and she thinks of herself as a hard-headed businesswoman. She has built a small, community-based organization into a sprawling empire, with meticulous attention to detail. She takes pride in keeping her costs below those of any other agency in town.

Carbonell has a vision of a quality child care enterprise that would link the generations in Miami's Cuban community. The need for such care is acute among low-income families in particular, who today can afford little more than group babysitting. Plus, there is a long tradition among Cubans that grandparents play a role raising their grandkids. This tradition has been strained by the dispersive forces of American culture; a day care operation staffed partially by seniors would help restore it again.

Carbonell calls this vision Project Rainbow. She has taken a large first step, with a model center at Little Havana's main building. The project is close to her heart. She wants to expand. But her great frustration is that the limits of what she can do depend, for the time being, on what help she can coax out of state and local officials to keep the concept afloat. This is the dilemma of social service executives like herself who deal in problems—in this case, low-income families in need of quality child care—the commercial market rejects, particularly if money alone defines the resources at hand.

But Carbonell has another resource. She played a large role in rescuing Miami's Time Dollar program from the bureaucratic graveyard. Now she is using Time Dollars to help staff her model center. The concept is not a cure-all. But it brings her several steps closer. While it helps balance the books, it also helps fulfill the dream of bringing the generations back together in a nation that seems to pull them apart.

With that center in place, Carbonell is now laying the groundwork for a much larger step. She wants to upgrade hundreds of mom-and-pop day care centers in her community and bring them into a network that would turn them into first-rate operations. They would get training and resources. The kids would get the kind of care usually reserved for the well-to-do. Project Rainbow would be in every neighborhood, sometimes every block.

Such endeavors take capital, and Carbonell has to raise money. But she doesn't need as much, because she has Time Dollars as well.

A NEW-OLD DEFINITION OF ENTERPRISE

Entrepreneurs were the new darlings of the 1980s. Ten years before, few would have predicted that a book on business management would dominate the best-seller lists. Yet, *In Search of Excellence*, by two management consultants, Thomas J. Peters and Robert H. Waterman, Jr., topped the lists for weeks on end. Individuals like Stephen Jobs, who started Apple Computer in a garage, and Donald Trump, the real estate mogul, became folk heroes.

At one level, such entrepreneurs seemed a bulwark against the Japanese, reassurance that America had not lost its productive juices. Then, too, the economic attitude of the Reagan administration suddenly made it okay to get rich and enjoy.

But something deeper was at work. In a nation dominated increasingly by institutions and bureaucracies, enterprise came to represent the frontier. It suggested setting out on your own, taking risks, doing life your own way; it had some of the romantic appeal of the counter-culture in the 1960s, with money as a bonus.

Twenty years before, John F. Kennedy had claimed this rugged frontier spirit on behalf of doing good. His "New Frontier" had a cutting edge, grass-roots quality that began with the Peace Corps and carried over to the domestic front, with initiatives like VISTA (Volunteers in Service to America) and the original Legal Services. But in the years since, those social ideals had gotten bogged down—in the public mind at least—in the sludge of bureaucratized social service. The New Frontier of the 1980s was making money.

Yet for all the adulation heaped on business in the 1980s, another kind of entrepreneur was slowly entering the scene. Many of these new entrepreneurs looked much like the kind the nation was reading about in *Business Week* and *Forbes*. They started businesses, took risks, set out on their own in the wilds of the market. But there was one crucial difference. They were not interested primarily in making money; rather, they wanted to sustain a business that would do some good.

These are social entrepreneurs, and they are reclaiming the frontier on behalf of good works. Many are mainstream businesses that grow out of social values. The nation's largest supplier of recycled writing papers, for example, is a company called ConservaTree based in San Francisco. It was started by a former foundation head who decided that the most effective way to encourage conservation was to get into the business of doing it. Similarly, a mail-order company in Vermont, called Seventh Generation, sells products for the home—from toilet paper to recycling bins—that are environmentally sound.

Through the 1980s, the list kept growing. Perhaps the most inventive was an effort to reroute the underlying flow of money. A San Francisco-based company, called Working Assets, developed a new kind of credit card that has good works built in. A portion of each purchase goes into a fund that gets distributed to worthy causes at the end of the year. (Cardholders vote on the recipients.) Working Assets also has a long-distance telephone company, with a portion of each long-distance charge going into the same fund. Why wait for Congress and the politicians? If you control a piece of the economic plumbing, the way conventional banks and credit card companies do, you can tap into the economic flow yourself.

FROM HUSTLING GRANTS TO SELF-SUFFICIENCY

Such efforts are all rooted in the market. They start with the daily functions of buying and selling, and seek to make them more benign. This can raise money for good causes, and be part of those causes.

But there is a whole realm of social problems that lies outside the market. Community health problems, child care for women in poverty, care for the indigent elderly in their homes—even socially conscious businesses can't do much with these because there isn't any money. (If the people had money, they wouldn't be social problems.)

Traditionally, these have been consigned to government. But in recent years, people have been bringing the skills and energies of enterprise to this realm of family and community as well.

In the past, the entrepreneurial energies of good-works groups had gone mainly into hustling grants from foundations and government. They packaged and repackaged their programs to suit the latest funding fads and panaceas. They mastered the nuances of grant-writing lingo. They played political patronage games and courted incumbent office holders to get grants renewed.

Little of this was aimed at building the kind of independent base that economic entities like businesses and labor unions have. It seemed the government and foundation money would last forever.

But it didn't. Even the direct-mail well has been getting low. So good-works groups are thinking more and more of self-sustaining bases.

One of the leaders in this social enterprise movement—and this will be a surprise to many—is Ralph Nader. Since the 1970s, Nader has been virtually a synonym for government regulation. But this son of a small-town immigrant baker has always been an entrepreneur. His original capital was a damage settlement from General Motors, arising from the company's investigation into his personal life after his early attacks on the Corvair. He used this to build a cohort of activist groups in Washington, D.C., which he sustained largely through his speeches and writing, with some foundation money and later direct mail.

UNITING FORCES FOR MUTUAL BENEFIT

Then, in the Reagan 1980s, Nader shifted his focus from government regulation to consumer self-help in the market. An example is Buyer's Up, a residential fuel-buying club now operating in several states. By combining their purchasing power, ordinary homeowners can get the low prices and extra attention that big corporate customers get. Nader also moved from lobbying Congress to direct voter initiatives, such as the law California voters passed to bring down car insurance rates.

Now Nader is attempting to activate time that market forces leave dormant, on behalf of social betterment. (Actually, he has spent his life trying to activate citizens, but now he's doing so on a more targeted basis.) His first target is what he calls latent institutions, such as college alumni groups, which generally function as little besides cash cows for their alma mater. Starting with his own class, Princeton '55, Nader is trying to turn these into a positive social force. He feels that many of his peers have probably climbed as high up the corporate ladder as they can or care to and are ready to use their knowledge to make a contribution to a world they may have helped pollute.

The founders of another group, Habitat for Humanity, have come closer to a dynamic that mobilizes time outside the market on a self-sustaining basis. Through Habitat, volunteers contribute hours to build or rehabilitate houses for people who can't normally afford them. These people pay a nominal amount—$20,000, say—and their payback record would be the envy of any S&L or student loan operation. More to the present point, each person who gets to buy one of these houses pledges to help build a house for someone else.

The system works much like the house-raising process of frontier communities in which neighbors gathered to build houses for one another. The output has been impressive: hundreds of thousands of units built in locations all over the globe (at differing prices, of course). The sun never sets on the Habitat empire of good works.

Habitat is a form of what used to be called change work. You help me, I'll help you. It is really time barter. Time Dollars are the next step. They do for the informal economy of helping what money did for the commercial economy of barter; they free it from the tandems of you-and-me relationships and enable this time exchange to grow into a community of good works. They become a kind of scaffolding on which to rebuild the informal, household economy.

And like money, Time Dollars open up new channels for enterprise. They link supply and demand the way the market does, in a fluid and self-adjusting way. But they activate supply the market rejects and demand the market ignores. Like the market, Time Dollars offer rewards, but for behavior that advances humane ends. Also like the market, Time Dollar programs have an inner growth dynamic: Each time someone earns a credit by helping another person, that person takes on an obligation to help someone else.

Perhaps most important of all, the Time Dollar concept includes the excitement of the market for those who get the bug: the opportunity to build and risk and dream. And they set these dreams free of the market's tyrannical command to deploy resources where the monetary return is greatest. Instead, entrepreneurs can begin to deploy time where it does the most good.

A RAINBOW LINKS THE GENERATIONS

That is how Josefina Carbonell was thinking about her Project Rainbow to link elderly Cubans with working mothers in need of child care.

Not too long ago, Carbonell thought she had the answer to her resource problem. It was the concept of double duty. Locate the child care center on the premises of a senior center, and the two could ride almost for the price of one. The facility was already there, though substantial public funds were needed to renovate it to comply with licensing requirements. The nurses, dietitian, and other staff were already there, too, along with buses for transportation. Best of all, there was a ready supply of seniors, who had time to spare and were eager to play a role in the lives of the children of their children.

The extended family was important in Cuban life before the mass exodus from Castro's regime. Children grew up around their grandparents, who played a significant role in their lives. In the 1960s and

1970s, however, the second generation dispersed from the old neighborhoods, following any number of ethnic groups before them. The older folks felt deprived of the contact with their grandkids, and this has continued to be an issue in Cuban life.

Carbonell had in mind much more than a babysitting operation. She wanted a model child development center, with the best in professional staff, combined with the tenderness and care of the older generation. Political clout gained the capital grants from the state. But she needed cash to pay the professional staff; and most of the families she wished to serve couldn't begin to pay enough to support those salaries through fees. The state provided some money for this, too, but Time Dollars became an increasingly important part of the business equation. They turned the free time of the seniors—generally considered a social burden—into a resource for the center. And they provided a way for low-income parents to pay these seniors back.

The senior center was already a daily gathering place for hundreds of elders from the surrounding Cuban neighborhoods. And many of these were already members of the Time Dollar program in Greater Miami. So enlisting these workers as staff was a very small step. It was a very important one, however, for the seniors involved.

Project Rainbow is a warm, cozy wing on the rear of the Little Havana headquarters, in the middle of the old Cuban district. It has the feel of a well-equipped kindergarten or rumpus room, with toys and posters and miniature mats for napping on the floor. There are little boxes along the walls, where the children keep their personal belongings.

There are four to five Time Dollar workers at any particular time, who work under the teacher and assistant teacher. They help in every aspect of the program, freeing the teachers to focus on actual instruction and the developmental work for which they have been trained. "The program really has been good for me," says Julia Perez, who has been working there a few weeks. "I keep busy with the children. It makes me feel useful and needed."

Ruben Alvarez, a sturdy retiree with a sweet, charming manner is equally enthused. Alvarez has been working at the center for 1½ years and it is a high point of his life. "I love them and I feel loved, too," he says. "I feel needed and appreciated."

The real beauty of the Time Dollar concept is that the generational healing doesn't stop there. Most of the parents of kids at the center can't afford to pay much money. The state pays for some, under the welfare reform act that helps welfare recipients get back to work. But these parents can also pay in time; and by doing so, they can fill some of the center's gaping needs. The center is only open during the week, for example. On weekends, many of the seniors sit alone in dingy apartments waiting for Monday. Some have little to eat, because they depend on leftovers from Little Havana's hot lunch program during the week.

Why couldn't parents bring their kids to visit during the weekend, to brighten those lonely days and bring a little food—as family rather than as charity? The time the seniors give to the children would then come back in time given to themselves. This hasn't happened yet. But when it does, it will open yet other possibilities. Time Dollar markets grow like the commercial kind; except they don't have to manufacture needs, because the needs are already there.

WHY STOP WITH A SINGLE CENTER?

By most measures, Project Rainbow was a success. The seniors were happy. The children were happy. The center was keeping its head above water financially. But Carbonell wasn't satisfied.

One center didn't begin to meet the needs of the Cuban community. For every family the center could help, there were thousands more who still needed day care at a price they could afford. "I want it to be a beacon of hope for the entire Cuban community, not an island of privilege in a sea of misery," Carbonell said. "No way."

First, she tried to raise money to build a similar facility at another of Little Havana's senior centers. Despite her pull in Tallahassee, the money just wasn't there. That meant she had to find another way. So Carbonell called her kitchen cabinet together and asked them to explore an entirely different approach.

Most low-income mothers in the community use mom-and-pop day care that is really just babysitting in someone's home. It is a cottage industry: cheap to start, free of regulation if under six kids are involved.

. The quality of care often leaves a lot to be desired. The providers can't afford to do much on what the parents can afford to pay.

So rather than build an expensive new center, Carbonell thought, why not try to build on what was already there? Use Project Rainbow as a kind of training hub for these mom-and-pop providers. And build an entirely new kind of business plan, with Time Dollars an integral part. Seniors could be trained at the center as kind of adjunct child development staff, to help the mom-and-pop providers and fill in when they came in for training or were sick. They could give the service credits they earned to their own grandkids, to help them get care, too. This would bring the generations back together in yet another way.

The scope of this new concept could bring in more state money. If Carbonell could bring the small operators up to legal standard, they would qualify for money under the state's workfare program, funded under the federal Family Support Act. This in turn gave the idea an economic development twist.

Carbonell's theory of the Cuban community's economic success is that once a dollar enters, it never gets an exit visa. It just keeps circulating, as Cubans buy from their own, causing what economists call a multiplier effect. Carbonell had in mind a central purchasing arrangement, through which Project Rainbow could buy supplies in bulk for all the mom-and-pop centers. They could have a central lending library of toys and books and educational materials; they could buy gas for Time Dollar workers who drove other Time Dollar workers to day care sites. All this would cut costs and keep the federal dollars multiplying in the community.

In business terms, Project Rainbow would become a kind of child care temp agency, a purchasing agent, a center of quality control. In social terms, it would meet the needs of three generations of Cuban Americans.

WORK WITH THE MOM-AND-POPS

Carbonell's team came back with a report that made her concept seem all the more imperative. The mom-and-pop centers run on incredibly tight margins, the report said. And what the kids get is little more than custodial care.

To be sure, the start-up costs for these operations are very low. This is one reason that mothers with small children see them as a way to make a little money at home. Looking after four kids can seem little different than looking after two. On the other hand, expenses add up quickly: from food and office supplies to wages for fill-in caregivers, and insurance. Collecting payment from parents is a major problem. Sickness can be a disaster. (What do you do if you wake up sick one morning and the kids are coming in 30 minutes?)

Not surprisingly, the returns are low—less than minimum wage in many cases when you reckon in the time really spent. And the care is often what one would expect at that wage level: Put the kids in front of the TV and leave them alone. Some caregivers are warm and nurturing, but that depends on the luck of the draw.

Despite all this, most of the day care in America is home-based care. And that is likely to continue, given the lack of funds for new centers like Project Rainbow, unless a way can be found to upgrade them without increasing the amount they take out of the family's income. Many working parents prefer home-based care. It is flexible, low cost, and it comforts parents to know that their children are in a home. This gives Carbonell's project a new dimension of importance. If home-based care is the continuing trend, and if it is in such marginal shape, then a practical way to upgrade this care could be a model for the entire country.

It turned out that Ford Foundation projects had already developed most of the business plans and training manuals for home-based day care. So Project Rainbow is now raising the money to put these into effect. Time Dollars are going to help to make it happen.

Ruben Alvarez was one of those who lost the chance to be involved with his own grandkids in the 1960s and 1970s. Now Project Rainbow is providing a second chance.

"I had children, but I was never able to bring up my own grandchildren," he says. "These kids whose parents have to work—I can be a grandfather to them." It is not customary for men to volunteer at day care centers. Some might think it a woman's role. But to Alvarez, that's why his being there is all the more important. "They have a lot of mother figures but they don't have father figures. The boys need that."

12

Centro San Vicente: From Ability to Pay to Willingness to Give

When Phyllis Armijo scheduled a retreat in early 1990, the mission of the Daughters of Charity health clinic in El Paso seemed in jeopardy.

The Order, known for the charity hospitals it operates around the world, had already been forced to sell Hotel Dieu, the one it had operated in El Paso for nearly a hundred years. To keep faith with the poor of the city, the Daughters had opened the clinic, Centro San Vicente, in the poorest, most underserved part of town. Now it, too, was in trouble.

The staff of 15, plus 30 volunteers, consisted of sisters from the Order and community people. They had recruited Armijo, the dynamic public affairs officer from a local hospital, to be director.

When the center opened in November 1988, expectations were high. By some measures, the results were promising as well. San Vicente, as the clinic was known, served over 7,000 needy residents during the first year and a half, with services ranging from immunization to prenatal care. The clinic pioneered an award-winning health program for diabetic women.

Yet for all these efforts, the community's medical needs remained staggering; the more Centro San Vicente did, the more it seemed to fall behind. The lack of basic sanitation made the area a breeding ground for disease; the needs of the residents were matched only by their inability to pay for care.

The Daughters of Charity run a lean operation, and the nuns on staff work for a pittance; their reward comes from the service itself. Still, they found themselves caught in the classic dilemma of medical aid to the poor. Needs were escalating out of control, yet there was no money to pay for the care already delivered—despite increased revenues from donations, clinic fees, and foundation grants.

It was the old debate. You cannot fulfill your mission if you do not survive; but if you focus on survival, you can easily lose sight of your mission. The board had put it bluntly: We will continue to provide a subsidy; but if you don't stabilize your income and balance the budget, you must be prepared to close up shop.

As a last resort, Armijo and the staff at Centro San Vicente began to think about Time Dollars as a way to bridge the gap between resources and needs. The result was better than anyone hoped for. Today, Centro San Vicente is a case study of how a clinic serving the poorest of the poor integrated Time Dollars into a conventional accounting system. This step changed the fee structure in a radical manner. The old approach was to charge according to "ability to pay"; now, Centro San Vicente looks at "ability to give" as well.

The story of Centro San Vicente also shows how Time Dollars can help turn consumers of health care—even the very poorest—into producers, altering fundamentally the definition of care.

SERVING THE POOREST OF THE POOR

El Paso is the poverty capital of the United States. Almost two out of four residents fall below the poverty line. Lower Valley, the area directly outside the city, is even worse. This strip of land between Interstate 10 and the Mexican border is filled with shanty settlements called *colonias*. There is no water, no sewerage, and no transportation between the city limits and the border. And that means no access to medical care, schools, or jobs. No jobs means no tax base to finance schools or other community needs.

Locals call it Zip code 79915, the way one might say "Stalag 17." Health problems here are legion. Diabetes, anemia, malnutrition, substance abuse—the list goes on. By the time children from the *colonias* are school age, most have had hepatitis. Eighty percent of the babies in the *colonias* are born to teenage mothers, resulting in many premature infants. The cost of caring for one is $10,000 the first day and $2,000 per day thereafter, with an average hospital stay of 45 days. Many of these don't live long, despite the care and expense.

The medical needs of the *colonias* are compounded by the patients' lack of money to pay for care. Only a quarter of the physicians who practice in El Paso County will accept Medicaid/Medicare patients. Many of the people whom Centro San Vicente serves are not eligible for either federal program anyway, or else they have not applied. One in three of Centro San Vicente's clients come from families earning under $5,000 a year; four out of five families are below the poverty line.

When the Centro San Vicente board met in 1989, the burning issue was the fee schedule. Considering the volume of service rendered, the clinic was not generating much income. Why couldn't fees be raised, the board wanted to know? Why couldn't collection rates be better?

The obvious questions. But all the answers led to the same dead end: Don't increase the fees, and the red ink continues to flow; increase the fees, and San Vicente's mission is violated. Most clients can't pay the fees anyway; they pay what they can—30 to 40 percent of the actual cost of the service, at best. Possibly, a few clients could be signed up for Medicare, but the number of eligibles would never be great. Moreover, their clientele is particularly wary of entanglements with the federal government.

After a meandering discussion, the board did what boards often do; it dumped the problem back in Armijo's lap. Improve the collection process, they said.

Armijo is a slightly built woman who wears her hair pulled back from a delicate face. She avoids flamboyant clothing, but there is always an understated feeling of old tapestry in the dresses she wears or the shawl wrapped over her shoulders.

Armijo greets visitors to the clinic as a gracious hostess, with a warm smile and a charming deference. In action, however, she moves like quicksilver through the clinic, speaking quickly, noting every detail, greeting every patient individually and warmly. In an auditorium, standing small behind a tall podium, she can hold an audience spellbound with phrases alternatively soulful and stirring, fiery but somehow gentle. One of her weapons is the knowledge that others will underestimate her determination and staying power.

In Armijo's office is a dog-eared paperback book bearing the dry title *Community-Oriented Primary Care*. This collection of essays, her bible, was published in the mid-1970s. That was the era when the Baby Boom began to descend upon the nation's medical schools, and the problems of medical care in poor and rural areas became a fashionable subject. The result was a new approach to medicine that looked not just at sore throats and tumors but also at underlying social problems such as malnutrition. Somehow, the focus had to shift from treatment to prevention and from individual to community.

But how? A sole practitioner, working in a hamlet of Appalachia, was hard-pressed to handle the cases in his or her waiting room, let alone address "underlying social problems" such as isolation and lack of sewers. No one had figured out how to make community health care work on a practical level.

Phyllis Armijo was still committed to the ideal, however. She had pioneered a nationally acclaimed program, Paso a Paso—Step by Step—in which female volunteers led diabetic women through an intensive course of exercise and education. Armijo wanted to expand the approach. The question was how, when she didn't even have enough money for the day-to-day operations of the clinic.

Three months after the stormy board meeting over fees, San Vicente held a weekend retreat for its board and staff. Finances and the fee schedule were still very much on everyone's mind. But a new factor had been added. Armijo and several of the board members had seen an article in *Newsweek* magazine about the Time Dollar program. This new currency appealed to an intuitive sense that the people they served could be a resource instead of a burden.

Armijo began the retreat with a simple question: What would happen if the clinic were to accept Time Dollars for its services instead of, or in addition to, regular dollars? What would it mean when clients paid with their time instead of just with money?

Not surprisingly, the finance people immediately brought up the implications for the budget. Of course, they wanted to expand the clinic's activities, but wouldn't this new program require money? And wouldn't it reduce revenues even more? If people could pay with time, why would they part with even the few dollars they pay now? Then, how could the clinic buy vaccines and other needed supplies?

PATIENTS AS PARTNERS

Maybe they wouldn't pay *entirely* in Time Dollars, Armijo countered. They could use the new currency for the part of the bill that they didn't have the money for. She was groping along with everyone else. But somehow, Time Dollars seemed to offer a way for people to contribute *something*.

Armijo wasn't just talking about another form of payment. She was looking for a fundamentally different way for the center to think about its mission. It was clear that there would never be enough money from the Daughters of Charity or from the people they served, so patients would have to become partners in their own care, by producing some of the health services they needed.

What kind of services could patients provide other patients? The traditional model meant case-by-case treatment: Get people to the clinic. Give them shots. Screen them for diabetes or cancer or TB. What could people do in that context to pay for their treatment? And where would San Vicente get the resources to launch this new program when they were already in the red?

Well, one possibility was transportation. People have to get to the clinic before they can get treatment. So other patients could earn Time Dollars for driving them. And fewer "no shows" at the clinic might mean more revenues.

With Time Dollars, Centro San Vicente could expand to include counseling and prenatal care for expectant mothers, as well as help after the babies were born. This is a proven way to reduce infant mortality and child abuse. Armijo had wanted to do it all along; she just didn't have the money. She could pay the counselors in Time Dollars and they could use the currency to pay their own fees at the clinic.

Soon the ideas were flying thick and fast. Why not a babysitting service for the sick children of working parents, who can't afford to stay home and lose a day's pay? A neighbor-to-neighbor program for the elderly could provide them with companionship and shopping and help around the house. Maybe volunteers could help provide better and cheaper child day care; some volunteers might even work by maintaining the cars used in the Time Dollar car pool program.

Gradually, the staff and board members began to realize how many not-strictly-medical things people could do for one another and thereby help Centro San Vicente do its job more effectively. If people paid Time Dollars for medical services, Centro San Vicente might have less money, but it would also have less need of money.

The possibilities could be even broader. If the clinic were to take on health problems at their source, it could contemplate a whole new range of activities—digging wells or removing lead-based paint, for example. If clients could provide rides and babysitting, why not undertake projects such as these? Just the previous month, elderly volunteers in El Paso had completed a major survey of sources of potential water contamination that identified several thousand potential sources of pollution. Already the volunteers had formed a task force to work with the city and county on groundwater contamination. Wasn't that just the sort of thing Centro San Vicente could do?

Dropping her voice to a quiet, matter-of-fact level, Armijo posed the question that seemed to flow from everything else. "Doesn't this mean our idea of mission has to change?" she said. "If we are talking about health, then the real mission of El Centro has to be to create a *community.*" Nobody was sure what that implied. But they knew one thing: Dispensing more and more medical services was no longer enough. It was a means but not an end. Organizing to dig a well, mobilizing a march on the city council, was as much their job as vaccinating people. This was a way to turn community-oriented primary care into something more than theory.

A NEW STANDARD OF PAYMENT: ABILITY TO CARE

The first reaction from the Daughters of Charity was "No." They couldn't afford more expansion and they couldn't afford a request for more funds. Besides, they couldn't simply forgive the bills of Centro San Vicente's clients.

Armijo needed to explain why this new system wouldn't hurt revenues. She sensed that the basic problem lay in the concept of ability to pay. Without money, you couldn't buy services. Anything else was charity, and that was limited by the amount of money at hand.

"We can't be limited in our vision by the amount of money we have," Armijo said at the time. "Ability to pay can't determine our decision to give medical care. Can't we find a different standard? What about a standard based on ability to care or ability to give?" she said. If you can pay money, pay money; if you can give care, then give care. Armijo decided to get some data from her business manager Jaime Villegas.

It turned out that the cashiers in the business office had no way of verifying what the clients said about their income, so the billing process turned into a bargaining session. The patients were poor; Centro San Vicente was poor. But the patients were much poorer. So the clinic ended up absorbing a loss of 58 to 68 percent on every bill. Those who lied about their incomes paid less than those who told the truth. Taking into account the likely amount of lying, Centro San Vicente probably had given away more discounts than necessary.

Villegas says the Time Dollar concept is a way to stabilize this discount process *and* increase revenues. For example, the clinic might limit the low-income discount to 50 percent of the bill. Some might get 10 percent, others 20 or 30 percent. But 50 percent would be the maximum. "Right now, we are giving away an average of 58 to 68 percent," he said. "And that's the average. Some of the folks make such a fuss that the cashier just gives them a 90 percent discount."

With a new system, the clinic would have a position for bargaining. It could offer a larger discount—up to another 25 percent of the bill, for example—to those willing to help the clinic. Some would do it; some wouldn't. But that would help weed out the deadbeats.

Either way, Villegas felt, the center came out ahead. If a family was willing to help, the center could save money. If they would pay, that would be great. "At least this way, they would stop using us," he said. Centro San Vicente would never turn patients away just because they couldn't pay, but patients who had no willingness to give were another matter. A line had to be drawn somewhere—an ethical, not just an economic line.

And once people became personally involved in the clinic, they might have a different attitude toward paying. "They will not only earn Time Dollars," Villegas said, "They will want to pay off their bills, a little at a time, because the clinic will be more like family to them."

IMPOSSIBLE PROGRAMS BECAME POSSIBLE WITH TIME DOLLARS

There were a lot of details to work out. How exactly do you incorporate time into a fee structure based on money? Since Time Dollar systems don't use market rates for wages, how much would each credit be worth for purposes of paying off the bill? San Vicente was literally inventing a whole new way of thinking about prices and payment.

Armijo began to plan new programs that would be impossible without Time Dollars. Infant and maternal mortality are big problems in the community, and from the start, the clinic has provided prenatal care. Time Dollars opened the way for a much more vigorous approach. For one thing, San Vicente decided to give expectant mothers an incentive to come in for prenatal care. The sisters designed a program that allows expectant mothers to use Time Dollars to reduce the charge for prenatal care from $250 to $75. In addition, they can use Time Dollars to get help taking care of the new baby from an *abuelita* (granny) pool. How will the pregnant women earn these Time Dollars? From a baby shower, of course, at which friends will bring pledges of hours as well as more traditional gifts.

At a time of bank failures, budget deficits, and general gloom, things look a bit brighter for many in the Lower Valley. Maybe actual cash income won't go up, but if people can get rides and tutoring and babysitting and other help from their neighbors, money will count a little less.

Money gets you one of two things: someone's time or products such as TVs. With Time Dollars, you get the first and you get the second, too, because the money you have goes further. No one in the Lower Valley will get wealthy. Time Dollars hardly substitute for the jobs and public services that the area desperately needs. But a sense of community and health are not bad starting points in a locality that has neither.

One day during this period of planning and struggle, Armijo opened up a note that had been pressed into her hand by a patient who had served as a volunteer health worker. It was an old saying among her people, she explained. "If you do not live to serve," it said, "you do not deserve to live." Phyllis Armijo felt she was back on home territory.

13

Michigan and Missouri Let a Hundred Flowers Bloom

In the early 1980s, Missouri was in budget trouble. Other states were, too, of course; but the Missouri governor had a novel idea. He wanted a volunteer program that had some real traction. "Something like a blood bank," he told his staff.

Missouri became the first state to enact Time Dollar legislation. In contrast to the bureaucratic sludge that mired the Florida program, Time Dollars in Missouri got sun and air. "I'm in the bureaucracy but I hate the bureaucratic paperwork process," says Joanne Polowy, an official with the Missouri Department of Human Services. "I felt it had to be a neighborhood grass-roots thing."

The state didn't even bother to issue regulations the first year. They just got local groups involved and watched the concept grow. "I just played Johnny Appleseed—going from place to place, talking to groups, planting the idea," Polowy says.

If Florida showed how hostile officials can kill a program, then Missouri—and Michigan—showed how committed state officials can help bring one to life. Time Dollar programs don't really need state help. Most are going it alone. But states have many reasons to want to get involved. If they do it right, both sides gain.

Michigan's program took shape after an assistant to a Republican state senator named Connie Binsfeld (now the lieutenant governor) saw a syndicated column on Time Dollars in a local newspaper. The bill had a Democratic sponsor in the House, and was signed by a Democratic governor, which suggests the broad appeal of the concept. Then it went to Eric Berry, the state's Director of Senior Resources.

Michigan's bill was focused on people who care for frail seniors in their homes. By providing relief (or respite) for these people, the state hoped to forestall burnout and a resulting need for expensive nursing home care. Berry, a Republican, took a decentralized approach, seeking out local groups that could use Time Dollars to expand existing programs. Sixty were interested; he chose ten, and most of a $250,000 appropriation went to them rather than to the bureaucracy in Lansing.

Berry brought all the directors together once a month; this boosted morale and also inspired a bit of healthy competition between the programs. In Michigan, too, the state took nearly two years before getting around to issuing regulations. "We wanted to avoid the complications in Florida," Berry said later.

In this supportive atmosphere, the programs grew quickly. When the pilot phase of the law expired in 1990, the legislature enacted it as an ongoing state endeavor, with a mandate to serve all the elderly in the state. In the fiscal crunch of the early 1990s, the Time Dollar program emerged from some complicated horse-trading with a modest increase. But more important, Berry opened up the program to virtually every volunteer organization in the state. He also established a kind of statewide automated teller network, through which a Time Dollar earned at any participating organization could be spent at any other. The program is no longer limited to respite care; and so long as one party in a transaction is over 60, the other party can be any age.

MISSOURI MEETS OBSTACLES MASTERFULLY

In Missouri, meanwhile, obstacles were met with practicality and finesse. Like Michigan's legislation, for example, the Missouri bill was confined to respite care; but it left in limbo the friend or family member who cared for a senior who lived alone. Could they get respite, too? Florida officials might have blown a fuse. To Polowy, no big deal.

"We got around that one," she says. "If there was a neighbor who looked in regularly, we just designated that person a 'psychological caregiver' who needed respite. So the credit earned went in the state's bank, guaranteed."

One of Missouri's major programs is at Grace Hill Neighborhood Services, a settlement house serving over 40,000 disadvantaged people in St. Louis.

Grace Hill was struggling with budget problems around the same time the state was. Independently, it started groping toward a kind of service "blood bank" to build a mutual-aid network among its members. Step by step, the effort has led Grace Hill to a whole new sense of what it's doing. Now it sees its main mission as enlisting residents as participants in the community's well-being.

Grace Hill went through a cycle familiar in the 1960s and 1970s. There was a great surge of federal funds, starting with the Great Society, only to be followed by the drought of the Reagan years. In this case, however, the way in proved to be a way out. Grace Hill had always worked on the premise that people with needs are also people with assets; and this view, faced with a severe budget crunch, led the staff naturally to explore ways that its clients could pool these assets in a barter network, without the mediation of money.

Grace Hill's story is instructive on several levels. It illustrates how conditions in the early 1980s, much as during the Depression, literally pushed social service agencies toward a rediscovery of time barter and self-reliance. It shows how Time Dollars can claim back for ordinary people the life roles that credentialed experts have monopolized.

But perhaps most important, the story of Grace Hill shows how a Time Dollar program, once started, generates a growth momentum as people see how time can take the place of money.

SATISFYING THE SPECIAL NEEDS OF THE ELDERLY POOR

Grace Hill began early in the century as a settlement house in a neighborhood of working poor. For the first 50 years or so, it functioned in the traditional manner, providing recreation and social work to a community that was becoming increasingly poor and black. All that changed with the War on Poverty and the flood of funding that came suddenly from Washington.

Like similar groups all over the country, Grace Hill quickly mastered the skills of grantsmanship, inventing new programs, repackaging old ones, casting these in the jargon of graduate schools of social work. Its mission expanded from mere one-on-one helping to a larger focus on community development. In the 1960s and early 1970s, there was money for low-income housing, a health center, and a Head Start program. Then, in the mid-1970s, the federal government discovered the elderly, thus opening a whole new arena of expansion.

It was also, of course, an arena of acute and growing need, tied directly to the erosion of the second economy of home and community. People were living longer, and the Medicaid program, enacted in the 1960s, provided somewhat for their medical needs. But few had given much thought to the care of the elderly outside the doctor's office: How do you *get* to the doctor, for example, if you can no longer drive or walk to a bus stop (assuming there is a bus)? Or how do you eat if you are too frail to go out shopping? Previously, friends and family provided such help, but they didn't seem to be there anymore.

A growing specialty called gerontology seized upon the problem, and daily life functions became the subject of expert measurement and concern. There was much discussion of ADLs (activities of daily living, such as dressing and washing) and IADLs (instrumental activities of daily living, such as shopping or writing letters). Chilly as such parlance may be, at least people were focusing on defining the support functions that the household economy had traditionally provided. Typically, Grace Hill was in the forefront, with a program to integrate medical care with this new range of services. The goal was to help the elderly live at home, away from nursing homes. In the acronymic fashion of the day, they called the program STAES, System to Assure Elderly Services.

In essence, elderly people coming to Grace Hill's clinic would be evaluated on their ability with ADLs and IADLs. Others would be enlisted to conduct a survey door-to-door to identify the elderly in the neighborhood. In addition, local beauty parlors, drugstores, and the like would be asked to keep an eye out for older customers who were having trouble getting around. Then staff social workers could contact these folks and try to find help for their needs. Grace Hill linked up with settlement houses serving two adjoining areas, thus broadening the base for the new assessment program.

This expanded base got Grace Hill staff to thinking. Lots of seniors contacted in the survey would prove to be reasonably healthy. Why let that contact go to waste, they thought, when they might be enlisted as volunteers to help those who showed greater need? Thus was born a new volunteer program in which seniors helped other seniors. Grace Hill hired staff to match volunteers with elderly recipients and to monitor the care they provided.

AFTER THE MONEY STOPPED

STAES prospered in the first couple of years. But then, in the third year, the Reagan administration cut the funding abruptly. Grace Hill found itself with 750 frail persons on its hands, some 500 of whom would go to nursing homes if they didn't get help at home. Pushed to the wall, the Grace Hill leadership took their previous thinking one step further. If volunteers could work with the needy one-on-one, why couldn't these same volunteers be trained to run their own programs? They could help the needy deal with government agencies, and generally step into the roles formerly held by paid staff.

That role followed the latest trend in social work circles, something called case management. This is the social work equivalent of the professional shopper. The case manager contacts various government and private agencies on behalf of an elderly person, trying to assemble funds and assistance to help that particular person. By necessity more than design, the STAES team leaders became, in effect, volunteer case managers. But they could do so only because they were building on a groundwork that the staff specialists and caseworkers had already put in place.

Grace Hill still faced a hemorrhage of funds: job training, housing, food stamps, child care—all these were in jeopardy. Its budget dropped by almost a third, and various agencies it worked with lost their funding completely, leaving Grace Hill to serve their clientele. "We had fewer dollars but suddenly had more people because other agencies closed their doors," recalled Richard Gram, director of the organization. "And we decided that if we just reduced our programs, they wouldn't be viable." The only way out was to extend the volunteer approach, and try to find a way to make it dependable and solid.

A Grace Hill board member who worked at the PET milk company arranged a day of free management consulting, to help the staff think through their dilemma in the focused manner corporations use. It was an intense day-long session, 15 people in a closed room, developing a whole "package" (in marketing parlance) from services to acronym. "We told them we had to find a way to make less more," recalled Betty Marver, now director of Grace Hill's Time Dollar exchange. "And that's what we came back to at the end of the day—MORE."

Today, MORE stands for Member Organized Resource Exchange, defined as "a self-help service that creates solutions for neighbors through the exchange of members' resources and abilities." Grace Hill staff read that theme statement with the conviction of corporate managers quoted in the book *In Search of Excellence*. It provided an organizing focus for the lean years. It also proved the old saw that fortune shines on those who help themselves.

Around that time, Missouri was starting to formulate its Time Dollar program. When the state began looking for sites in St. Louis, Grace Hill's MORE initiative was a Cinderella's slipper. The settlement house was already committed to mutual self-help. Why not enlist these same volunteers to provide respite care and bank their hours in the state's new service credit bank?

The concept could go much further. Grace Hill had a full panoply of programs, spanning the generations, and this could be the basis for a whole Time Dollar economy, for which respite care was just a starting point. Kids could shovel snow and work in teams on heavy yard work for seniors. Elders could babysit or help at day care centers. Adults could staff a driver pool or do light home repair. They all would become contributors to something worthy of being called a community. The state signed on, as did the Robert Wood Johnson Foundation, which pitched in a three-year grant of around $200,000.

Grace Hill had groped its way into something much bigger than it first imagined. A computerized time bank meant people could find help quickly or could match up with others who needed their help. This made the whole district operate a little like the old kitchen table or side porch; it turned people into neighbors, even though they might live several miles away. In addition—and this has special relevance to the underclass—Grace Hill's programs were breaking down the artificial barriers to helping work.

In the market, tasks tend to move in one direction: toward credentialed professionals and experts. A social work degree might be required to run a volunteer program or visit an elderly person at home. Time Dollar programs move work the other way, toward the lowest possible level of specialization and training. You don't need an advanced degree to visit homebound seniors and help them do their laundry or fix lunch. This means more opportunity for the needy in providing those services—a redefinition of work that is likely to feed back to the world beyond volunteer and Time Dollar programs.

PUTTING TIME DOLLARS IN VOLUNTEERS' HANDS

Today, MORE volunteers put in roughly 100,000 hours annually in helping work. Close to 250 team leaders check up on over 1,500 frail elderly in their communities each day. Trained volunteers put signs in their windows informing neighbors that theirs is a home they can turn to for help. Most MORE participants are still working on a straight volunteer basis, without the reciprocal exchange of a Time Dollar bank. Grace Hill's goal is to use Time Dollars gradually to integrate all of Grace Hill's programs into a single volunteer exchange.

The effort is going slowly. Even in social service agencies, programs become hard to change once they are established. In its early phases, the Time Dollar exchange is operating on a relatively modest scale: a little over 400 workers, roughly a third of whom had never volunteered before. A survey of these workers found that over 90 percent say they are in the program "to help others," while less than a third said they are interested in earning credits. It was significant, however, that this third tended to be the most needy; Time Dollars feel like a real currency for those who think they may need help down the line.

Step by step, Grace Hill will deploy Time Dollars throughout its system — to the young, to welfare mothers, to training programs, to housing programs. They will even accept Time Dollars in their health clinic as part of a sliding-scale fee system, so that people can pay with their care as well as with money.

Initially, some volunteers were suspicious of the credit approach. They may have survived a serious cancer operation, for example, and felt that "God spared them to do something for others," in the words of Mary Hamilton of the Grace Hill staff. But they are starting to see the credits in a different light.

The very day that Hamilton was talking about the program, a man came in to report 300 hours for working with two people who are terminally ill. This man had survived triple bypass surgery; he had resisted the credits on the grounds that when he was sick, people cared for him. But then he realized that the credits do precisely that — bring visitors to those who otherwise might have none. "Time Dollars made him think of money," Hamilton says. "But that's just the term we use to distinguish the program."

THE QUESTION OF A GUARANTEE

Missouri was the first state to guarantee Time Dollars earned in the respite program. If people hold Time Dollars and can't find another volunteer to help them, the state will pay for that help instead.

To Florida officials, a state commitment raised the specter of liabilities growing out of control. In Missouri, people handled it with aplomb. To the extent such a threat exists, Polowy thinks it could provide a useful goad. "Then maybe they would make sure [a program] was running in every county and district in Missouri," she says. "That's what I'd like to see."

But Joanne Polowy also defuses the guarantee issue with a little common sense: consider the plus side of the ledger before getting too gloomy over a hypothetical minus. "I guess they figure that regardless of how much money they have to spend," she said of the legislature, "they will have saved thousands more by enabling families to keep taking care of their own, rather than sending them off to nursing homes."

Paul Marshall could offer testimony to that. Marshall was one of the first people in the state to call upon the Time Dollar program, and he represents another plus on the program's ledger that is often overlooked. If Time Dollars are part of a state's debt, they are one that people actually desire to pay.

WHEN PEOPLE WANT TO PAY FOR SERVICES

Few people who get a service from government—street cleaning, for example, or a traffic cop at an intersection—rush down to city hall with check in hand. Most people grumble over taxes, no matter how much service they get. They pay only what they have to, avoid whatever they can. When help comes from another person, by contrast, the whole dynamic changes. People *want* to return the favor, even if to a third person. Since Time Dollars embody that relation, they are obligations people want to pay, even more than to receive.

Marshall lives in a small rural community called St. Joseph, where the main bank still has a bootscraper at the entrance for getting the manure off of boot bottoms. The stockyards and the holding pens are deserted now. Swift & Company closed its meat packing plants and moved south when the unions demanded higher wages. St. Jo (as residents call it) has never recovered from that loss.

In the fall, trucks still stand waiting at the grain elevators, stretched as far as the eye can see. Farmers still store their wheat and corn, hoping that the market will rise enough to cover their interest payments on the equipment they bought when prices were high. But the farmers are older now; the young people have up and left, those who could, drifting away to the sun belt and jobs. A whole generation is left as it pushes past 60, not knowing who'll be there when they need some help.

The point man of the Time Dollar program in St. Joseph is a man named David Berger. Dressed in tweed sports jacket, puffing between sentences on a handsome briar pipe, Berger runs an interdenominational senior service program called Interserve. Berger had gambled on Time Dollars to meet the needs of people like Paul Marshall, and on this day he was complaining about a provision in the state law that did not permit people under 60 to earn the new currency. It was giving him a real problem, he said. Just then, the problem walked in the door, brightly clad in a clown outfit, complete with pointed, tasseled jester's shoes that jingled with each step.

THE CLOWN MAKES A DEAL IN GRATITUDE

Marshall reached out with his left hand, holding on to his mother with his right. Despite the white make-up, red nose, and huge red mouth, he was blushing with embarrassment as he launched into his story. He took over the family restaurant after his father died, he said, but then sold it after his mother got sick. His wife wanted to continue working, so he stayed home to look after his mother and the two kids. Then his mother started showing signs of Alzheimer's disease.

Standing next to her son, Lottie Marshall was a thin, sprightly woman. Her eyes were bright and she smiled the whole time. The only time she interrupted was when Paul mentioned that they were coming to the Halloween luncheon at the center. "I only eat home-cooked food," she said. "I won't eat that other stuff." What she really seemed to be saying was: "I don't want charity."

It was unnerving to talk about Mrs. Marshall's condition as if she weren't there, even though she stood there looking as though she understood every word. But Paul continued.

"I don't know what we'd do without this [Time Dollar] program," he said. "My wife and I got to go out twice since Mattie's been helping us. One time we were able to drive into Kansas City to eat dinner out at one of our favorite restaurants. Another time, we went to the movies. The movie was really rotten—but just getting out made it a big event."

Paul confided he was feeling drained. His mother's memory was so bad that she couldn't be left alone for a moment, lest she turn on a stove, say, and then totally forget. He was worried. He *wanted* to help her, but sometimes he just got so exasperated. "I'm terribly afraid I'll lose control and say something to her and that will be the last words she understands," he said. "And I'll never forgive myself for (pause) . . . for the rest of my life. That's what this is saving me from."

But that gave Paul another problem. He wanted to repay, but the program wouldn't let him. He doesn't have much money; he dresses up in the clown costume for children's parties to earn a few dollars, which was why he was wearing it that day. So he wanted to pay by helping someone else. But the Time Dollar program the state enacted was only for people over 60. He didn't care if he earned a credit, he said. He just wanted to make a gift of his time, as a way of saying "thanks."

Finally, he and Berger made a deal. Marshall and his mother would carry meals to housebound seniors in his truck. It would be a special outing for his mother, where she could socialize with the people who got the meals. And Paul could repay his debt. "Some of those meals are going to be awfully cold," Berger laughed. "But it really doesn't matter."

Later, Berger drove his guest to visit Mattie Schneider, the Time Dollar worker who had been helping to care for Lottie Marshall. She was out of town that day, volunteering (though not for service credits) at a small day care center. While the children napped, she told how nice the Marshalls were to her and how she mainly just visited with Lottie.

"It's not like she's a lot of trouble," she said. "But she just forgets about things and she has to be watched. Sometimes she starts looking for her husband in the next room. He's been gone for years. Or she'll go out on the porch to get the Saturday evening paper. That doesn't exist anymore. Or she'll want to serve me some cake she just baked and she'll go looking in the icebox for a cake she must have baked a long time ago. She'll take food out of the freezer and just leave it there."

The visitor asked whether the service credits made any difference. Schneider looked at him sharply, taking the question in. The look lasted for as long as it would take to drink half a glass of water, Berger said later. "I can't say it doesn't matter," she finally said. "Like insurance. The best kind is the kind you don't have to use."

14

The New Politics of Time

In 1984, Sargent Shriver, the generalissimo of the War on Poverty in the 1960s and a Democratic vice presidential candidate, received a copy of a document entitled "Surplus People," an early exposition of the Time Dollar concept.

"It's wonderful," he responded, with his trademark enthusiasm, after he had perused the document. "This could mean the rebirth of the Democratic party." Then he paused, adding thoughtfully: "Or its demise."

Most proposals that enter the political debate are marked ideologically before they arrive. School vouchers, workfare, paid leave for new parents—even casual followers of national affairs know that conservatives will favor the first two and liberals the last. The Time Dollar, by contrast, does not fit the standard groove. It has elements that appeal to the Right, elements that appeal to the Left; and overall, it's an idea that lies in a frontal zone that is unclaimed by either side.

LIBERALS CAN LIKE THE CONCEPT . . . BUT

Liberals can like the idea because it addresses the problems of the needy. It draws on the 1960s values of local empowerment, grass-roots involvement, and freedom from stifling bureaucracies. But therein lies a rub. The national Democrats have not developed according to those values, but rather along the New Deal/Great Society model of top-down bureaucratized programs. They tend to fixate on the notion that progress lies in the deployment of government agencies and experts upon a problem.

The Democrats' core constituents, moreover, include those tied to these programs: public employees, organized recipient groups that get grants, and the "helping professionals" that serve as consultants and advisors. Time Dollar programs don't necessarily mean fewer jobs for public employees (see chapter 15). They could well mean better, more productive, and rewarding jobs. But they can appear threatening never-theless. They question the assumption that needy people are victims requiring professional intervention, and have no resources or desire or need to help themselves. They question, too, the assumption that family and community self-help are forms of backwardness, awaiting the ministrations of professional social workers, educators, and so forth.

For these very reasons, the Time Dollar concept has obvious appeal to conservatives. Volunteering and family and neighborhood are things that warm the conservative heart—often because polemically, they don't cost money. Time Dollars make human helpfulness look more like a marketplace—more like economics—and hence more congenial to the conservative mind.

But underneath the comforting self-help model, there are depth charges for the conservative mind as well, and these will separate the real conservatives from the economic opportunists who often populate the Right. Specifically, Time Dollars raise basic questions about the facile equation of self-interest with the public good. They raise questions, too, about motivation and value: If people are spurred to effort by a desire to help and a need to be needed, as well as by a desire for gain, then supply-side economics—with its glib connections between tax cuts and individual endeavor—goes largely out the window. It becomes a narrow special case, rather than the universal one its proponents claim.

Perhaps most threatening of all, Time Dollars challenge the political Right's claim to have it both ways: free market fundamentalism on the one hand and traditional home and community values on the other. The concept brings into focus how the commercial marketplace, left to its own devices, uproots these traditional values by invading the life functions that are the soil in which they grow. Values aren't hydro-ponic; they don't grow in conceptual air. Values of home require a home that *does* something besides consume. Community values require communities that serve a real function—that don't depend on things bought from a corporate marketplace or from government for their entertainment, recreation, security, and so forth.

In practice, the Right pushes an economy that undermines the very bonds of family and community that it espouses. The family dinner table may yield to McDonald's, childhood may become just another arena for marketing (TV ads aimed at children continue to soar). In all this, the Right can see nothing wrong. Someone is making money. The "invisible hand" is about its benevolent work. If families and communities are falling apart, the reason must be Planned Parenthood and rock lyrics and the late Robert Mapplethorpe's controversial photos.

NO LOYALTY TO COMMUNITY OR COUNTRY

The Time Dollar concept would force the Right to choose—between the corporation and community, between the family and the market. Major corporations are now on record that they feel no loyalty to community or even country. "There is no mindset that puts this country first," an executive from Colgate-Palmolive told the *New York Times*, in an article headlined "U.S. Businesses Loosen Link to Mother Country." Now the Right needs to choose, too, whether values like loyalty and trust come first, or the economics of the market. This choice, put into practice, could disturb its prime constituents, the corporations, whose nightmare is an America in which people want to do for one another rather than to buy.

This ambiguity explains why political support for Time Dollars has come from legislators at all points of the political spectrum, but neither party has embraced the concept in an organized way. There is one place, however, where the battle lines are clearly drawn. Legislators tend to like the Time Dollar idea because it offers a real way to address problems without large expenditures of money. And administrators often dislike the concept because it jars them from established routines.

It requires them to deal with the unwashed masses rather than with licensed professional staff. It makes them enlist the needy as full partners rather than as subordinate recipients of services.

With occasional exceptions, administrators tend to see problems as an opportunity for more staff and more funding. Time Dollars, by contrast, mean more empowerment for someone else. It is the rare administrator—Missouri and Michigan are noteworthy exceptions—who regards this as a happy prospect.

THE PROBLEMS ARE UNIVERSAL

The budget problems at every level of government are becoming so intractable, however, that these habits are going to have to change. The underlying political debate will have to change as well. For all their differences, the Right and the Left in America share one central belief: that a growing economy will wash most social problems away. Jobs will end most poverty; and the tax revenues generated by growth will provide ample relief for the rest. The possibility that economic growth itself can cause problems, thereby creating *more* needs rather than fewer, is simply beyond the pale of the conventional political debate.

That point has been driven home, of late, because Japan, Germany, and Sweden have all sent teams to examine the Time Dollar programs. That came as a surprise. These countries are not beset by the same budget deficits as is the United States; taxes are at a higher level; the balance of trade is favorable. Yet, they are encountering the same resource shortages in meeting the needs of the elderly and the young that we are. And they are projecting greater shortfalls as they move toward the year 2000. This suggests rather that the problems do not necessarily stem from a weak economy or a party in power that seeks to cut social programs. It suggests that the problems we face are built into the growth dynamic of virtually every major industrial nation.

At least one nation is confronting the problem head-on and has given it a name: chronopolitics. This country may provide a preview in some respects to what is coming in the United States.

AN IDYLL APT TO TOPPLE
IN A GENERATION

Imagine, if you can, a country where the people have been willing to tax themselves at levels exceeding 50 percent of national income, so that no citizen is needy and every citizen has access to housing and education and medical care. And imagine a country where, nevertheless, the work ethic is strong, unemployment rarely exceeds 3 percent, and economic growth has been generally healthy. Trains and airlines are on schedule. Meetings start on time. The newspapers are blissfully free of headlines on brutality and corruption. And on the average, people live to be 80 years old.

This country is Sweden, and to a visitor, it appears almost as idyllic as the statistics suggest. Stockholm, the capital, is a picture-book city of cobblestone streets and houses dating back to the 1600s, with a subway system that is modern and immaculate. The winters are cold, but most people can afford a vacation in Florida or Spain—especially with the five-week vacations that are a universal right.

But amidst this cheery picture, an economic time bomb is ticking. The Swedes know it. They talk about it, study it, debate how to defuse it, with the grim fascination of a small town when the local steel mill is on the verge of closing. The basic problem is familiar: The population is getting older, the demand for services is greater, and a country already taxed to the gills cannot keep pace with the claims on these revenues. The good life as they know it cannot last much beyond the year 2000, without a break from the past that is far more radical than the reduction of the social safety net that conservatives are always advising. "To continue in the old way will soon lead to economically disastrous consequences," a government report has acknowledged.

The Swedes view government in a far different way than does most of America. For them, government exists to solve problems, meet human needs, plot a rational course for the future. (The state of Minnesota, known for orderly and progressive government, and populated heavily by people of Scandinavian descent, is perhaps the closest comparison in the United States.) Until the recent election, they were willing to back the decisions of government as expressions of a broad-based assent. And so, with typical prudence and with a genuine desire to confront the problem, the government called upon its Secretariat for Future Studies—the very existence of which says much about the Swedes—to articulate the problem and identify the options.

DANCING AS FAST AS THEY CAN

What emerged was not of crisis proportions by American standards. But it represented an ominous trend downward in a country in which living standards are the highest priority. Many of the problems cited, in fact, were the result of the longer life span that society so ardently sought. While medical expenditures septupled over the last 20 years, helping to keep people alive longer, the social structure to support those lives was failing. The number of persons aged 85 and over will grow by 70 percent by the turn of the century, for example; and such persons spend ten weeks a year on the average in hospitals and nursing homes, largely because of a lack of care at home.

Meanwhile, the safety net was growing faster than the enterprise that supported it. Between 1960 and 1980, employment in enterprise fell by about 15,000 annually. At the same time, the care sector was enlisting almost 30,000 new employees a year, most of them women. If the growth rate of the safety net were to continue to the turn of the century, employment would double and costs would quadruple, without a proportionate increase in care.

The major stumbling block boiled down to one familiar word: money. Deficits were growing, and nobody was doing anything about it. "Putting it drastically," the commission stated, with a candor unthinkable in official reports in the United States, "the problem could be said to be that politicians are afraid to jeopardize their electoral following by demanding full payment for a service that they dare not reduce. Nor can they instigate the production which could solve the balance of payments crisis."

The Swedes are not eager to dismantle their state-funded safety net, though the last election showed a desire to slow its growth. The Swedish welfare state is designed around rewarding the work ethic: The level of services is based on past contribution. That is why Swedes are willing to pay tax rates in the 50 to 60 percent range. They "earned" their benefits, the old-fashioned way. Swedes are not lazy; Swedish productivity earns high marks; the rate of growth of the gross national product compares favorably to other industrial nations.

The problem is the explosion in demand for services—services to the elderly and children in particular. This growth in needs threatens to outstrip any affordable increase in government-provided services. In others words, Sweden cannot afford to maintain the social compact it has with its own citizens, a social compact already paid for by the elderly and now being honored by an exceptionally hard-working labor force.

Some will argue that England's Mrs. Thatcher had the answer: Cut back the safety net and let private business expand. But even if this did generate more jobs and revenues, it would not alter the underlying dynamic of industrial societies, which is that social problems increase as the society ages and, at the same time, more of life gets drawn into the commercial sphere. Even Japan, that paradigm of pro-growth economics, is encountering the gap between social needs on the one hand and resources on the other.

WE MUST ORGANIZE "TIME TO CARE"

The fall of Communism in the East Bloc has induced a dangerous complacency. That the other guy is wrong does not make us right. The question is not whether market economics have been vindicated; they have been, for what they do well. The question for the industrial democracies is how to adapt that market system to address the problems it causes and the ones it neglects.

While prevailing over Communism, the market economy has also prevailed over something else: the nonmarket economy of family and community, which was the built-in safety net of capitalism. The West—and America in particular—was so obsessed with outstripping the Russians, that it lost track of what it was doing to itself. Now the challenge is to repair the damage from the war.

The Swedes have come to realize that their remedy of tax-supported professional care can't carry the repair load anymore. And they have realized as well that without money, they have to get back to basics. "Care and welfare in the end have to do with time," the report stated.

"We will not be short of time in the future, and so the focus of this discussion is how we will organize our time so we have 'time to care.'" Unlike the United States, moreover, Sweden has a relatively weak tradition of volunteer care.

And so the Swedes leaned naturally toward a state model: compulsory community service. "Just as we need a taxation system to raise the necessary funds for public social commitments," the report said, "we believe that compulsory social service will be needed in the long run to provide all the care and welfare services that are required." This highlighted something about Time Dollars that is easily missed until the concept goes abroad. The concept is a distinctly (though not exclusively) *American* solution, open and fluid like the market, harkening more to the frontier tradition of voluntary, neighborly helping than to the statist traditions of other countries.

This is one reason that it became a minor media event when, in late 1990, a visiting American introduced the concept in Sweden at a seminar of state officials and policy makers. Public policy gets that kind of attention there. The Swedes had not considered that market incentives could be combined with volunteerism through a hybrid currency.

WOULD TIME DOLLARS CUT INTO OTHER PROGRAMS?

In private conversations, the Swedes acknowledged that the problems of their welfare net went deeper than a simple lack of funds. The complex system of supports left people feeling helpless and confused, even though they perceived the system as basically benign. Social work had low status and pay, and there were significant shortages of direct service providers, despite the influx of foreign workers overall.

The Swedes were intrigued at how the Time Dollar plan eliminates status distinctions by valuing all hours the same, regardless who does what for whom. They were positively enthused at the underlying principle that everyone has something to offer, and that a society ought to expand the opportunities for people to function productively outside the traditional market setting.

Yet they were still skeptical of the volunteer model. Given their sophistication and intellectual openness, the ensuing dialogue reached the velocity of intellectual jai-alai. And it rehearsed in many respects the debates that are likely to arise in the United States.

First off, the panel was worried that Time Dollars could become an excuse for cutting back on public funds. Sometimes the issue was stated candidly as the possible loss of jobs for government-employee unions. The answers took them aback. If people are doing what they can to help themselves, then they have a *stronger* claim to public funds. If loss of union jobs is a worry, then organize Time Dollar workers just as you once organized government workers. Dues could be paid in Time Dollars and used to care for other members who were retired or sick. And, if you stop thinking of the elderly as essentially useless, and see them instead as productive workers, it should be clear that these workers can go on strike, just like any others.

The panelists who wanted to posture as militant defenders of the elderly had something to chew on for a while. But what of those in society who are too frail or disabled to earn credits for themselves? Would they be left by the wayside, just as they are in the marketplace? The answer was that Time Dollar programs all require "pump priming" at the start, because nobody has credits when the system begins. Some have to get credits from the central bank, just to get the system going. The unspoken understanding is that the first generation of recipients doesn't have to pay; but that each succeeding generation will take care of those coming before it. Then, by spending the credits they earn, they will get the care they need from the generation coming behind.

Because of the family feeling of these programs, nobody objects to the oldest getting "free" help at first. Would you deny your grandmother a ride to the doctor because she couldn't pay? And besides, through Time Dollar programs many grandmothers discover that they *can* pay, if only through participating in a telephone assurance network. That prospect brought nods of assent in a country where dependence on a welfare bureaucracy is so widespread.

The question of taxes opened yet another dimension of the issue. If one felt that, in the interest of fairness, Time Dollars should be taxed like any other income, then levy the tax in Time Dollars. In other words, participants could get a net income of 8 credits for every 10 earned, the other 2 going to pay administrative expenses, help the needy, and so on. The redistribute-the-wealth camp now had something to chew on, too.

THE PERENNIAL PROBLEM OF THE FREELOADER

Sooner or later the specter of the potential freeloader arises, and it did here. Wouldn't some people ask for help simply because they were lazy and wanted someone else to clean the house? This conjured up the prospect of a large bureaucracy checking on need and policing the system for abuse. But part of the beauty of the system is that it is self-policing, somewhat like a family. The family member who constantly imposes on others will be tolerated for a while but will be gradually shut off; Time Dollar workers send the same signal by simply declining to help a particular individual.

It was noteworthy that nobody was worried about guaranteeing the credits. This question preoccupies public officials in the United States; it is understandable to a point, given the wave of bank failures and overall level of public distrust. In Sweden, there have been no bank failures in memory, and people trust the government even if it doesn't always work very well. But the Swedes did worry about a possible run on the bank. What would happen if everyone decided to cash in at once?

This raised an important point about the demographics of Time Dollars, at least where the elderly are concerned. Those who earn credits are generally around 65 years old, while recipients of their services have been closer to 80. This is not surprising; the younger give and the older receive. Given mortality rates, there should always be more "young" elderly (a happy designation for those at this stage) than older ones, so the possibility of a run on the bank becomes remote. Besides, programs can control build-ups of Time Dollar accounts by limiting the number that can be carried over from year to year, somewhat the way employee vacation plans stipulate that a certain number of days must be used each year or lost.

When the session ended, it seemed a corner had been turned. Skepticism and even outright hostility had given way to curiosity and enthusiasm. Participants understood the symbolic importance when a representative of the Swedish Red Cross declared with great solemnity that he differed with his American counterparts on this issue. "I don't care what the American Red Cross thinks about this idea," he said, speaking of that group's opposition to the concept. "I am prepared to go on record for the Swedish Red Cross in support of the idea and in support of developing and testing a Swedish model."

The Swedish Council of Local Governments decided to develop and test a Swedish model of Time Dollars. They committed funds to a study of the willingness of elderly Swedes to participate in such a program, and to develop a how-to manual. Perhaps most important, a test site was selected: a retirement community located on a green jewel of an island called Lidingo, not far from Stockholm. The selection came from the bottom up, not top down, by vote of the pensioners group there.

The next day, the conveners of the conference visited Lidingo. One elderly resident wanted to ask a question that had bothered her greatly. Her eyesight was going, she said. She did not know how long she would be permitted to remain in her housing unit. But her primary concern was whether the credits could be used after her death to help tidy up her apartment and pack her belongings so they could be sent on to her children. The "yes" answer put her mind at rest. One tentative supporter had become a convert to the cause.

15

Taxpayers into Citizens: How Government Can Spend Less and Help More

Advocates of reform always end up saying that government should fund it. And we say that the government should fund these reforms with Time Dollars.

We're all born with the power to choose how to use the ultimate personal asset each of us has: time. But the government can make it easier and more appealing for people to act on their best impulses. And it can assist organizations that utilize Time Dollars to rebuild family, neighborhood, and community. In this sense, government can empower people to mint this new money by eliminating impediments, by recognizing and honoring those who earn Time Dollars, and by giving them preferred access to public goods and services. Time Dollars represent a psychological and monetary reward for rebuilding the non-market economy. Public policy and programs can reinforce that reward, enhance its value, and facilitate new ventures between the non-market (household) economy and the public and private sectors of the market economy.

Government can set a moral tone by reinforcing the self-approval that comes from helping others. But it also can do much more. It can help—as Missouri and Michigan have done—to legitimize Time Dollars. Government can reward those who give their time to public needs in the same way it assists those who serve the nation in times of war. And the reward can come at any level, from federal to state and from county to neighborhood block association.

A TRADITION OF PARTICIPATION

The idea of citizenship as a responsibility goes back to the founding of the Republic. Jury duty and volunteer fire departments are all remnants of a day when government was something people *did*, not just paid for.

Scattered hints of this attitude still exist. The federal government has made community service a condition of certain scholarships: for a while, young doctors were required to serve in rural areas in exchange for tuition help in medical school; teachers accepting difficult assignments were once eligible for loan forgiveness. Governmental licensing and accrediting power confers a quasi-monopoly, presumably to serve and to safeguard the public interest. There is no reason why the issuance or renewal of licenses and governmental franchises should not be conditioned on evidence of having actually furthered the public interest by participating individually or institutionally in Time Dollar programs. Courts appoint private attorneys as officers of the court to help impoverished defendants, for example, which is a kind of lawyer draft. All of these stress participation and reciprocity: You get a benefit, you give something of yourself back.

Increasingly, restitution and community service are required as a form of rehabilitation. Persons found guilty of misdemeanors often do community service work in place of going to prison or paying a fine. In New York City, persons found evading the subway fare are put to work cleaning the subways. We might go further than merely exacting service. We might create opportunities for such offenders to serve as role models by actively helping to rehabilitate others. Youth courts in which former offenders and addicts become eligible to serve as jurors, prosecutors, and public defenders are more than a road back; they enable those who once violated the law to become role models for others.

EXCITING WAYS TIME DOLLARS CAN HELP US NOW

This is the spirit of Time Dollars as government policy. The concept isn't a way to get services cheap or a desperate way to patch the budget gap. Rather, it provides a vehicle to reaffirm social bonds, and it can work in a variety of circumstances and needs. Here are some examples of how it can work.

First, if we do not wish to tax industry and other economic elements more heavily, why not create a new tax to meet basic social needs that can be paid either in dollars or in Time Dollars? At the very least, why not create special tax districts to experiment with the idea? Is the present tax system working so well that no further experimentation is necessary?

Second, we already dispense large amounts of financial aid in the form of guaranteed student loans, tuition grants, work-study money, and other benefits. So why not set aside a portion of those funds for students who earn some minimal number of Time Dollars? Shouldn't those who serve be first in line when the benefits are handed out? Then, after graduation, these students could pay back portions of those loans with Time Dollars earned using the knowledge and expertise gained in school.

Third, if we want to help our fellow citizens meet their basic needs, why not enable them to purchase at least minimal subsistence, shelter, and educational opportunity with Time Dollars? Then they'd be giving as well as getting; and virtually everyone can earn Time Dollars. Homeless people could pay rent for different levels of shelter with Time Dollars earned helping others and building community. They could get basic nutrition, health care, and educational opportunity in the same manner.

Fourth, if we really think people ought to be more involved in their own education, safety, and healing, then we need to redefine the role of professionals as persons skilled in getting help from those they help. In education, that means that professionals ought to be incorporating home and family and peers into the instructional process. In juvenile justice, it means more experiments in which teens take responsibility for the processes of justice. They can serve on juries, for example, imposing sentences of constructive community work and restitution; they can supervise those sentences and bring the weight of their disapproval to bear on their peers.

In health, people should be able to pay part of their health insurance premiums with Time Dollars earned by providing supportive and health-related services to others. Since people who volunteer tend to live longer, participants in such programs should be classified as *better* health risks. And they should get that designation, too, by following regimens of exercise, nutrition, and prevention that make them active co-producers of their own health.

In crime prevention, it means enabling citizens to earn Time Dollars by serving in crime watch and citizen alert patrols. Such participants would be entitled to preferred insurance rates and access to a volunteer victim assistance program that provides tangible assistance to victims of crime.

In general, there should be incentives for citizens to do more than the bare minimum. Regardless of income, every citizen—welfare mother and bank teller, truck driver and middle-class matron—could become a "public benefactor" by making an additional contribution to the public, with due honor and recognition. Time Dollar donors could get the kind of special treatment now reserved for large campaign contributors or patrons of the local symphony: luncheons, special meetings with officials, a hotline number for straightening out problems with government agencies, even front-row seating at various cultural and athletic events. Imagine the boost to volunteer efforts if parking spaces were reserved downtown for those who earn the public service equivalent of Frequent-Flyer credits.

PAY TAXES BY PROVIDING SERVICE

As taxpayers, we know we're lucky to get even 50 cents worth of service for every $2 the government collects in taxes. But if we reverse that equation, pay part of our taxes by providing services to others, we feel a bit different about the entity we call government because we are part of it. And we help create a volume of service that can transform our lives as citizens.

The issue should not be *whether* important needs are met. The issue should be *how* we meet them, and whether we do it ourselves or fork over money to pay someone else to do it for us. Each agency has to ask, How much of the payroll is spent paying people to do things that the family, household, or neighborhood could do better, if it had the money? The government creates money, and we say it's this money that prevents us from meeting our needs—because we don't have enough of it! Why wouldn't government support the creation of a different kind of money that would make it possible to meet those needs? Here are a few ideas for how that new money might work.

> **PROPOSAL 1. Create special tax districts and authorize them to impose, by referendum, a service surtax that gives every person the option of paying in Time Dollars or regular dollars. Require Time Dollar budgets from public agencies.**

We need to ask, What are our total "needs" and how do these needs translate into actual "hours" of labor? How many of these hours could be bought with Time Dollars? How many have to be bought with Federal Reserve dollars?

When you ask these questions, budget deficits and revenue shortfalls take on a different aspect. Deficits caused by paying for services that could be purchased with Time Dollars, could be eliminated without hardship to taxpayers. Residents might prefer a tax increase to cutbacks in needed services—*if* they could pay the increase in Time Dollars.

Here's how it could work. Let's say a neighborhood street has potholes. Costing out for repairs is done by government in terms of hours per task times market wage. Then the cost is apportioned as a special assessment for fixing the potholes. You could sign up for a neighborhood work crew to fill them and get paid in Time Dollars, which you would then use to pay the tax.

Or, you could earn Time Dollars by providing transportation to the elderly, then satisfy your tax bill by paying those Time Dollars to the city. The city then hires teenagers (paying them in Time Dollars) to fill the potholes. The teenagers then use their Time Dollars to purchase tutoring from senior citizens . . . who then use the same Time Dollars to buy more transportation.

Frequently, state legislatures authorize counties or cities to increase taxes by some stated percentage. Similarly, a state could authorize school districts and the like to levy an alternative tax. The tax authorized could be earmarked for a special purpose: to improve education, for example, or to aid the elderly.

A tax on professional services was adopted in Florida recently, then repealed because of massive lobbying by professional groups. A Time

Dollar tax might be more politically palatable—and equitable. The tax could apply to specific transactions such as lawyer and doctor fees. That way, professionals, wherever they live, would be obliged to contribute (preferably with their time) to the community in which they work.

A tax levied on real estate transactions could be earmarked for neighborhood improvement and crime prevention projects. A tax on drivers' licenses could be designated for improved access for persons lacking private transportation or physical mobility. An education tax levied on all local employers could be earmarked for education in order to improve the local labor pool.

Are Time Dollars anti-union? No. Nothing prevents a union from organizing Time Dollar workers—and collecting union dues in Time Dollars. Those dues could then be used by the union to purchase child care or elder care or other services for their members, including retirees.

> **PROPOSAL 2. Make new fringe benefit packages including elder care, child care, and support services for public employees and Public Service Corps volunteers.**

Employees often have to take sick leave to take care of children or elder parents. But those employees with informal networks of friends and relatives are less likely to miss work for such reasons. Also, they are better insurance risks because people with home support have less need for institutional care if illness strikes. Active membership in a Time Dollar program could entitle a public employee to a special fringe benefit package that reflects the lower risk associated with having this informal support network.

Membership in groups like the AARP (American Association for Retired People) or the American Bar Association has long provided access to special, low-cost group insurance plans. In the same way, a Public Service Corps whose volunteers are paid in Time Dollars could enable its members to secure quality health insurance at low rates. The members would include people who have historically been excluded such as female heads of households.

Elderplan, a Health Maintenance Organization in Brooklyn, and South Shore Hospital in Miami have pioneered elements of such a program. Elderplan permits members earning Time Dollars to pay one of its quarterly insurance premiums with Time Dollars.

Another approach is suggested by South Shore Hospital's patient discharge planning program. Many know too well that Medicaid and Medicare—as well as virtually all commercial insurers—won't pay for more than one month of registered nurse care. That is utterly inadequate for people such as stroke victims and cancer patients who need long rehabilitation. It is equally inadequate for people who only need the help of a practical nurse or homemaker. Membership in South Shore Hospital's Time Dollar program includes access to these critical services.

There is nothing new about giving a special health care policy as a benefit to volunteers. VISTA volunteers now get a stipend of $400 per month plus free Blue Cross/Blue Shield coverage. As research data accumulates showing that Time Dollars volunteers are better risks, health insurance costs could be reduced and benefits could be improved.

Fiscally beleaguered municipalities need to test for whether productivity can be increased (and absenteeism reduced) by instituting a Time Dollar program for public employees. The program might offer day care services, babysitting for ill children, and companionship for older relatives under the care of the employee. Funding to cover the cost of such a pilot might well come from organizations like the National Alliance for Business or an independent insurers trade association. Indeed, support for a pilot program might come from any industry plagued by high absenteeism.

Finally, governments dealing with cutbacks and layoffs have already tried experiments in job sharing, flex-time, and part-time employment in order to spread the pain of fiscal austerity more broadly and more thinly. It's possible to augment the "income" of such employees directly with Time Dollars.

Similar results could be achieved by creating a new category of public employee who would work two or three days for Time Dollars and two or three days for Federal Reserve dollars. The Time Dollars could be used to buy quality child care, care for elder parents, superior health insurance coverage, and even municipal parking privileges. They could also be used for other employment-related benefits: premiums for special insurance packages, increases in the number of vacation and sick days that could be carried over from year to year, and preferential vacation and holiday scheduling.

PROPOSAL 3. Set up special initiatives for the homeless.

Communities spend substantial sums on food and shelter for the homeless. The needs keep growing. And political support for such expenditures wanes because of suspicion that the homeless are just preying on the public's sympathy. Why not launch a program that enables the homeless to earn Time Dollars that can be used to purchase shelter and food? A Time Dollar "rent" charge could be established for minimal shelter, dormitory shelter, semi-private rooms, and even an apartment for a family.

The homeless could earn Time Dollars by undertaking various municipal projects such as renovating abandoned houses, cleaning up neighborhoods, and beautifying parks. They could then buy meals with Time Dollars at a kitchen staffed by the homeless. Ideally, such a Time Dollar program would be co-sponsored by a public employees union. The union could run a kind of hiring hall where homeless persons looking for employment could come to be recruited for work crews.

Such a program could also offer literacy and job training sessions and provide special tutoring and day care for children of homeless families. Groups serving the elderly could train homeless people to work as live-in companions, earning only Time Dollars at first, then, a combination of Time Dollars, free rent, and a stipend. It would help to rebuild a sense of community if municipalities sponsored such Time Dollar programs jointly with churches and groups already working with the homeless.

PROPOSAL 4. Create student aid/loan forgiveness programs.

In Japanese elementary schools, pupils do custodial chores. This not only saves money; it also builds a sense of connection between the pupils and the school. At Berea College in Kentucky, students are required to do maintenance and other work as part of their tuition. This helps break down status barriers between wealthy and less affluent students. It tends to put them on a more even financial footing as well. At many schools, students receiving work-study financial aid end up doing low-paying jobs at school, while their well-to-do classmates take high-paying jobs downtown. The Berea system eliminates this disparity.

Everyone has to contribute, with time as well as tuition, to making the school function. It represents a principle that the educational system should adopt much more broadly.

Some states already insist on some form of community service as a high school graduation requirement. Many colleges and universities offer field placements, internships, and practicums for course credit. It is possible to earmark certain pots of financial aid, such as work-study and guaranteed student loans, exclusively for students earning Time Dollars. This would give preferred access to financial aid based on community service.

Taking this idea further, students could qualify for different categories and amounts of financial aid based on the number of Time Dollars they earned. Upon graduation, students could have the option of signing on for varying amounts of loan forgiveness in exchange for serving in Time Dollar programs.

PROPOSAL 5. Use Time Dollars to start a more effective upward mobility and child development program and for enforcement of child support decrees under the Family Assistance Act of 1988.

The Family Assistance Act of 1988 directs states to initiate programs that require some form of work, education, or training in exchange for financial assistance to poverty-level households with children. While these objectives reflect a healthy desire to strengthen families, the reality is that both the child care and the training elements of the program are likely to remain underfunded. Time Dollars can help to remedy foreseeable deficiencies.

A Time Dollar program aimed at providing quality child care is already in operation in Miami; several others are in different stages of development. The basic model uses Time Dollars volunteers to augment child care staff, to implement an effective child development curriculum, and to reduce costs. It can readily be used to improve programs launched under the Family Assistance Act. (For more information on this model, see chapter 11.)

Time Dollars can be used to help with the educational and job training needs of welfare mothers. Currently, lack of money limits both quality and duration of job training for female heads of households.

The push is to show good numbers—to generate the maximum number of "job placements" to get women off welfare and into the labor market. The minimal requirements of the act can be satisfied simply by sending a trainee to earn a GED back at the high school where she failed. That is normally a formula for failure.

Much more is possible. Experience in California and elsewhere indicates that the educational and skill potential of trainees can be better realized in special programs at community colleges. The problem is that attendance at community college-sponsored programs may require more time and support at home than welfare mothers can get. Just as students can secure educational loans for tuition and other costs, these mothers could get Time Dollar loans to pay for evening and weekend child care and, if necessary, personal tutoring. Time Dollar systems could be integrated with the Family Assistance Act in ways like this to boost the program without increasing costs.

Various welfare and public assistance programs call for enforcement of child support obligations of the father. Under certain circumstances, noncompliance will result in imprisonment. Yet, there will be situations where the father can't find a job or must work for pay too low to allow for adequate support payments. There is no reason why an unemployed father cannot earn Time Dollars to be paid to the mother for use in purchasing child care and other needed help. This should not be an excuse for evading child-support obligations. But earning Time Dollars might at least help fathers to meet enough of that obligation to avoid penalties. Where appropriate, the father might also be encouraged to enroll in a program that would impart parenting competencies; he could earn additional Time Dollars serving in a Big Brother program as a surrogate father, so that the future need not be an endless replay of the past.

PROPOSAL 6. Redefine measures of national economic activity and growth.

In this society, nothing is taken seriously unless it can be put into numbers. This is why economists monopolize the public policy debates. They have numbers and all anyone else has is words and sad stories. With Time Dollars, we can have numbers, too. They give us a way to quantify the damage the market economy does to the non-market economy. We need to start to use this tool.

Our present methods for assessing the economy provide a distorted image. The gross national product (GNP) treats every loss of a function by the nonmarket economy as a gain in national productivity regardless of the damage done to the nonmarket economy of family, neighborhood, and community. When mothers go to work, when kids go to day care, when professionals are enlisted to undo damage done by the loss of time invested in family, the GNP grows even though the functions of family are diminished. There is no reason why economists cannot modify their indicators to reflect the loss side of the ledger.

Our economic indicators should tell us when apparent gains in the market economy mask corresponding losses in the nonmarket economy. At the simplest level, for example, when both parents work, their income must be weighed against household and community functions that go neglected. If we can quantify the cost of rebuilding Kuwait or restoring a community leveled by a hurricane, we can at least approximate the cost of rebuilding our households. We need to figure the cost we incur as the household economy becomes "depopulated." Latchkey kids, abandoned elderly, children giving birth to children, and a peer culture that discourages achievement are part of this legacy.

Once such tools are developed, we need the equivalent of an environmental impact statement for household and neighborhood economy. We need to reassess economic policy, regulation of business, and government social programs in terms of the costs these may impose on the informal safety net, which we have taken for granted for too long.

16

The Long Shadow of the Future

By now we know that the use of money as the exclusive medium of exchange has certain consequences, some desirable, some undesirable. Thanks to money, strangers can deal with each other. But also, because of money and the wondrous workings of the market economy, neighbors have been turned into strangers and an informal economy based on trust and reciprocity has been badly ravaged.

We have also seen how a different currency can have very different consequences. The Time Dollar rewards and reinforces those very things that money generally doesn't: caring for friends, family, and neighbors. To use the economist's phrase, this new currency appears to increase the "competitive value" of relationships of trust, in relation to use of monetary gain. It is important now to understand how such a currency, if used widely, could change fundamentally the dynamic of the culture in which we live.

Most of us remember how differently we acted in school, when a substitute teacher was in the room. It was like a vacation day. We goofed off, passed notes to our friends. We knew the teacher probably would never be there again, so there was no reason—in a kid's mind, at least—not to have a little fun. There would be no connection between what we did that day and our grade at the end of the year.

Much of life is like that. We act differently when we know we are together for the long haul. In small, stable communities, people trust one another in ways that people from cities find astounding. People leave their doors unlocked, their keys in the car, have accounts at the hardware and grocery store that they pay at the end of the month—no credit card required. Nor is this necessarily a function of class and wealth. Immigrant families on New York's Lower East Side, then the most densely populated area in the world, kept their apartment doors unlocked even into the 1930s and 1940s.

The reason is that when people are together over a long time, they know their acts have consequences. "Do not do to others," said an early version of the Golden Rule, "what you would not have done unto you." Somebody just might!

COOPERATE OR GO IT ALONE?

There is a game called The Prisoner's Dilemma that illustrates how people act differently toward one another when they think they are engaged in a one-time encounter.

Here's how the game works. Two prisoners are trying to escape. If they cooperate, each will get 3 points. If one prisoner cooperates and the other doesn't, but betrays his partner instead, the first will get 0 points and the betrayer will get 5 points. If neither cooperates and both go it alone, each will get only 1 point. No matter what the other does, defection yields a higher payoff than cooperation.

In this situation, one does better by betrayal than by cooperation; except that if both betray, then they do worse than if they both had cooperated. That is the dilemma. Do you take the risk of cooperating and trust the other will follow suit, even though he could play you for a sucker and get 5 points to your 0? Or do you play it safe and act selfishly, knowing you will at least get 1 point, and the other guy will get no more?

The answer lies in a crucial factor: time (leaving aside the possibility that some will cooperate just because they think it's right). Robert Axelrod, a political scientist at the Massachusetts Institute of Technology, ran a tournament in which the players submitted strategies; Axelrod then tested these through computer simulations. He discovered that the game turns out differently, depending on how many times it is played.

In a one-time encounter, betrayal wins. But if the game goes on and on into an indefinite future, then a different strategy emerges as the clear long-term winner. Players begin to feel one another out, to cooperate tentatively in a phase the author calls "Tit-for-Tat."

WHAT WILL THE RELATIONSHIP BE?

In this feeling-out phase, the first player *offers* to cooperate. If the other doesn't, then the first defects in the next game as a form of retaliation. A kind of social norm begins to evolve. Actions become signals that are sent and received, accepted or rejected. "The players might meet again," Axelrod concludes. "The future can therefore cast a shadow back upon the present and thereby affect the current strategic situation."

Axelrod cites a remarkable example from the trench warfare in World War I. These were among the most gruesome encounters in the annals of war; yet for that very reason, the troops in the field adopted a policy of "live-and-let-live." Facing one another for weeks or even months across a narrow strip, they worked out modes of cooperation: cease-fires at dinner time, then informal truces.

When the high commands got wind of these and tried to stop them, the troops worked out unspoken rituals. They established fixed artillery routines, for example, so each side could stay out of the way. Both sides cooperated; both got 3 points instead of likely death. The artillery behind the lines had less stake in these rituals, however. Their war had no long shadow, and so sometimes they didn't go along. Once, a salvo came unexpectedly from the German side while the British were out of their trenches. A German soldier appeared immediately on a parapet to apologize. "We are very sorry about that. We hope no one was hurt," he shouted. "It is that damned Prussian artillery."

The high commands finally disrupted the truces by ordering the soldiers out of their settled positions in trenches, to go on raids. The raids threw the situation back into the first phase of the Prisoner's Dilemma tournament. With no pattern of long-term dealing—no long shadow of the future to act as a restraint—the two sides turned into marauders. American corporations operate much like that.

The Long Shadow of the Future

187

MOVE ON TO MOVE UP

Our world today does not have that many stable positions, where people are thrust together for the long haul. We are either ordered on raids, or else we are the ones raided. As much as we might like more stability, we feel a need to remain mobile and disengaged, fearful of being taken for suckers.

Money is conducive to such a world. It tends to sever the connection between present and future. Pay and be gone: no further relationship required. Money tends to reward the very behavior that pulls the social bonds apart. Deserting the family can pay. Moving from the community pays. Leaving a small congregation for a more lucrative and prestigious pulpit pays. Skipping from job to job pays. Executives do it. Pro athletes and sports teams do it.

Corporations—the social structure of the business world—do it most of all. They are disengaged from any commitments except to the mandates of profit and loss. They put their factories up for sale to the highest bidder. Wherever the taxes and wages are lowest, the freebies like sewer hook-ups highest, they tend to go. The locality, the state— it makes no difference.

Increasingly, the nation where the corporation is based makes no difference either. Even as wage rates abroad approach U.S. levels, corporate leaders have no intention of returning. They will go where the money is. "If the best markets for any product develop overseas, then I would not hesitate to switch the operation abroad," Richard Ayers, the chairman of Stanley Tool, an old New England firm, told the *New York Times.*

It is instructive that Japan and the European countries endeavor to keep industry at home, at least to some degree. Economists denounce such efforts as "protectionism"—tax breaks, local content laws, import regulations, and so forth. These practices deviate from the economist's model of "perfect competition." But at least they recognize that industry is part of a social structure; and society can't stay together if too many important pieces are flying apart. "Only American companies are really doing it," said a former trade negotiator in the Reagan administration, speaking of the trend of abandoning the mother country.

A society in constant flux is like the Prisoner's Dilemma without the long shadow of the future. That flux is built into the medium of money. It has no locality, no loyalty, no roots. It is highly unlikely that anyone will find a way to put the genie back into the bottle. People can't all go back to small towns, where the hardware stores let them run up accounts. In many families, it isn't feasible for one spouse to suddenly stop working, to repopulate the kitchen table.

But we can begin to introduce a dynamic that values connection and loyalty and trust as much as money rewards their opposites. We can begin to rebuild a sense of future that reinforces our best instincts instead of our most acquisitive ones.

MEANINGLESS PAST, MEANINGLESS FUTURE

In urban society, we live as strangers, even if we live on top of each other. Neighbors pass each other daily—and remain strangers. People ride together in elevators every day to the same floor, and if they are especially daring, they comment on the weather. On subway cars, it is deemed a violation to make eye contact with another person. The prevailing convention is to act as if every meeting is the first meeting and as if there will never be another.

The result is a loss of the sense of social causation. There is little connection between what we do today and what might happen to us tomorrow. Upon moving to a new city, many have the distressing feeling that what they did before doesn't count any more. If they are escaping an unfortunate past, that may be to the good. But it also means that favors to neighbors and work with the Cub Scouts that gave them self-esteem—the goodwill they could draw from in their home-town—are lost in the wind. A society without connection perpetuates that feeling. Why bother to build the web if it's just going to come apart or be blown away?

A J. Walter Thompson poll found that almost three out of four Americans don't even know the people who live next door. Not surprisingly, two-thirds said they never give time to community affairs. How can people even begin to solve problems together if they have no connection to one another, and no shared sense of tomorrow and the day after that? Vance Packard, the noted author and social observer, once wrote a book called A *Nation of Strangers*, in which he interviewed corporate executives who were transferred frequently and who went along with these frequent moves to advance their careers. "You haven't time to get involved in the community so you don't really *care*," one such executive said. "When we lose touch with our [local] governmental roots, we begin to have that helpless feeling."

There is also a loss of a larger sense of justice and reciprocity—that rewards come to those who deserve them, and that people who betray others sooner or later pay for their actions. The bureaucrat or the credit card official may abuse us, and what can we do in return? As the Prisoner's Dilemma shows, one answer is to lengthen the time frame. If they know they have to deal with us again and again, there is at least an inducement to act differently. We sense this intuitively, when we ask the name of a billing clerk or customer service rep when trying to straighten out a problem. They know this means we can get back to them personally—or to their superior—if they don't follow through.

Consequences need not come immediately, but they must come sooner or later. When we have to live with the consequences of our actions and when we perceive what the costs may be, then we tend to act differently.

The Time Dollar concept offers a way to bring a sense of future back into the present. It provides a long shadow that moves people to cooperate in the Prisoner's Dilemma game. Participation in these programs is not a one-time exchange. Rather, each good deed begets a credit, which begets another good deed. The bank that records these deeds functions a little like the social memory of the neighborhood or small town. The result is a linkage between past actions and future reward.

Time Dollar programs do more than provide a way out of our social Prisoner's Dilemma. They also have the winning strategy built in. One can't use a Time Dollar to "defect"—as Axelrod puts it—or to take advantage of another. Money can defect: A corporation can take dollars out of a poor community and use them to invest abroad. With Time Dollars, every credit stays in the game. The result is continuous activity among persons who previously were strangers. No one worries that by offering to cooperate he might be taken for a sucker. The reciprocity is built into the currency that they use.

Historically, money has been a way to *avoid* trusting people. "Give me cash" means "I won't have to trust you by extending credit and I never have to see you again." Originally, coins were minted with gold or silver or other things deemed to have inherent value. That way, one didn't have to trust the giver (except to check against counterfeit). One could trust instead the value in the market. In time, paper money transferred that trust from metals to the promise of a government to stand behind its paper. Now, money is proliferating in so many forms that we vest our trust in pieces of plastic and electronic blips, and in the institutions we know little about that stand behind these.

The Time Dollar is money that is almost anti-money. It provides a practical way to restore and validate trust; and it makes community institutions, rather than corporations and government, the nexus of this trust. It is a way out of the Prisoner's Dilemma. Now that we have trusted gold and governments and plastic and computer blips, is it really so outlandish that we try to trust our neighbors?

PART II

You Can Start a Time Dollar Bank

Time Dollar programs have grown up in all shapes and sizes, from the small version in a senior citizens building to a coalition of more than six major organizations operating at over 30 different program sites. They all have one thing in common, however—a commitment to transform a group of strangers into a community.

In many cases, people know what they want to do, what services they want to provide, and whom they want to help. Many are already affiliated with organizations that might be willing to start a Time Dollar program, so they are not interested in discussions of how to choose a base. They want more nuts-and-bolts materials.

Starting a Time Dollar program in many ways is like starting a business. You need to decide what services you want to offer, who will provide them, who your customers will be, and how you will reach them. You need to develop a strategy to recruit your work force. You need a marketing plan to attract organizations and institutions that may need your services for their

SOURCE: Adapted with permission from *Essential Information* from The Compleat Time Dollar Kit, by Edgar S. Cahn.

clients or members. And you have to worry about paying for things like rent, phone bills, photocopying, and the cost of whatever core administrative staff is needed to manage the enterprise.

The only thing you don't have to worry about is finding money to pay your "workers"; they earn Time Dollars. Most of them do, at least. You may have to secure the services of someone who has to be paid in dollars for at least part of his or her time. But more about that later.

The Time Dollar is a currency that literally turns time into money. If you belong to a Time Dollar program, you earn credits for the time you spend helping other members. One hour of service earns you one credit—a service credit or a Time Dollar. With that credit you can "buy" an hour of a particular service that you need. If you don't need all the credits you earn, you can save them up. Or you can donate them to someone you know. Or you can give them back to the "bank," so that the people who run the program can make sure the members with the greatest needs get all the help they require.

Unlike traditional volunteer programs, Time Dollar programs recognize that people who need help can often help others, too—just in different ways.

Start by funneling your enthusiasm into some basic thinking about your aims and how to achieve them. You will want to include these major stages.

- Planning and organizing the program
- Completing the preparatory work and running the program—day to day
- Sustaining and securing a long-term future for the undertaking

17

How to Plan the Network

There are six steps to be completed before your concept can become a reality. Let's consider each of them in some detail.

IDENTIFY NEEDS YOU'LL MEET, SERVICES YOU'LL PROVIDE, AND THOSE YOU'LL SERVE

No doubt you already have some idea of the particular need or social problem you want to address. That may mean more than you think it does. It means you suspect that a significant part of the need can be dealt with by peers or family or friends or neighbors provided their time can be mobilized on a sustained basis.

It means something else: You have an intuitive, gut sense of what you personally want to be involved in. Time Dollars will enable you to make a difference if you are willing to make the commitment yourself. So now you know what your "mission" is. The question is: How do you accomplish it?

You must now ask what these people who work with you will want to buy with their Time Dollars. If you produce child day care and they want child day care for themselves as well, then you need only produce that one service. If you produce home care for the elderly or transpor-

ASSESS YOUR COMMUNITY'S NEED

Several groups meeting over a period of months asked themselves two questions: What do people need? What kinds of services would people want to buy with the Time Dollars they earn? They came up with the three categories below. The list serves as a practical guide in choosing areas of service to pursue.

It was understood that it would take several years before all of these services could actually become available. But it was useful to make projections because people could see how, over time, their Time Dollars would become more useful.

Service to Elderly	Service to Children	Educational Services
Adult day care	After-school day care	Arts and crafts
Advocacy	Babysitting	Certificate programs
Companionship	Child development	Citizenship
Escort	Home visiting	Entitlements
Excursions	Latchkey	Entrepreneurial/man-
Gardening	Preschool	agement
Home repairs	Prenatal	Establishing a day-
Homemaker services	School support	care business
Letter writing	services: cafeteria	Exercise classes
Light housekeeping	aide, classroom	First-aid
Meal preparation	aide, library aide,	Literacy/English
Pet care	monitor, teacher's	Literacy/Spanish
Post-hospital care	aide, tutor	Parenting classes
Reading	Sick-baby day care	Sewing classes
Religious visitations	for working parents	Special courses: avo-
Respite care		cational, continu-
Shopping		ing education,
Telephone assurance		weekend institutes
Translation		Teen pregnancy
Transportation		
Typing		

tation or translation services and that is what they will want, you need go no further. But if you think they will be more willing to help you if they can use the Time Dollars to purchase a different kind of service, then you have to find a way to make that happen. You can either add that second service to what your program provides or you can search for another person or group or organization to do so. Possibly, you will be able to buy the services in exchange for what you produce.

Intergenerational exchanges are clearly the next frontier for Time Dollars. Many elderly don't want to work with other elderly people; they want to pass on their affection and their traditions to the young. The need for affordable child day care is critical and growing. The synergy is there. It is bound to happen. The potential for home-based day care rather than care rendered at a center is great.

The table on the opposite page not only helps you decide what to produce, but it suggests what other services should be produced elsewhere so your "workers" can spend the Time Dollars they earn on something they really need or want. There may be some exciting possibilities you overlooked. Think about it. Brainstorm with others. Work with other groups. Trust your collective judgment.

A *word of caution:* Start with a limited range of services (2 or 3) that you are relatively sure you can deliver. That way people come to know the program, rely on it, and can identify it with a particular need. Do *not* try to launch an all-purpose, social service barter system to provide every conceivable kind of service and meet every conceivable kind of need. It won't work. You can't mount 15 new lines of service at the same time.

CHOOSING AND SECURING A BASE

The base of operations you choose depends on what you want to do. For example, you could operate out of your own home or apartment if you planned to provide a neighbor-to-neighbor type service. But there are reasons why you might prefer to set up elsewhere.

Logistics

Time Dollar programs recruit volunteers, receive requests for service, match volunteers and recipients, keep track of hours, provide some form of quality control. All of this requires logistical support. Organizations and institutions normally have certain built-in capacities: phones, office space, staff, recognition, and record-keeping ability.

They can usually provide support with little or no additional cost. Your own place of employment or worship or social activity may be just such a base.

Constituency Orientation

Organizations are usually built around a mission. They have a client base, a membership, and a constituency that can be tapped. Congregations have elderly members; senior centers serve meals and provide services to the elderly; senior housing complexes have a built-in pool of volunteers and recipients; hospitals often discharge elderly patients who need a variety of nonmedical support services. Securing an organizational base greatly facilitates the job of recruiting volunteers and generating requests for service.

Philosophy

Time Dollar programs are more than a service delivery system; they are a vehicle for recreating a sense of community. They tend to have names like Friend-to-Friend or Member-to-Member. No matter how long we live in one place or how close we live to one another, we often live as strangers. If you choose an organization as a base, you will be increasing the rewards and benefits of being associated with that institution. Creating a Time Dollar program means increasing the ways in which people can relate to each other. The base can be almost anywhere: a religious congregation, a veterans organization, a senior center, a community college, a community-oriented public school, a membership club, or a block association. Time Dollar programs rebuild community. They tend to spin off efforts and activities for which people do not earn Time Dollars, like crime-watch programs, food banks, and informal neighbor-watching-out-for-neighbor systems. Here are some options and considerations when choosing the organizational base.

Start with One Organization or a Coalition? Most of
the original Time Dollar programs started by finding one organization with the interest, capability, and energy to make a program work. In Miami, however, the organizers decided to create a coalition (they

called it a consortium) in order to involve organizations from diverse ethnic groups, with sufficient geographic spread to offer county-wide coverage. The coalition method was slower getting off the ground but has proven to be more successful at pulling in other organizations because no one group "owned" the program.

In another community, some 19 organizations have banded together because they knew that, in combination, they had the clout to secure a grant from the local community foundation. They chose this route even though they were already in competition with each other on separate grant applications!

Which route should you take? The choices are not mutually exclusive. Follow whatever strategy will tap the most energy fastest. The depth of commitment and excitement from the leadership or from a particularly energetic staff member can make all the difference in launching a successful program. Enthusiasm and energy are major considerations. Hopefully, there will be several sources. If only one group is ready, go with it. But do what you can to keep the door open. And involve other groups in the planning so they can come into the program when they are ready or when resources permit. A successful program generates imitation; other organizations want to join or set up their own.

What Organizations Might Be Sponsors? Organizations now sponsoring Time Dollar programs include a nonprofit community hospital, a Health Maintenance Organization (HMO), a community college, a senior center network, a state social service agency, various churches, and a community-oriented primary care clinic. It is important to appreciate that they are involved in a way that advances their own institutional mission. In securing a sponsor or base, you would do well to think through ways in which *your* vision of a Time Dollar program could advance the institution's own agenda and mission. Sometimes the incentives are intangible; sometimes they are very tangible.

Community-oriented nonprofit hospitals are sponsors because they want to say to their patients: "We care about you *after* you leave the hospital." That is good business because it fills hospital beds. It also makes it possible to discharge patients who don't need hospital-level care, yet must have some support system when they return home. That can help cost-containment efforts that in turn affect hospital finances.

Churches and synagogues are becoming involved because helping others is basic to their mission. But they also understand that membership will grow and member loyalty will increase if membership means more than simply weekly worship services.

Twelve-step programs like Alcoholics Anonymous have begun to express interest. Members sometimes find themselves pushed to the breaking point. Existing support structures may not be enough. Time Dollar programs provide a way to mobilize help and yet spread the burden.

Some organizations need volunteers simply to fulfill their mission. In order to receive payment from the federal government, hospice organizations need to enlist volunteers. Other organizations often have to demonstrate (in competitive bidding situations) that they are cost effective. One organization secured a major foundation grant based in part on its proven ability to mobilize volunteers.

Whatever their particular reasons for sponsoring a Time Dollar program, organizations of all kinds find that launching one gives their members something to be proud of and enhances their image in the community. So consider all possible organizations: retiree associations, chambers of commerce, veterans associations, condominium and tenants associations, unions, fraternal organizations.

Build around Strengths In picking a base, the basic principle is: Build around its strengths. First, get the support of the leadership. That may mean key board members; it may mean the executive director. Someone at the top must share your vision and must believe that Time Dollars offer a special opportunity for the organization to fulfill its mission. If no one of influence believes that, if you feel you are just being tolerated, this may be the wrong "home" for the program.

Second, some institutions and agencies have "captive" memberships: senior housing projects, congregate meal sites, patient discharge units in hospitals, congregations, student bodies. The program's design for recruitment and for identifying service recipients should "piggyback" on those internal features.

Example: Senior centers that serve federally subsidized lunches offer an ideal audience for recruitment. If they also operate a home-delivered meal program, they have a natural source of demand. Offices that plan patient discharges from hospitals have to arrange for a full array of support services for patients about to go home; membership in a religious congregation can become a source of mutual assistance; senior housing projects have regular tenants' meetings where people understand that their neighbors are still "strangers."

Third, structure your program around the natural flow of the organization.

Examples: To build a transportation pool, a health clinic may assign one person to remind people about their appointments. That person can also inquire if the patient needs a ride or can give a ride to someone else in return for Time Dollars.

As people go through an intake or waiting room, you have an ideal opportunity to show them a video about the program, sign them up, and identify what they are willing to do for each other.

Some health clinics have a cashier's office that administers a sliding-fee scale based on ability to pay. Others simply send out bills. Either system provides a vehicle to tell people about Time Dollars. In El Paso, the cashier's office is establishing a procedure that in effect will enable clients to use Time Dollars to pay part of their bill. And one HMO permits members to pay one of their quarterly premiums with Time Dollars. Although the policy decision has to be made at the top of the organization, implementation is built into operations.

If a "regular" fails to show up for several days at a congregate meal site, the staff finds a Time Dollar member who is a neighbor to look in on him or her and deliver a meal.

If expectant mothers tend to drop out of prenatal programs, one program will offer them an incentive to finish in the form of a "free" grandmother (earning Time Dollars) to help with the newborn.

A *word of caution:* If you find that the "base" you chose already has a volunteer program, avoid conflict or competition. Schools, hospitals, churches, and synagogues all have volunteer organizations. That's great. They can still add a Time Dollar program. But in trying to persuade them to do so, do not denigrate volunteer programs. They fill a real need and they provide special, meaningful opportunities for people to serve. There are few enough people who give selflessly; the last thing you want to do is put them down.

If there is a volunteer coordinator, he or she may feel threatened by a Time Dollar program. It is a whole new undertaking. She may feel overwhelmed by the number of tasks entailed. The coordinator of a hospital volunteer program who was very interested suddenly became concerned about whether starting a Time Dollar program meant that she would now have to pay Time Dollars to the volunteers who run the gift shop and to the candy stripers who visit each patient daily and wheel in a cart with magazines and candy.

The following suggestions may prove useful.

- Distinguish volunteer programs that operate within an institution, augmenting that institution's staff capacity (like volunteers running the gift shop), from Time Dollar programs, which tend to give one-on-one service in people's homes or in settings where volunteers have not been heavily used before.

- Time Dollar programs should *add* to the programs and resources of an institution, not substitute for existing volunteer programs. For example, a Time Dollar program might enable an institution to stay open nights and weekends or take on additional service components. Your best bet is to start by making the Time Dollar program separate. Do not try to incorporate it into any ongoing volunteer program, at least in the beginning.

- Retain flexibility on whether existing volunteer programs should be included in the Time Dollar program. Make the decision on a case-by-case basis and avoid making any decision until you have contacted people in ongoing programs and had the benefit of their experience and intuition in sorting out the pros and cons.

ESTABLISHING BASIC POLICIES AND PROCEDURES FOR THE PROGRAM

Establishing policies and procedures couldn't be simpler. This is because a procedure manual has already been developed as part of the Compleat Time Dollars Kit (see the opposite page). Familiarize yourself with the procedure manual, then put it aside until a problem arises. Check the manual for guidance and modify it as experience dictates.

If you become part of a coalition, you have to work out certain administrative, fiscal, and governance issues. Who will be fiscal agent for the coalition? Where will records be kept? Above all, what mutual obligations do each of the coalition members have to each other for

THE COMPLEAT TIME DOLLAR KIT

The Compleat Time Dollar Kit includes the full manual "How to Grow Time Dollars," $15; a systems and procedure manual available either in hard copy or on diskette (in WordPerfect 5.0 format for customization), $10; and a Time Dollar grantsmanship manual, $15. Also included is a 10-minute video segment introduced by Ralph Nader, which aired on network TV, $12, and a user-friendly computer program (with forms) for keeping records, making and tracking assignments, and compiling reports, $45.

This kit can be used and modified for individual cases as problems arise. The key is to understand the basic, then refer to the manuals on an as-needed basis.

For ordering information, see the coupon at the end of the book.

Time Dollars earned by individuals associated with one group or another? (See "Sample Sponsorship Agreement" on page 230. You may not want to use it but it gives you a starting point for identifying the issues.) Details have to be worked out in advance; for example, can one organization gain access to the membership lists of another in order to fill an urgent need for a volunteer? It is best to work out such issues in advance to avoid any charges that one group is "raiding" another for volunteers.

FINDING A COORDINATOR (OR DIRECTOR) AND ESTABLISHING BASIC STAFFING PATTERN

These are among the most critical decisions you will make in establishing a Time Dollar unit, so choose carefully. The choices you make could be the difference between success and failure. Here are some tips to follow.

Choosing a Director

The best programs have people with a kind of contagious warmth and enthusiasm that make others feel welcome and appreciated. They are excited by the idea of the mission and by its potential. They do not need to be professionals. They *do* need to be self-starters who are not easily discouraged, who have lots of energy and a warm smile of approval always ready. They do not need to be extroverts; they can be low-key and modest.

Those who have this kind of "people touch" are often reluctant to spend time at record keeping. They are fantastic at making presentations, recruiting, responding to phone calls and hand tooling assignments that match just the right volunteer with the right recipient of service. It is best to make full use of those talents. However, there must be a clear understanding that the director is responsible for seeing to it that somehow the hours get recorded and the volunteers get their monthly or quarterly bank statements.

Building a Staff

There are three standard possibilities here: full-time, part-time, and volunteer staff. One way or another, some mix of these is needed to make sure that everything that needs to be done, is done.

At least one program is being run almost entirely by volunteer staff who earn Time Dollars for the time they spend running it. Many other Time Dollar programs rely on member volunteers as part-time staff. Naturally, the more all-volunteer the staff is, the cheaper the program is to run.

The decision as to which mix to use depends on the answers to three questions. First, how much are people associated with this organization—you, for example—willing to do? Second, how much will others do to help you? Third, how much can this organization pay to have the work done?

Increasingly, programs are turning to a federal agency, ACTION, which operates a program called VISTA (Volunteers in Service to America). This program provides stipends of approximately $400 per month for "full-time" volunteers. Miami uses 12 VISTA positions to recruit, match providers and recipients, make presentations, and oversee the 32 locations out of which the program runs. The St. Louis program run by Grace Hill Neighborhood Services has just received several VISTA slots. Centro San Vicente in El Paso, Texas, has been awarded 6 VISTAs who will coordinate the transportation element of each of the Time Dollar initiatives they are launching.

Such VISTA grants can be renewed for up to four years. Until longer-term funding strategies are implemented, this support is proving helpful. (A copy of one of the funded VISTA applications is available as part of the Compleat Time Dollar Kit).

There is a tendency to feel that a program has to have paid, professional staff to be effective. Most Time Dollar programs have at least one paid staff person as director. Those running Time Dollar programs really are candidates for burn-out because they are totally committed to what they are doing but they give so much of themselves. That means that over the long haul, you need to plan for some fund-raising strategy that will provide pay for at least the core staff.

Whether you have paid staff or not, you have to divide up some of the responsibilities. If you rely primarily on volunteer staff, you probably have to start with a core group of committed individuals, parsing out tasks to other members as the program grows.

One valuable resource for you to create in the beginning is an organizational chart—a list of people (positions) in the organization, and the tasks each is responsible for. Organizational charts don't have to be fancy. They are most useful when they clearly assign the tasks individuals are responsible for, so everyone (whether paid or volunteer) can see at a glance who's supposed to be doing what. (See "Sample Organizational Charts" on page 236.)

While you can run a program with only one person, it's a good idea to have a back-up in the wings. This not only gives the main person help and relief, but it gives the program room to grow.

Several programs have steering committees made up of staff, members, and funding sources. These committees generally set broad policy for the program, such as whom the program will serve, who is eligible to earn credits, who is eligible to spend them, and whether any major new initiative is to be launched.

RECORD KEEPING TO RUN
A TIME DOLLAR PROGRAM

There are three basic kinds of record keeping.

1. Bank Records: This credit-and-debit system records credits earned, credits spent, and credits given away.

2. Volunteer Assignments: Someone has to search the pool of volunteers to find someone available nearby, willing to do needed tasks and, if necessary, able to negotiate steps or speak a language other than English or drive at night or tolerate being in the same room with a smoker. A tentative match has to be made, then confirmed with both parties.

3. A Quality-Control System: Put this in place early to track performance, provide follow-up, check on whether things are going well, and deal with complaints.

At first, some people thought that a computer was essential to these tasks. It turns out that one can make do with a regular index card file, though it gets more cumbersome as the numbers pass 50. Records do have to be kept. Volunteers have to be matched. A small program can be run out of a shoe box. And even with large programs, it turns out that there are two ways to create one.

BIG = BIG

or

SMALL + SMALL + SMALL = BIG

Time Dollar programs are not intended to create an impersonal monolithic army of volunteers to be "matched" by some form of computer dating service. The program directors who are most effective get involved personally in the matching process, to make sure that helpers and recipients will get along, at least, and possibly even bond as friends.

Computer programs can match people by ZIP code, task, availability, experience, and so forth. They are helpful in narrowing the list of candidates, but this is less critical than the personal touch, particularly when programs are getting off the ground.

The need for a computer grows as the program grows in size and when there is staff turnover. New staff have to make matches among people they don't know. Here, the computer can help greatly.

Eventually, computer programs will assume a more important role as the numbers become massive and as people start spending more credits than in the beginning. Computer programs can be particularly helpful in making sure that volunteers whom a program director might not know personally get assignments. There is a natural tendency to keep using the volunteers who have proven reliable. A computer program will help identify members who have not had an assignment recently, an essential factor in keeping effective, enthusiastic volunteers.

Everyone knows tales of woe about the early efforts to develop a user-friendly, yet powerful, computer program. Now you can set a program with screens in English and Spanish that requires no computer expertise, can be used on any IBM-type computer, and keeps the records, helps with matching, tracks assignments, and generates reports. The program and forms are available as part of the Compleat Time Dollar Kit.

PREPARING YOUR BUDGET

How much does it cost to operate a Time Dollar program? The cost of Time Dollar programs varies depending on a number of factors.

- Do you have paid or volunteer administrative staff?

- Is the paid staff full-time or part-time?

- Are you required to pay volunteer insurance?

- Do you have to rent office or meeting space?

Although no program has yet succeeded in being self-sustaining (no outside support), some programs have come very close and have a lot of ideas about how to get closer still.

In the years 1985 through 1987, it took investments of between $60,000 and $100,000 to launch the first Time Dollar programs in Washington, D.C., and Missouri. In 1988, the state of Michigan proved you could start a program with grants ranging from $10,000 to $20,000.

Today, it should be possible for anyone with access to this book to launch a program for $100 or so, if they are prepared to work full-time (and overtime) without compensation (and maybe even wangle help from their friends). Access to an IBM-type computer makes things considerably simpler—but is not essential.

Of course, you really do have to have some things before you can start a Time Dollar program. You can buy them, find someone to donate them, or donate them yourself. The process of preparing your budget starts with thinking through how you're going to obtain these basic resources:

- Office space

- A place to meet, train, and socialize

- A coordinator or director (preferably full-time, whether paid or unpaid)

- Clerical and record-keeping help (to answer phones and record Time Dollars earned and spent)

- Other staff

- Phone and answering machine (experience indicates that much of your contact with members regarding services they need and services they agree to provide will take place by phone)

- Office furniture, such as desk(s), filing cabinet(s), lamp(s)

- Extra chairs (members have to have somewhere to sit when they're filling out their membership application forms or when they're talking over their experience assisting another member)

- Supplies (pens, pencils, paper clips, stapler, paper, stationery, envelopes, stamps—it's amazing how fast these little things add up)

- A brochure explaining the program (which could be as simple as a single sheet of paper)

- Membership applications

- Forms to track member requests for services (and debits to their accounts)

- Forms to track services provided by members (and credits to their accounts)

- Photocopying/printing (for brochures, fliers, forms, notices)

- Volunteer insurance and in certain limited situations, workmen's compensation; volunteer insurance is available for $3 per volunteer per year. (See the discussion of insurance on page 213.)

- Refreshments, special events, awards, certificates

- Reimbursement of travel expenses for care providers (optional)

- A computer and printer (optional, depending on the size of the program and whether you want one. However, computers provide an efficient, safe means of tracking Time Dollars earned and spent and providing an accounting to members.)

The budget items listed below can add up to a lot or almost nothing, depending on how formal you make them. While you need the various plans listed, they might consist of only a few handwritten pages, costing nothing more than the paper they're written on. Even the kits and materials listed can be fairly informal, although they should be neatly typewritten.

- Plan for recruiting/servicing members and membership kit

- Volunteer training materials

- Fund-raising plan and materials

- Publicity plan and press kit

- Administrative policy and procedures manual

All of these items are listed in "Sample Budget" on page 238. You can use it as a starting point for your own budget. Once you've worked through what you need to start your Time Dollar program, you can start writing up how much you expect each of the things to cost. If you can get things, services, or space donated, just write "donation." If there are items you don't think your program will need, just write "N/A" for not applicable. There are blank lines at the bottom of the budget where you can add items not listed.

18

How to Launch
the New Currency

Now you're ready to blast off and put your good inten-
tions into practice—help the elderly to go shopping, provide child care
for working mothers, see that the sick have transportation to the doctor,
and more. But first, there are some things you have to do. Fortunately,
many others have done these already so you can profit from their
groundwork to save time and effort.

DEVELOPING AN INFORMATIONAL PACKAGE

There are several elements such a package should contain. Check
this list.

- One page handout (See "Sample Handout for a Local Program"
  on page 239.)

- A set of Q & As (See "Sample Questions and Answers" on page
  240.)

- Brochure (See "Sample Brochure Coverage and Layout" on
  page 242 and "Sample Flyer" on page 244 for two samples.)

- One or two newspaper or magazine articles so that people know
  that the idea has been tried elsewhere and has worked (See "A
  New Slant on the Golden Rule" on page 248.)

Your brochure can be as simple or fancy as you want to make it. If you have access to a computer with a word-processing program and laser printer, you can usually make a brochure at very low cost. If you have access to a photocopier as well, you can make a lot of brochures for next to nothing. If you're not up for creating a brochure, a one-page handout will do. A brochure needs to contain answers to these questions.

- What is the program's name?

- What are Time Dollars?

- Why are Time Dollars important?

- What does the program do?

- What services does it provide?

- Who can join?

- Why should I join?

- If I want to join, whom should I call? Where should I go? What can I expect?

Feel free to take any text from this book and from the samples in the appendix. Note that one of the brochures includes some testimonials. As soon as you can, you should add testimonials from members of your program who have received help and from others who have provided service. Eventually you will want to incorporate these testimonials into the brochure itself; but until you do, just print them on a separate sheet of paper and tuck them into the brochure. Remember, people are often convinced by testimonials even when they're not convinced by your assertions, no matter how eloquent. After all, you're selling something. Testimonials are proof that what you're selling is worth buying into.

DEVELOPING A "SALES PITCH" OR PRESENTATION

There are some basic points you will want to get across in talking to groups and individuals. Your own personal enthusiasm is more important than any specific information you want to convey. When you're trying to recruit volunteers into the program, the last thing you want to say is that they should earn Time Dollars against the day they need them. People don't want to think about that grim possibility, especially seniors. They certainly don't want to join a program where that's what people are thinking about. As Terrie Raphael, director of the Elderplan program observed, the insurance industry discovered long ago that they had to sell "life insurance, not death insurance."

It's the same with Time Dollar programs. You have to sell people on the personal satisfaction, the sense of being needed and the new friends they make in helping others. People want to build networks and they want to cease being afraid of strangers. They want to be less alone, and they want to know that they have something to offer that others value and need. And they will like the idea of being part of the wave of the future, especially when it means recapturing the best of their past. These inducements, coupled with human interest stories and personal testimonials, are most effective.

Anna Miyares who heads the Greater Miami Service Credit Program includes three elements in her recruitment pitch that are extremely effective.

First, she reminds people of their roots, asking whether they remember a time when neighbors helped neighbors. Then she tells them that this is what the Time Dollar program is trying to bring back. She couples this with a reminder about budget cutbacks in services and how we need to be able to cope with these.

Second, she asks how many are now helping someone or have helped someone during the past year or so—shopping, fixing a meal, babysitting a sick child, helping move or clean. She gets them to raise their hands if they have done any of those! They do and somehow, that means they have crossed a certain line from passive to active, from audience to participant. It amounts to a tentative commitment.

Third, she says that in this program, they will do the same kind of thing, but for a *new friend*. That addresses their fear of not knowing what to do (since they are already doing it) and it emphasizes that Time Dollars help you renew and expand your circle of friends and acquaintances.

You will find a sample "pitch" laying out different points you may want to make on page 251. A 10-minute video introduced by Ralph

Nader and shown on network TV is available from "Essential Information," part of the Compleat Time Dollar Kit. It explains the idea, shows several programs in action, gives people a feel for how a program actually works. It helps to break the ice and generate discussion.

DECIDING ON THE SOURCE AND NUMBER OF RECRUITS

Think small: Five or seven is more than enough. You and a friend ought to be able to drag that many acquaintances in to get things going. From that point on, it gets easier and easier because they give testimonials, and you use what they are doing to give examples to others to get them interested. Here, the choice of a base, or site, may be essential. One announcement at a meal site for seniors is likely to net you more than you can handle, particularly if a staff person or the head of the organization introduces you and "endorses" the idea. Make sure you can give them an assignment within two to three days. "Use them or lose them" is really true about volunteers (see "Sample Information Form" on page 256 for member information forms designed to provide the information in a format that can then be transferred to a computer). In identifying the initial volunteers, take advantage of the base you have selected and build a program around the "natural flow" of the organization.

IDENTIFYING AND SECURING SERVICE RECIPIENTS

This particular task is more difficult than most people think. It is critical that you not underestimate the difficulty.

First, people generally don't like to accept charity. Even though Time Dollar programs are self-help programs, not charity, you have to convince them of that.

Second, people might need help, but that doesn't mean they'll ask for it. Frequently, they equate asking for help with begging on street corners.

Third, people are afraid to invite strangers into their homes. They are warned by their neighbors and children not to open their doors to strangers, and with good reason, considering some of the scams that have been perpetrated in recent years. So be prepared to demonstrate to both the prospective member and his or her family and friends that your program is legitimate and that the volunteers coming to the recipient's home are trustworthy.

It may help if you explain to the person receiving help that she has something to offer to the program and that, as soon as possible, you will expect her to be earning Time Dollars. Even if she is still confined to bed, she can be part of the telephone assurance pool that makes contact with other members and checks to see if a service performed was satisfactory. That makes it clear to people that you don't view them merely as charity cases.

Your best bet is to identify one or two organizations or agency staff who always need help for a client and who can virtually guarantee to deliver some requests for assistance on an ongoing basis. Be creative in identifying these organizations. For instance:

- Make a pitch to organizations that provide home-delivered meals; they have a built-in list of people who need companionship, grocery shopping, and light meal preparation.

- Talk to hospital discharge planners; they know the recently discharged patients who require nonmedical support beyond what insurance covers.

- Organizations to which elderly and disabled people travel could use a transportation service.

- Prenatal care centers could use a "grandmother service" to help mothers with newborn infants.

- Hospice always needs more volunteers. And even though Hospice has intensive training requirements for those volunteers who work most closely with the family, they often need a volunteer who will just take the kids to the zoo or do some shopping.

The point to remember is this: We are a society where many who need help are reluctant to ask for it. Channels for seeking help informally have disappeared for many. So be prepared to invest extra time in generating requests for help.

ARRANGING INSURANCE FOR GIVERS AND RECIPIENTS

It is essential to carry insurance that will cover any injury to a Time Dollar volunteer or to a person receiving help from a volunteer. Accidents happen; people get hurt and you don't want anybody to be worse off for having participated in the program. A special insurance program for volunteers has been offered for over 20 years by CIMA (Corporate Insurance Management Associates), 216 Payton Street, Alexandria, VA 22314. Phone: (703) 739–9300. The annual premiums are phenomenally low; $3 per year (personal liability, 50 cents; accident insurance, $2.50) buys $1 million in coverage for injury to the volunteer or the recipient. An additional $3 buys excess automobile coverage for volunteers using their cars. The carrier is INA (Insurance Company of North America). In some states, volunteers to state agencies are covered by workmen's compensation; Pacific Presbyterian Hospital in San Francisco covers all of its volunteers with workmen's compensation but does not require that the organizations in its Time Dollar coalition do likewise. Check out the applicable law. But regardless, get the private insurance.

ARRANGING FOR MEDIA COVERAGE

Sometimes editors actually read press releases and make assignments. More often, releases get thrown away. Make some personal phone calls to local reporters and editors. Contact them early and provide regular updates as the program gets off the ground. Also, try to get a public service announcement on the radio. Ideally, you want a story that simultaneously announces the start of the program and describes one or two of the first assignments that members are carrying out. That, in turn, becomes part of your handout packet at meetings and for new volunteers. Local TV news likes this kind of story: Producers can film at their convenience and use it as "filler" on a slow day. A story about a new Time Dollar program has the feel of a "hard" news event that stays current for days if not weeks.

CONDUCTING TRAINING AND MAKING ASSIGNMENTS

You will need a packet of orientation materials and forms. (See Sample Information Form on page 256 that new members need to fill out.) The orientation materials include:

- A statement of rights and responsibilities (see "Rights and Responsibilities of the Time Dollar Volunteer" on page 258).

- A summary of dos and don'ts (see "Dos and Don'ts for the Time Dollar Volunteer" on page 261).

- A code of ethics for members (see "Code of Ethics for the Time Dollar Volunteer" on page 262).

TRAINING: WHAT WORKS BEST

All programs provide some kind of basic orientation. They need to gather information on new members, to introduce them in greater depth to the Time Dollar concept, and to provide a briefing on the code of ethics and dos and don'ts. (The "don'ts" are important: Don't try to lift someone; don't administer medication. People trying to be helpful can sometimes exceed their own physical capability and their own knowledge without realizing it.) Beyond that initial orientation, programs differ greatly in their approach.

Some provide a great deal of training. Most directors have found that training turns off many volunteers because they have already helped out neighbors or raised children or done the things they will be asked to do in the program. So, effective programs disguise the training by incorporating it into regular social events and gatherings. Pot-luck lunches where volunteers engage in joint problem solving are an example. They stimulate insights, identify resources, and create a new kind of social setting for volunteers. This kind of informal exchange is probably the best kind of training, particularly when a resource person is available. A team approach where volunteers are paired for an assignment provides a kind of safety margin for the service recipient; supervision, back-up calls, and spot checks provide additional margins of safety during on-the-job training.

Many programs have evolved into informal but highly effective referral systems, enabling people to get tangible help and services they did not know were available. Over time, programs assemble materials in a kind of Yellow Pages for social services helpers: what agencies provide what kinds of service, whom to call to get what, and the like. You will probably want to do that, but not right off.

In the meantime, ask your local United Way or area Agency on Aging or hospital discharge planner if you can use its resource handbook.

Other programs insist on training because they want Time Dollars to provide a new opportunity for life-long learning and for the acquisition of new skills. Participants in Elderplan's peer counseling program, for example, take real pride in their counseling skills. All programs seem enthusiastic about providing a kind of continuing education on subjects of interest to members—such as sessions on financial planning, entitlements, insurance, and the like. If you build in substantial training, award certificates. If it can be done in a community college setting, so much the better.

The principal conclusion is: Don't be doctrinaire about the need for training. If people like it, if it builds morale and a sense of family, that's great. If it turns people off and they tend to drop out, then cut the training and get them involved, preferably teamed up with a more experienced volunteer at first.

19

How to Sustain the Bank

Before you even get started, people often ask how you plan to survive over the long haul. They wonder what will happen after the initial funding gives out, or who will carry it if you should disappear. There *are* answers—even though there are *no* guarantees.

They may not realize it but they are actually asking two questions:

1. How do you envision the program's evolving to further the organization's mission? In other words, what are your *long-range ideas on the program?*

2. How do you propose to get the program on a *stable financial basis over the long haul?*

This section shares ideas on both questions. But one thought first.

The Time Dollar is a new idea. The very *worst* that can happen is that some people will help some other people and feel proud that they did so. And some people will get help they would have missed, and they won't feel they were begging for it or taking it from someone else who needed it more. Those are not exactly terrible things even if the program "fails" and dies. The "downside," the so-called worst-case scenario, is still better than doing nothing.

The upside is really exhilarating. If the program succeeds, then new possibilities open up in virtually every sphere of social activity. Where we count upon the student, the patient, the family, the neighborhood, the community to carry part of the load, there is a new way of rewarding and stimulating that effort without vast increases in taxes or expenditures. Time Dollar programs hold out the possibility of tapping a vast reserve of human energy and hope that neither the market economy nor appeals to volunteerism nor threats of being "terminated" from some program have been able to touch. Time Dollars give your organization a chance to get in on the ground floor, to be innovators and social entrepreneurs.

So don't get defensive. The worst that can happen is good. The best that can happen is that we can begin to dream and hope and trust again. That's worth some effort and even some risk. Now for the more concrete answers.

LONG-RANGE PROGRAM DEVELOPMENTS

Programs have to take root and grow. Increased self-sufficiency is a radical notion in an economy built on specialization and mutual dependence. There are two applications or extensions of the concept that will be tested soon. If they prove viable, it might mean that Time Dollar programs could be incorporated in the warp and woof of every institution and every organization.

How to Generate Reciprocity

Many social service agencies are funded to provide free services. Some organizations like health clinics and child day care programs are required or obliged to charge a fee but have flexibility to set up a sliding-fee scale based on ability to pay. Such agencies are typically overwhelmed. The people they help almost invariably come with a bundle of problems unrelated to what the agency does or outside the scope of the agency's sphere of operations. Time Dollars offer a way to turn the time of clients into a resource with which to address those problems. Any agency that gives free or subsidized service should give serious consideration to charging a fee to be paid in Time Dollars by those whom they help. There are two reasons.

First, charging a fee to be paid in service transforms the helping relationship from one of subordination between professional and client (with the taint of charity) to one of reciprocity. It assumes that the person being helped has something of value to give to others.

Second, enlisting clients as part of a mutual help network enables the agency to mobilize resources that its clients desperately need, often as much as anything the agency itself can provide. If every agency giving away services could use those services as a catalyst to create a resource bank of people prepared to do anything from babysitting to engaging in a neighborhood crime-watch program, then many of the problems that bear on the agency's mission could be addressed. People who are isolated need a way to create informal support networks. Providing services for a Time Dollar fee can trigger the creation of such networks. That may actually rebuild community and create a sense of extended family with the capacity to address problems far more effectively than any single-purpose agency.

In addition, that one Time Dollar fee will trigger more service when the client helps another person, then that person in turn can be asked to "pay back" with Time Dollars for the help received. That turns the efforts of paid staff into a chain reaction that just keeps going. There will be exceptions of course: people who can genuinely not pay back. Yet, even in such cases, there are often family or friends or fellow members of a congregation who will happily pay back for such a person. Even bedridden people can be part of a telephone visiting program.

The presumption ought to be that everyone has something to give. If we act as though we believe it, we will find out that faith is vindicated. If we act as though people are worthless and simply manipulating the system, they will probably confirm our worst fears. So set the right tone. A Time Dollar fee-for-service policy can trigger major social change.

Employee Time Dollar Programs

Except for the once-a-year United Way drive, employees rarely have reason to give thought, as employees, to finding ways to do community service as an extension of their employment. Dreaming up a project of your own requires an extra effort and an extraordinary degree of initiative. Dr. Martin Luther King's statement, "Everyone can be great because everyone can serve" is true—but few of us act on it personally as we head home to the kids or dinner or the bills or undone chores. Instead, budget cuts, layoffs, reorganizations, office politics, career options occupy our attention before, during, and after the work day.

Yet, there is a basic decency that keeps coming out, as when a fellow employee is injured or has problems in the family. We don't know the potential for good in all of us—until we give it a chance and a reason to come out.

Why not institute a Time Dollar program as an option for every employee at every work site? Participation should *never* be imposed as an obligation. But employers could make participation easy and even attractive by offering:

- Time Dollar volunteers the opportunity to participate in a flextime program that would permit them to work 40 hours in a four-day week, if they spent part of the fifth day earning Time Dollars

- On-site day care, free or at reduced rates (staffed in part by Time Dollar volunteers)

- A volunteer to help out at home for women employees in the sandwich generation (simultaneously raising children and caring for an elderly parent) in return for Time Dollar participation

- A first chance to pick holiday and vacation scheduling for Time Dollar participants

- Access to a program where Time Dollar participants could pool their sick leave and thereby gain access to more in case of major, prolonged illness

- Preferential access to training programs for Time Dollar participants

- Increased leave time or sick leave carryover for Time Dollar participants

- Special computer training courses or tutoring by employees for the children of Time Dollar participants

- Special health packages for Time Dollar participants because participation gives them an informal support network that puts them in a preferred risk category

Employees have personal lives too. They need family and support systems and neighbors and a sense of community. In their book *Rein-*

venting the Corporation, John Naisbitt and Pat Aberdeen talk about how corporations are trying to create a community so that work and personal concerns are no longer so polarized.

There is no reason why the employer and the employees cannot seize the opportunity to convert their work site into a base from which to build community, neighborliness, and a sense of extended family. And there is no reason why every employer should not endeavor to convert an agency, corporation, or institution into a good citizen contributing tangibly to the civic health of a community.

LONG-TERM FINANCIAL SURVIVAL

We can anticipate that the short- to middle-term survival of some programs will depend upon creative fund-raising that runs the gamut from bake sales to grantsmanship of the most sophisticated kind. This will be coupled with efforts to get private sector contributions where philanthropy might have a positive effect on business. Thus, banks and other businesses are an obvious starting point. Studies indicate that they lose a considerable number of employee days because a work force composed largely of women is struggling to cope with child care and parent care problems, often simultaneously.

Three basic strategies have emerged to generate long-term revenue streams necessary to support Time Dollar programs.

Institutionalizing the Program

Grants are great but they provide only short-term funding. Where it is clear that a Time Dollar program generates net revenue or reduces significant costs to an institution, then it is worthwhile for that institution or organization to absorb the cost as part of its basic operating budget. That means the program's survival is no longer contingent on hustling short-term support.

The Miami program, for example, has generated numerous referrals to South Shore Hospital and resulted in billings to government Medicare and Medicaid programs estimated to be in excess of $1 million. The Greater Southeast Community Hospital in Washington has used its Time Dollar program as part of an advertising campaign to project its image in the community as a leader in health care. Elderplan in Brooklyn uses its Eldercare program as a selling point to seniors in a hotly competitive market for Health Maintenance Organizations. (See "Sample Flyer" on page 244.) If Time Dollar programs could reduce maintenance and security costs in housing projects or improve student performance in schools—to give just two examples—that would make the case for building administrative costs into the core operating budget of those institutions.

Servathon: Using Time Dollar Volunteers to Raise Cash Dollars

All of us have heard of walkathons: friends, merchants, employers pledge a certain amount to charity for each mile a participant walks. That often gets hundreds and even thousands of people out walking as a way of raising money for a good cause. Why not adapt the basic concept to Time Dollars? Why not solicit pledges of $1 for each hour of service that people provide through the program?

Employers whose work force includes large numbers of mothers who both raise children and care for an elderly parent might like to give a donation pegged to hours spent providing relief for working mothers. Local merchants might want to do the same for grocery and shopping services for the elderly and infirm. Agencies funded to stimulate volunteering as part of their mission (e.g., local area Agencies on Aging) might like to give a commitment of funds based on the increase in service delivered *to* or *by* the elderly. Public schools might like to promote mentoring by the elderly or peers by committing a sum of money to reward the organization that mobilizes those resources. And so on.

The arithmetic is simple: 100 Time Dollar volunteers averaging 4 hours per week for 50 weeks would generate 20,000 hours a year. Multiply that by $1 an hour and the organization could raise $20,000 by helping others while its members earned Time Dollars for themselves.

That's $1 an organization would earn for every hour spent running errands for the elderly, taking them for medical check-ups, providing day care for preschool children, running an adult-literacy program, providing job training and meals for the homeless—doing whatever its Time Dollar program does.

If the organization needed start-up funds, it could ask for an advance on the first quarter of the money in order to hire the coordinator and get the program launched. The understanding would be that it could not get the next installment until volunteers had generated enough hours to "earn" the first installment.

A variation would be to sign up two organizations willing to provide matching grants of 50 cents per hour of service (or 4 organizations at 25 cents, and so on) if the program meets its stated goal.

Legislative or Public Sector Support

During the next two to five years, ongoing programs of any magnitude will require a funding source for both the core operation and for expansion and innovation.

Here, the public sector can play a critical role; given budget constraints, government at every level will want Time Dollar programs to succeed and to expand. *Who* in government will want this?

- Legislators? Yes. They want to address constituent problems without spending lots of money.

- The chief executive? Yes. A mayor, governor, and perhaps even the president want to find cost-effective ways to meet needs.

- Heads of agencies with jurisdiction over the problem? Not always. By and large, they desperately need increases in appropriations just to avoid imposing cutbacks. They will give a polite audience, appear to be very interested, but unless they are peculiarly innovative or mavericks, they will tend, regardless of party or ideology, to regard Time Dollars as a very mixed blessing indeed. The original fiasco in Florida (see chapter 9) provides a classic bureaucratic case history.

Executive Branch Discretion It is entirely possible that right now, the head of an agency dealing with elderly problems or youth problems or welfare problems has the administrative discretion to earmark funds available under some authorization to test the applicability of the Time Dollar approach to some particular need. This is done usually by issuing an RFP—a request for proposals. If you or a grass-roots group with which you are involved have entrée to an innovative, open-minded administrator, then see if he or she would be willing to issue such an RFP. This was done in New Jersey when a particularly creative administrator (previously with the Robert Wood Johnson Foundation) was in charge of Human Services. An RFP was issued, proposals were received, and grant awards were made to four programs. Unfortunately, after this administrator left, his successor was not able to keep that particular pot of money. A copy of the New Jersey RFP is available as part of the Compleat Time Dollar Kit. (A grants-manship manual for Time Dollar programs is also included in the kit.)

VISTA Volunteers Grants   There is one federally funded program that has proven so consistently valuable to Time Dollar programs that it should be singled out: the VISTA volunteer program funded through ACTION, the federal volunteer agency. VISTA volunteers are paid a small stipend ($400 a month plus health insurance). Sometimes funds are available to pay part of the time for an administrator or coordinator. The grant can be renewed for up to four years. An initial cadre of VISTA volunteers can get your program off to an incredibly fast start. They provide roving field program managers, recruit, make presentations, and do a hands-on job in matching volunteers and service recipients. The VISTA applications are challenging to fill out and require that you understand what they are looking for. For this reason, a copy of a successful (i.e., funded) VISTA application is included in the Compleat Time Dollar Kit. If a VISTA grant is of particular interest, you should also contact those programs that have been successful in obtaining VISTA volunteers: Miami, El Paso, and St. Louis.

Legislative Action   Legislators in many states are interested in Time Dollar programs. Both Michigan and Missouri have demonstrated that grass-roots programs funded under state legislation can work.

The Missouri law is the simplest and has been copied by other states. It provides:

SECTION 1. The division of aging of the department of social services may establish . . . a program under which persons who are sixty years of age or older may volunteer their time and services to an in-home service or voluntary agency serving the elderly which is approved by the division and receive credit for providing volunteer respite services, which credit may then be drawn upon by such elderly persons when they themselves or their families need such respite services. The division shall establish a registry of names of such volunteers and shall, monthly or as often as it deems necessary for efficient management of the program, credit each of such volunteers with the number of hours of service they have performed for agencies approved by the division. No person serving as a volunteer pursuant to any program established by the division under the provisions of this section shall be credited more than ten hours of volunteer service under this program per week.

SECTION 2. At such time as a person who has done volunteer work under this program established under section 1 of this act shall need assistance himself, he shall so notify the division and, if the division shall determine that such person is in fact in need of such assistance, which need shall not be based on financial need but on the social and medical condition of the person in question, such person shall receive the assistance of a volunteer. If no volunteer is available to assist a person entitled to assistance under this section because of his participation as a volunteer in the program established under section 1 of this act, and such unavailability has been verified by the division, the division, or an agency approved by the division, may obtain paid assistance for such person. Such paid assistance shall be at a rate which is no higher than the prevailing reimbursable rate established by the state for a unit of in-home services. The cost of such paid assistance shall be paid by the state if the person in question is not eligible for Medicaid from in-home service funds appropriated to the division.

SECTION 3. The division of aging shall submit a report to the general assembly on January 1, 1987, indicating the number of volunteers recruited through the program established under section 1 of this act and the number of credit hours of service.

As a starting point, the Missouri statute has the virtue of simplicity. But it is unduly restrictive. You may wish to include language that addresses the following issues.

Augmenting Types of Service Rendered   For the elderly: "homemaker and related services," or any service that enhances the capacity of the recipient to maintain self-sufficiency or improves the recipient's quality of life.

Intergenerational programs: infant care, child day care, tutoring normally involve the provision of services by older persons to younger persons; but gardening, running errands, shopping, home repairs, and driving may involve services from younger persons to the elderly.

Demonstration or pilot programs: innovative applications to a variety of social problems—Alzheimer's victims, AIDS patients, adult day care, preschool day care, hospital discharge-related services.

Redefining Restrictions on Participants   Age is not necessarily a desirable restriction for earning or spending credits. Handicapped persons, adolescents, people of all ages all have something to offer and have needs that others can fill.

Restrictions on Transfer Recipients for Time Dollars
Persons related by blood or marriage ought to be able to transfer credits to each other, and a person ought to be able to give Time Dollars to a local, charitable membership organization. This will ensure that Time Dollars are used to strengthen family and membership in community-based organizations. It will prevent transfers to local merchants or use as a form of payment for drugs or alcohol.

Expanding the Nature and Scope of "Guarantee"
Demonstration programs should be required to develop contingency plans to deal with situations where a volunteer fails to show. If a program is being phased out, persons who have earned credits should have a reasonable period to use them or give them to someone else. A "guarantee" can also take the form of preferential access to publicly funded programs, provided that people with *greater* needs do not get bumped. *If the guarantee proves to be a stumbling block, eliminate it in any form and just require that local programs make contingency*

plans, trying to make sure that people who earn credits get the services to which they are entitled.

Eliminating Preconditions to Spending Time Dollars
Avoid at all costs any imposition of a formal determination of "need." People who have earned Time Dollars should be able to get help when *they* determine they need it. There is some possibility of abuse—but that is best remedied informally. There should be *no* financial means test. Regardless of income, all should be able to give and receive help.

Establishing an Advisory Committee
It helps to have such a committee established to oversee the program, to act as its informal advocate, and to encourage innovation and expansion. Members should be drawn from relevant government agencies, provider organizations, charitable institutions, and beneficiary groups.

Setting Up a Computer Program
State-run computer systems are often too complicated to modify—and instituting a new data-collection system can take months and even years. Legislation should provide express authorization for the state to contract with a local group to maintain records specified by the state. Confidentiality should be maintained. And many programs feel strongly that participants should *not* give their Social Security number to prevent invasion of privacy.

Securing the Proper Insurance
Insurance should be required that protects both the provider and the recipient. Licensed occupations and professions are normally excluded from volunteer insurance. No attempt should be made to require workmen's compensation.

Establishing Tax Exempt Status
The rulings from the Internal Revenue Service make it clear that Time Dollar programs should give rise to no "contractual" rights enforceable by either party—either to the provider who wants to redeem credits or the sponsoring

organization who wants to get a recipient to "pay back" for services received. In other words, these programs should be based on goodwill and trust, not on any sense of legal entitlement. There is nothing to prevent participants from being charged a membership fee or a pass-through charge for actual dollar expenditures (e.g., lunch in a child day care program).

Hints for Seeking Public Sector Support The *way* you go about getting the support you need often has everything to do with the success you have. Follow these tips.

Welcome support for Time Dollar programs from either or both political parties. So far, Time Dollars have not been the subject of partisan politics. Legislation has been sponsored by Democrats and Republicans and has been implemented under both Democratic and Republican governorships.

Don't let Time Dollar programs be used as an excuse for cutting (or refusing to grant needed increases for) other programs for older Americans or any other group in need. The function of Time Dollar programs is to rebuild family, neighborhood, and community. It is easy to bash bureaucrats and professionals; it is easy to attack public programs as giveaways. The fact is that there is acute need and that professional expertise, if used to reduce dependency and increase self-sufficiency, is invaluable.

Work to have government fund testing of the "servathon" strategy (mentioned earlier). It is not easy for a program to build up the requisite volume the first year—but following a one-year seed money grant, funding might be shifted to a "servathon" basis with payment made based on actual hours of service delivered. The government cannot buy an hour of delivered service for $1 so taxpayers would get a true bargain.

Fight means tests. Time Dollar programs must not be turned into a means-tested program for the poor.

Pinpoint prime areas of influence. There are targets of opportunity where Time Dollars can make a particularly significant contribution.

- Programs involving the elderly as recipient and provider
- Intergenerational programs bringing old and young together
- Peer tutoring and parent involvement programs in schools

- Home visitor programs to reduce infant mortality and child abuse
- Quality, home-based day care programs for children
- Programs to provide help to AIDS victims
- Programs of self-help for the homeless
- Programs providing useful roles for the handicapped
- Environmental monitoring and clean-up efforts

Some central themes emerge that legislators might listen to. Where breakdown of family or neighborhood results in problems that government is now obliged to address with funds, it makes sense for government to create an incentive (using Time Dollars) to restore the capacity of family, neighborhood, and community to do what they do better than specialized institutions and professionals.

Where there is evidence that some form of community service has a positive effect on education or health or crime or substance abuse, it is logical to fund experiments with Time Dollars designed to promote and reward community service.

In dealing with legislators and any other people of power and influence, careful preparation and well-thought-out proposals with contingency plans hold out the best chance for success. Further, having such a solid grip on the concept and the means for attaining it assures a steady course for the project throughout its early implementation and its maturity.

APPENDIX

Quick Reference Start-Up Tools

The items that follow are true working papers that were used to establish and continue actual Time Dollar units, ranging from neighborhood groups to community facilities and full municipalities. You are free to use them in any way that might help you create and operate a Time Dollar unit in your community.

The Sponsorship Agreement serves as a model to use in presenting the official purpose and position of your cause to a sponsoring group.

The organizational charts show essential assignments to duties that must be planned before the first staff member is recruited. A budget worksheet provides a model you can use as is or adapt to your own needs.

The brochures and handouts show you how to do it when you are ready to publicize your own group. You will want to reprint (with permission, of course) local newspaper features and others, like the piece from *Reader's Digest*, about your program to use as advertisements and enclosures in mailings.

Take every opportunity to speak out about your Time Dollar program to community groups of all kinds. The sample pitch provides guidelines for making your points effectively.

Volunteers you recruit will need to know their duties, what they can expect in return, and the rights of service recipients. The section on rights and responsibilities spells it all out for you. This group is followed by a list of important dos and don'ts, plus a basic code of ethics.

SAMPLE SPONSORSHIP AGREEMENT

If a group of organizations form some kind of consortium to launch a Time Dollar program, there needs to be some understanding of the respective responsibilities of all members. In Miami, this was handled by designating one agency as the "fiscal and administrative agent" for the consortium. That agency (which was called the Lead Agency) received the grants and did the centralized record keeping.

All other members were called Sponsors. Two categories of sponsors evolved: a "prime sponsor" which was an agency or organization with enough staff and administrative structure to take primary responsibility for operating "its own" program (consistent with the general policies of the Consortium); and an "Adjunct Sponsor" which might be a group or organization with virtually no staff where a volunteer serving as "team leader" kept the program going day to day and received technical assistance and direct back-up from either the Lead Agency or a Prime Sponsor.

An agreement, or Memorandum of Understanding, was drawn up that describes the responsibilities and liabilities of the Lead Agency and the Prime Sponsor. The Memorandum of Understanding provided below has been modified to provide a starting point for other communities. It is only a starting point; it should be adapted to local conditions and relationships.

MEMORANDUM OF UNDERSTANDING

_____ in its capacity as lead agency and fiscal agent for the Consortium and the Sponsoring Agency, _____, enter into this agreement to implement the Time Dollar Program as a condition of release of funds and assignment of VISTA Volunteers. The parties agree as follows:

In its capacity as Lead Agency and Fiscal Agent, _____
agrees:

(1)   To convene meetings of the Consortium and the Steering Committee in furtherance of the development of the Consortium and the Time Dollar Program and to provide a core staff for the Consortium.

(2)   To serve as fiscal agent for the Consortium; to ensure compliance by all participants with the conditions contained in any grants or other support by various funding sources; to receive, disburse and account for funds to funding agents; to make periodic payments to Sponsors based upon the terms of the grants received and the fulfillment by the Sponsor of its responsibilities under the grant.

(3)   To acquire and maintain such computer based system(s) as may be required for the day-to-day conduct of the Program, including the ability to match Service consumers with Service Providers from the pool of any of the Prime Sponsors.

(4)   To oversee and monitor implementation of the Memoranda of Understanding between the Lead Agency and Prime Sponsors and between Prime Sponsors and Adjunct Sponsors.

(5)   To mediate and resolve Program or contractual problems.

(6)   To undertake public information initiatives on behalf of the overall Program and in aid of such efforts by Sponsors.

(7)   To maintain appropriate administrative records regarding the overall Program as well as appropriate data regarding individual participants and Sponsors.

(8)   To endeavor through its best efforts to assure the quality and integrity of the Program through:

— the development of resource materials for the recruitment, screening and training of participants;

— monitoring and maintaining records on volunteer completion of core training program, in-service training and any specialized or advanced training designed to equip Service Providers to meet special needs of Sponsors or Consumers;

— the conduct of an on-going quality control follow-up;

— the development of mechanisms for periodic program review and evaluation; and

— the implementation of reserve and other requirements designed to insure the integrity of service credits.

(9) To maintain a separate participants pool for each sponsoring organization designating Full Participants, Recipients, and Donors involved in the Program through each Prime Sponsor. The pools will also designate program participants:

(a) with special skills,

(b) whose availability is flexible, and

(c) those willing to be designated "on call" who have agreed to provide services to individual consumers and/or eligible groups who are in the pool of another Prime Sponsor. The Lead Agency shall provide the names of such "on call" participants to assist Prime Sponsors to meet emergency and unusual situations. Except for "on call" volunteers or other situations where express consent has been given, the names of participants in one Prime Sponsor's pool shall not be shared with other Prime Sponsors to preserve confidentiality. The computer program shall be designed to keep the name and identity of participants confidential and available only to the Prime Sponsor with whom they are affiliated.

(10) To insure that Service Providers, Recipients and other program participants have been provided a full statement and

explanation of rights and responsibilities, obligations and limitations on obligations of all parties including Service Providers, Service Consumers, Prime Sponsors, Lead Agency and the Consortium.

The Sponsor, _____, agrees:

(1)   To designate a representative and alternate to participate in policy and procedure formulation through representation on and regular attendance at meetings of the Consortium and its Steering Committee. The representative shall have authority to speak for his/her organization on matters of policy and planning, and be able to seek, where necessary, approval from his/her particular Board of Directors in order to commit the organization's resources.

(2)   To operate a service credit program in compliance with the provisions of the Policy and Procedures Manual as a condition of receiving disbursements of funds allocated to the Sponsor under grants, gifts or contracts received in support of this program.

(3)   To provide work plans with time lines, target goals, projected numbers of participants and service hours generated.

(4)   To supply data necessary to determine progress under the work plan and to contribute to and assist in the compilation of reports needed by funding sources or for public information purposes.

(5)   To supply information on a timely basis needed to maintain and update the computerized management information system.

(6)   To provide prior notice and secure appropriate approval from the Steering Committee wherever the sponsor exercises the discretion reserved to it in the Policy and Procedures Manual to alter program design.

(7) To honor the five (5) day guarantee on all credits earned through its program, and to collaborate fully with efforts to assure the integrity of service credits earned throughout the Consortium.

(8) To provide a statement of steps taken and projected to meet reserve requirements.

(9) To honor credits earned elsewhere in the Consortium pursuant to policies and procedures jointly developed and promulgated.

(10) To comply with such additional terms as may be required by funding sources as a condition of obtaining or releasing funds.

(11) To insure that Agreements (if any) with Adjunct Sponsors conform with the policies and procedures of the consortium and to monitor the performance of Adjunct Sponsors to insure compliance with those Agreements and with the policies and procedures of the Consortium.

(12) To alert the lead Agency and the Consortium to problems that arise in implementation of the work plan.

(13) To give adequate advance notice to the Lead Agency and the Steering Committee of any situation that may involve utilization of reserves or may require the assistance of other consortium members in order to honor the five (5) day guarantee; this shall be considered as an obligation to be given utmost priority as a matter of urgency.

(14) To provide pre-service and in-service training as required and to monitor, track and record the progress of each Service Provider in training for purposes of quality control.

(15) To take all reasonable steps to assure:

(a) that Service Providers are adequately informed in pre-service training of the limitations on liability of the Consortium, Prime Sponsors, Sponsors and the Lead Agency;

(b) that Service Providers, Recipients and other program participants have been provided a full statement and explanation of rights and responsibilities, obligations and limitations on obligations of all parties including Service Providers, Service Consumers, the Prime Sponsor, lead Agency and the Consortium.

The Lead Agency and Sponsor both agree:

(1) to maintain liability insurance for themselves, their employees and volunteers engaged in this program;

(2) to indemnify and to hold harmless all other members, groups or organizations in the Consortium from claims, suits, judgments or damages arising from acts, failures to act and omissions of its employees, volunteers and other agents in relation to activities conducted pursuant to, under the direction of, or in cooperation with the Time Dollar Program.

Provided that entering into this Memorandum of Understanding shall not be construed to mean that either the Lead Agency or the Prime Sponsor accepts liability for the acts, failures to act, or omissions of other agencies or organizations for activities arising out of this agreement;

Either party may terminate this Agreement upon no less than thirty (30) days notice. Said notice shall be delivered to the party by certified mail, return receipt requested, or in person with proof of delivery.

Provided that termination of this agreement shall not relieve the Sponsor of full and primary responsibility for honoring all credits earned under its program component nor shall termination relieve the Lead Agency and the Consortium of responsibility to honor their "best effort" commitment (including use of reserves) to insure the integrity of credits earned and to honor the guarantees made to Time Dollar providers and recipients.

This Agreement shall be in effect from _____ to _____.

Lead Agency Project Director _____

Prime Sponsor Coordinator _____

SAMPLE ORGANIZATIONAL CHARTS

CHART 1

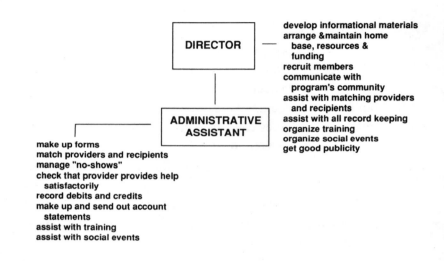

DIRECTOR

develop informational materials
arrange &maintain home
  base, resources &
  funding
recruit members
communicate with
  program's community
assist with matching providers
  and recipients
assist with all record keeping
organize training
organize social events
get good publicity

ADMINISTRATIVE
ASSISTANT

make up forms
match providers and recipients
manage "no-shows"
check that provider provides help
  satisfactorily
record debits and credits
make up and send out account
  statements
assist with training
assist with social events

CHART 2

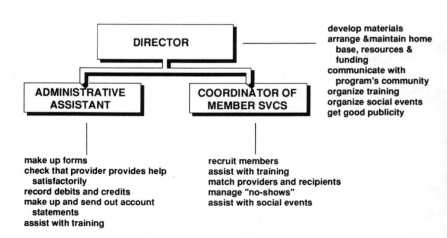

DIRECTOR

develop materials
arrange &maintain home
  base, resources &
  funding
communicate with
  program's community
organize training
organize social events
get good publicity

ADMINISTRATIVE
ASSISTANT

COORDINATOR OF
MEMBER SVCS

make up forms
check that provider provides help
  satisfactorily
record debits and credits
make up and send out account
  statements
assist with training

recruit members
assist with training
match providers and recipients
manage "no-shows"
assist with social events

CHART 3

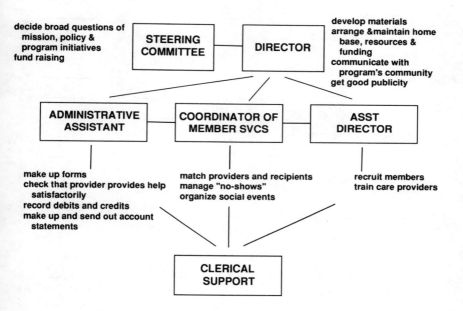

decide broad questions of
mission, policy &
program initiatives
fund raising

STEERING COMMITTEE

DIRECTOR

develop materials
arrange &maintain home
base, resources &
funding
communicate with
program's community
get good publicity

ADMINISTRATIVE ASSISTANT

COORDINATOR OF MEMBER SVCS

ASST DIRECTOR

make up forms
check that provider provides help
satisfactorily
record debits and credits
make up and send out account
statements

match providers and recipients
manage "no-shows"
organize social events

recruit members
train care providers

CLERICAL SUPPORT

SAMPLE BUDGET

YOUR BUDGET

                                                    annual cost

Office space   _____

Large meeting space   _____

FT coordinator/director   _____

"Bookkeeper"   _____

Other staff (position title _____)   _____

Other staff (position title _____)   _____

Phone/answering machine   _____

Office furniture, including extra chairs   _____

Supplies   _____

Brochure   _____

Membership applications & other forms   _____

Xeroxing/printing   _____

Volunteer insurance   _____

Refreshments, special events, awards, certificates _____

Computer & printer   _____

Plan for membership drive; membership kit   _____

Volunteer training materials   _____

Fund raising plan & materials   _____

Publicity plan & press kit   _____

Policy & procedures manual   _____

Local transportation, parking (reimbursement)   _____

Item: _____   _____

Item: _____   _____

Item: _____   _____

Item: _____   _____

                                   TOTAL   _____

SAMPLE HANDOUT
FOR A LOCAL PROGRAM

CENTRO SAN VICENTE SERVICE
CREDIT PROGRAM

On May 15, 1991, Centro San Vicente launched a major new program to serve this community. The program is called Service Credits. Service credit—or Time Dollar—programs are now in operation in Boston, Miami, San Francisco, Washington, D.C., Sacramento, and state-wide in Missouri and Michigan. But until now, such programs have been largely limited to elderly people helping other elderly people. This will be the first time that Service Credits have been operated by a primary health care program to involve the entire community in addressing its health needs.

Under this program, every member of Centro San Vicente will have the opportunity to earn this new kind of money by helping others. One hour of help given to someone else earns one credit. Members will then be able to use those credits to purchase additional services for themselves and their families—services like child care, care for the elderly, transportation, and even health care packages.

San Vicente has just been selected to receive a grant of six VISTA volunteers to mount a four-component program that will benefit the entire community. These six VISTA volunteers will create and coordinate a new transportation linkage system to enable this community to overcome the single greatest barrier it faces in addressing critical health needs: the lack of effective transportation to bring services to people, people to services, and people to people.

There will be four initial components:

1. A Member Transportation pool to enable members to get to appointments at the clinic.

2. A system to enable working parents with an ill child to avoid missing work and losing pay by getting help from a trained elderly member of San Vincente. This service will be particularly important for children who are sick for extended periods with chickenpox or colds—and whose parents cannot afford to miss a day's work.

3. A Home Visitor Transportation program that provides home visitation for women needing pre-natal care, for mothers with

newborn babies and for families at risk who need help, support or just plain relief in order to cope with crises. This should impact directly on health indicators such as infant mortality and child abuse.

4. A San Vicente Member Exchange program that enables members to help each other by exchanging services and provides both matching and transportation so that members can help each other as one community-wide extended family.

This new system issues in a new period of partnership between San Vicente and the community it serves. Together we can address the most serious health problems of this community with the most important resource we have—the time of our own people.

SAMPLE QUESTIONS AND ANSWERS

I. WHAT IS PROJECT INDEPENDENCE?

Project Independence is a private, nonprofit, grass-roots organization, headquartered in Norwich, Connecticut, providing in-home respite care, center-based respite care, and day care socialization programs for severely disabled children and adults. Our service area encompasses a town region of eastern Connecticut.

A. Goal:

The primary goal of the Senior Time Banking program is to enhance person-to-person, neighbor-to-neighbor relationships, keeping seniors in their own homes for as long as possible, while maintaining a high quality of life.

B. Concept:

Generally, most senior citizens are retired and living on fixed incomes. With prices for health care rising, people are having a great deal of difficulty meeting their medical needs. This program allows the clients to receive much needed help without inflicting a financial burden on them. Volunteers benefit by obtaining credits guaranteeing them help when they need it.

C. Who can volunteer?

Anyone aged 60 or older is eligible to become a Senior Respite Volunteer. All prospective volunteers are required to attend a brief training program prior to providing volunteer services.

D. Who can receive services?

Senior Respite Volunteers are provided to anyone aged 60 and older. Volunteers perform such services as: grocery shopping, accompanied doctor's visits, reading and writing, or just a friendly visit.

II. WHAT IS RESPITE CARE?

Caring for a senior loved one or a long-term chronically ill adult places a tremendous strain on family members. Such families need some time to themselves—a "time out," a break, a temporary relief from the demanding, exhausting, and stressful routine of 24-hour, around-the-clock care.

To help the family in this crucial effort, Project Independence conducts a senior volunteer program provided by trained companions, who are available on an as-needed basis to offer their services in the homes of clients. Our respite care services are designed to give needy seniors and their families the opportunity to receive some free help.

It may give caregivers of clients a chance to accomplish such daily matters as shopping, banking, dining out, going to a movie, etc. It may also assist families to meet emergency family crises or important family occasions.

SOURCE: Project Independence of Eastern Connecticut, Inc. Senior "Volunteer Time Banking"—A Source Book and Training Manual for the Respite Provider.

SAMPLE BROCHURE COVERAGE AND LAYOUT

WHY DO PEOPLE VOLUNTEER?

There are many wonderful benefits and rewards for being a VISCAP volunteer! Some of these are:

- Satisfaction derived from providing a much needed community service.

- Learning valuable new skills you can use your whole life.

- Making new friends and meeting colleagues.

- VISCAP banked volunteer service credits. (Volunteers, 60 years of age and older bank one (1) credit hour for each hour of service they provide. Volunteers under 60 and community groups can bank credits for a particular individual in need of services, rather than banked for personal use.)

- Volunteers with banked credit are given priority for services when they are in need.

- Insurance through Corporate Insurance Management (CIMA) provides accident and liability insurance for volunteers.

- Appreciation from your community for a job well done.

- Recognition from Kirtland Community College VISCAP at our recognition activities.

- And most importantly, the deep satisfaction of seeing older individuals being able to live independently

VISCAP

HELP WHEN NEEDED

Wilhine Roach

KIRTLAND
COMMUNITY COLLEGE
ROSCOMMON, MICHIGAN 48653

WHAT IS VISCAP?

In recent years, growing emphasis has been placed on the benefits of keeping the aging relative with their families rather than seeking institutional care. With this development has come an increasing public sensitivity that family caregivers should be recognized and assisted. To meet this need, VISCAP aims to create an awareness of the needs of the primary caregiver and to help provide volunteer support services in the recipient's home to give the caregiver relief.

WHO MAY BE HELPED?

The Volunteer Incentive Service Credit Account Program or VISCAP is a new program benefiting not only the caregiver, but the person being cared for.

The program seeks to help senior citizens, 60 years of age or older, and handicappers and disabled individuals to remain living independently and reduce the need for premature institutionalization by providing respite and/or support services to primary caregivers.

The legislation defines a primary caregiver as an individual responsible for a care plan to enable a person, 60 years of age or older, to remain living independently; or a person, 60 years of age or older, directly responsible for the independent living of a handi-

capper or disabled person.

Respite care is defined as part-time intermittent service provided by volunteers in the recipient's home to give the primary caregiver relief.

Reprinted from A.I.M. Michigan Office on Services to the Aging, September/October 1988.

WHAT MAY VOLUNTEERS DO?

Some of the support activities that may be provided by volunteers include: escort services, pet care, personal grooming, light housekeeping/heavy cleaning, exercise/recreation, letter writing/special correspondence, yard work, plant/garden care, meal planning/preparation, snow shoveling, telephone reassurance, companionship, errands, shopping, etc.

WHO MAY VOLUNTEER?

Anyone with a desire to help may volunteer.

Credit redemption is offered to volunteers, age 60 and older, for their personal use when they have need of respite and/or support services for themselves or their families. These hourly credits will be "banked" in a state computer-based system.

VISCAP is also an intergenerational program for all ages. Volunteers under 60 can bank credits for later use, or youth clubs,

service organizations and church groups can "bank" credits and donate them to individuals in need.

HOW IS THE PROGRAM FUNDED?

This program is funded through a grant from the Michigan Office of Services to the Aging to Kirtland Community College to serve the nine counties of Leelanau, Benzie, Manistee, Kalkaska, Otsego, Crawford, Roscommon, Oscoda and Ogemaw. VISCAP evolved from legislation sponsored by State Senator Connie Binsfeld and State Representative Maxine Berman.

HOW DO I OBTAIN MORE INFORMATION?

If you need the services of a volunteer or would like more information about volunteering yourself, call Carolyn Boone at Kirtland Community College, **275-5121 or 800-433-2517 Ext 264.**

No one shall be excluded from participation in any service or activity because of race, color, sex, age, national origin or handicap, for participation in, be denied the benefit of, or be subject to discrimination under this program.

SAMPLE FLYER

Member-to-Member
1276 50th Street
Brooklyn, N.Y. 11219-2539

ELDERPLAN, INC.

BUSINESS REPLY MAIL
FIRST CLASS PERMIT NO. 11, BROOKLYN, N.Y. 11219

POSTAGE WILL BE PAID BY ADDRESSEE

NO POSTAGE
NECESSARY
IF MAILED
IN THE
UNITED STATES

WHAT YOU GIVE AND WHAT YOU GET AS A VOLUNTEER

YOU GIVE - -
- - A few hours a week *at your convenience* in activities you enjoy.

- - Your life experience which is very valuable.

- - No previous experience required.

YOU GET - -
- - The option of a *free* quarterly Elderplan premium.

- - Training and on-going support in the Elderplan office.

- - The satisfaction of lending a helping hand.

- - The opportunity to join a group of terrific seniors like yourself.

- - Some help at home if you need it.

YOU CAN HAVE IT ALL!!!

Be a volunteer and get help at the same time! You can trade your skills for assistance with tasks that are difficult for you to manage. Call us to find out how you can give and get.

JOIN US TODAY!

If you need a helping hand . . .

. . . managing at home

. . . doing errands

. . . having a friendly visit

. . . sharing your feelings with a
trained peer counselor

We are here for you.
Give us a call.

WE WANT YOU

If you're a senior with a few hours to
spare . . .

If you have a skill you'd like to share ..

If the needs of others make you
care . . .

. . . Then you're invited to be a
volunteer in Elderplan's MEMBER-
TO-MEMBER program.

If you want more information about
becoming an Elderplan member,
please call
871-PLAN
If you want more information about
the volunteer program, please call
438-1593
Or
Return the attached postcard
No postage is necessary

MEMBER
- TO -
MEMBER

A Senior Volunteer
Program Serving
Elderplan Members

ELDERPLAN, INC.

(continued)

SAMPLE FLYER—*Continued*

HERE'S WHAT PEOPLE SAY ABOUT ELDERPLAN'S SENIOR VOLUNTEER PROGRAM

"It's like a family affair. Everyone works together. When I go to visit my partner and see the trust and satisfaction in his eyes, it makes me feel wonderful. This program does a lot for those who are sick and those who are helping."

— *Herbert, 75*

"At the beginning, it was difficult for us to accept help from a stranger, but Dorothy made it easier. She visits my wife weekly, giving her something to look forward to and allowing me to get out a little. It's really good therapy for my wife."

— *Joseph, 68*

"When you are old and sick, you have fewer and fewer friends. I am very lonely. My volunteer is a friend to me. She comes to visit. We just sit and talk."

— *Goldie, 88*

"I visit with a couple. My weekly visits provide them with an opportunity to talk with someone who will listen and understand. The program gives me a chance to keep busy with activities which are worthwhile."

— *Hope, 74*

WHAT THE PROGRAM IS ALL ABOUT

MEMBER-TO-MEMBER is a senior volunteer program serving Elderplan members. We match volunteers with people and projects needing help. And there's something special. Volunteers earn "service credits" for the time they spend helping - - one credit for every hour of work! And these credits entitle volunteers to special benefits.

MEMBER-TO-MEMBER works just like a blood bank or a volunteer fire department. It depends upon people being good neighbors the old fashioned way. You lend a helping hand - - and good things will come to you.

A program supported by The Robert Wood Johnson Foundation

HOW OUR VOLUNTEERS HELP

- Escorting people on errands or to the doctor.
- Shopping or doing errands for people who can't get out.
- Driving people who need a ride in the neighborhood.
- Making minor home repairs.
- Visiting people at home.
- Giving time off (respite) to people caring for relatives at home.
- Counseling people who need an understanding listener.
- Visiting Elderplan members in the hospital.
- Telephoning people who are lonely.
- Writing letters and paying bills.
- Sharing skills in music, woodworking, knitting, crocheting, needlepoint and other areas.
- Translating for people who need help with English.
- Doing office projects like stuffing envelopes.
- And any other areas that interest you.

TELL ME MORE . . .

☐ I am an Elderplan member and I would like more information about the volunteer program.

☐ I am not an Elderplan member and I would like information about Elderplan.

☐ I am not an Elderplan member and would like more information about the volunteer program.

(Please Print)

My name: _____

Address: _____

_____

Phone: _____

SAMPLE PROMOTIONAL REPRINT

The concept is simple: help a neighbor and a neighbor will help you

A New Slant on the Golden Rule

Condensed from WASHINGTON MONTHLY
JONATHAN ROWE AND STEVEN WALDMAN

FOR SEVERAL MONTHS in 1987 Elsa Martinez helped other senior citizens by shopping, cleaning and driving them around. For each hour she volunteered, Martinez earned a "service credit" at Friend to Friend, an unusual program run by Miami's South Shore Hospital and the Little Havana Activities and Nutrition Centers of Dade County. Then last year, at age 64, Martinez became unable to do things for herself. So she started spending her credits by requesting help. Fellow participants in the program—all earning credits themselves—kept her company and helped with chores.

On one level, Friend to Friend and programs like it in various parts of the country are simply updates of the old neighborhood baby-sitting club. Help a neighbor, and somewhere down the line a neighbor will help you. But the "time dollars," as the service credits are called, represent a radical new approach to the way Americans can help one another.

"The credit program uses market-like incentives, but it draws on altruism, a desire to help, a need to be needed," says Edgar Cahn, a professor at the District of Columbia School of Law and the leader of the movement.

Cahn started thinking about the service-credit approach in 1981 while recovering from a heart attack. Lying in a hospital bed, feeling helpless, he got a taste of what millions of Americans experience when they become old, sick or have unmarketable skills. Their time just sits there, like an enormous, untapped reservoir of oil only a few feet below the ground.

"The real wealth of a society is

the time of its citizens," Cahn concluded. "Why couldn't we create a new kind of money that pays people to meet the needs of society?"

Cahn eventually proposed his idea to the Robert Wood Johnson Foundation, which specializes in health-care grants. In 1987 the foundation issued $1.2 million in grants for programs in San Francisco, Miami, Boston, St. Louis, Washington, D.C., and Brooklyn, N.Y.

The basic mechanics of these programs are simple. A church, hospital or other organization establishes a computer record of volunteer work, acting in effect as the central bank. Volunteers report their hours and get credits they can draw on later. When someone needs help, he or she calls a program manager, who then assigns a volunteer interested in performing the task. Programs are as diverse as the communities they serve.

Often the elderly are forced into nursing homes not because they are hopelessly infirm but because they need help with tasks like washing dishes, cashing Social Security checks and cleaning the bathroom. In Brooklyn, the service-credit program, run by a nonprofit social and health-maintenance organization called Elderplan, helps seniors sustain themselves by providing assistance with these everyday chores.

Etta Goldsmith of Brooklyn has to take care of all the shopping because her husband is very ill. But she's having problems with her eyes, and shopping is a challenge.

Frank Vuolo, on the other hand, a former mechanic who loves to keep busy, has strong eyes and a humming automobile. Elderplan matched him with Goldsmith, and now every Thursday morning Vuolo drives her to the supermarket. "If it weren't for you," she confided to Vuolo, "I'd be lost."

Through some 120 volunteers like Vuolo, Elderplan is able to supplement its basic benefit package by providing help that otherwise would fall to home health aides or wouldn't get done at all. Participants can cut their health-insurance costs by using service credits to pay up to 25 percent of the annual premium.

The Friend to Friend program in Miami has recruited over 800 volunteers who work an average of 8000 hours a month. It delivers services for about $1.31 an hour, including overhead—a fraction of what the cost would be in the private sector or in the public sector if done by social-service professionals. Because most services are neighborly, with participants drawing upon intuition and common sense, there is little need for training.

The program, by encouraging an unusual level of cultural mixing, can help break down barriers that isolate people. In a racially tense Miami area, blacks and Hispanics who never communicated in their own housing projects are now bringing one another lunch every day. The only thing Boulos Chamoun, a 68-year-old Lebanese man, would seem to have in common with Eleuteria Alfonso, an 86-year-old Cuban-American woman, is that neither can speak English. But Chamoun's face brightened when Alfonso visited him at the hospital last December. Not long before, she had delivered a lunch to his apartment and found him collapsed on the floor. Now, as Alfonso leaves Chamoun's hospital room after another visit, she whispers to a friend, "I get so worried about him."

But is Alfonso really a volunteer? She is, after all, receiving a form of pay. Paradoxically, the credits do not seem awfully important to some of the people involved. "For me they mean nothing," Vuolo says. "It's my pleasure to help somebody in need." In fact, there are volunteers who aren't even cashing in their credits. Of the roughly 96,000 credits earned in Miami, only six percent have been spent.

Yet the credits clearly do make a difference to many. Volunteers flock to the programs, and dropout rates are very low compared with those of conventional volunteer programs. How can earned credits be both key and unimportant? Ana Miyares, Miami's program coordinator, explains: "Service credits provide the hook, but once people are here, they love helping."

Cassie Mae Brown earned low wages her whole life as a nurse's aide, but now she is the Rockefeller of service credits. On a typical day, the Miami volunteer rose before dawn to drive one man to his dialysis appointment, visited a woman who needed companionship and stopped by to see another woman in the hospital. Last year Brown won the Service Credit Volunteer of the Year honor for racking up 570 hours. The credits, she says, "make me feel like I'm somebody."

By accruing credits, volunteers will be more self-sufficient later, less dependent on their children. "We are like an insurance policy you take out," says Terrie Raphael, director of Elderplan's Member-to-Member program. "Except you don't pay with your money; you pay with your time."

In St. Louis this year, Grace Hill Neighborhood Services expanded its program to include participants of all ages. For example, a young husband and wife who help a senior citizen shovel snow can use their credits to get a baby-sitter. In Miami, senior citizens may soon help staff legal-service offices in exchange for free legal help.

The service-credit system gives recipients a sense of dignity. Instead of receiving charity, they are undertaking an obligation that they will pay back if they can. "You don't feel you're infringing on anybody," says Herbert Kilby, 66, who earned credits by driving another senior citizen to the airport. When Kilby recently had to have surgery, a volunteer drove him to the hospital.

"You help somebody," he explains, "and they help you."

SAMPLE PITCH PROMOTING
THE TIME DOLLAR CONCEPT

You have to remember to adapt this sales or recruitment pitch to your own experience, and to your audience. Don't speak more than ten minutes before you open the floor to questions. You might even prefer to speak for only two or three minutes, then show a ten-minute video, originally aired on the show 20-20, and available from **Essential Information, PO Box 19405, Washington, DC 20036.**

I.   Start with a personal story — how you first heard about time dollars; how time dollars have made a difference in your life; an incident that would have turned out better if you'd been able to lean on the sense of community time dollar programs provide. The audience can only identify with you (and ultimately with time dollars) if you reach them one-human-being-to-another.

Edgar Cahn, co-author of *Time Dollars*, tells his story. You must tell yours. A canned pitch does not work.

The hardest thing I ever had to do was to be a patient in a hospital. In 1980, I...

II.   Explain why you wanted to speak to this audience in particular, for example, because they have political power, a wide network, a lot of energy, respect in the community, positions of leadership, demonstrated compassion and concern for the problems your time dollar program addresses. Explain why it's important to you, personally, that they carry this torch.

A related statement is to remind the audience that you all share common values, commitment to improving our lot, mutual respect, mutual affection.

III.   Explain simply what time dollars are: Time dollars are a new kind of money. You earn time dollars helping other people.

You spend time dollars to get similar kinds of help for yourself or your family, or by giving them to someone who needs help. At the core is a very simple equation: 1 hour = 1 time dollar.

In many ways, a time dollar program is like a blood bank. You give a pint, and down the line, if you or someone in your family needs it, you can draw down on it. The difference is that this bank enables you to deposit time, *and everybody's time is equal to everybody else's time.*

AS AN ASIDE: I know that market wages for companionship are different from market wages for translating are different from market wages for driving somebody to the grocery store, but this program is not about market wages. I wouldn't ask my mother and you wouldn't ask your mother to go next door to scrub the floor for market wages. But I wouldn't hesitate to ask her to scrub the floor of a sick neighbor. The only issue would be whether I could get her to accept time dollars, and this is how I would do that. I would tell her that it's selfish to NOT accept time dollars, because if she doesn't accept them she can't give them away to someone who needs them.

IV. Time dollars are *local* currencies. You can start them up from any number of bases — community colleges, senior centers, businesses, clubs, community service organizations.

V. Time dollars work. The idea has been tried and tested. It's now operating in ten states across the country. In one city alone, it's generating 8,000 hours of service a month, involving 900 volunteers serving about 1,800 people.

VI. The IRS has ruled time dollars are tax exempt. And the reason is because this is like family doing for family and neighbors doing for neighbors; it's not a commercial barter system, for example, between dentists and lawyers.

VII. Mention the kinds of services your program provides. Mention some of the services other time dollars programs pro-

vide. Mention real people who get needed help from time
dollar programs. People like Mrs. Amaker, who gets around
on a walker. Although she can drive (she drives members of
the time dollar program to the doctor, or to the grocery store),
she needs someone to help around the house — to get up on
a step-ladder to put in a light-bulb, and to carry laundry
downstairs, where the machines are located.

People like Herbie, who is legally blind. He is almost entirely
self-sufficient, although he needs help with some house-
work, like defrosting his refrigerator. He earns time dollars by
helping people who are coping with increased eye difficulty
locate places to get books and newspapers in big print, how to
lay out the house to make it easier to get around, where to learn
to read braille, how to get books on tape.

People like Mrs. Wallace, a retired teacher, who teaches a
time-dollar sponsored adult literacy class. Sometimes her
student is an older adult who has always been ashamed to
admit he or she can't read. Sometimes it's parents who want
to learn to read so they can help their kids with homework.

VIII.   Underlying time dollar programs is the fundamental belief
that the real wealth of our society is the people who live in it,
and their time. There are real needs in this community. We've
gone through cutbacks [name some of them, and their effects
on the audience]. I'm not prepared to put our problems and our
needs on hold until the budget is balanced, and the trade deficit
is eliminated, and the dollar is stronger vis-a-vis the yen and
the mark. With time dollars we already have what we need —
time to spend helping each other.

Time dollar programs are about more than simply doing tasks
and delivering services. Somehow, time dollar programs are
able to turn strangers into friends, and neighbors into extended
family. Time dollar programs are about re-building community. And it seems to be able to transcend racial and religious
lines.

As Eric Berry, the director of the Michigan time dollar program said, "Society is not set up so that we can walk up to someone and say, I want to help you." Time dollar programs are like a letter of introduction. They give people who pass each other silently on the street or in the elevator a reason to finally meet, and say hello, and help each other.

IX.   Questions & Answers. Here are some points that might be useful to touch on when you're answering questions.

1.   The real reward of time dollars is feeling that we are needed, that what we can do matters in someone else's life. In most time dollar programs, people aren't yet spending a lot of credits themselves. But they like getting the time dollars because it makes their work "really count", as opposed to "just volunteer" work.

2.   There used to be a time, when you did good works in the community, it would remember, and take care of you if you happened on hard times for a while. However, today one out of every five Americans moves every year. Even ministers move. A time dollar program (supported by a computer system), acts as the equivalent of a community's collective memory.

3.   If you are speaking to an elderly audience, you might want to point out that society generally does not think the elderly have a contribution to make. Time dollar programs all over the country are proving we have a contribution to make.

4.   The only person to whom this program could conceivably be a threat is the producer of commercials for TV soaps — it might actually succeed in drawing a few people away from their TVs. But it doesn't take anything from anyone else.

Anna Miyares, who is the director of the Greater Miami Service Credit Program, includes three elements in her recruitment pitch that are extremely effective.

First, she reminds people of their roots, asks whether they remember a time when neighbors helped neighbors — and tells them that this is what her time dollar program is trying to bring back. She couples this with a reminder about cutbacks in services, and how we need to be able to cope with them.

Second, she asks how many of them are now helping someone, or have helped someone during the past year, with life's necessities — grocery shopping, fixing a meal, babysitting a sick child, moving to a new house, washing up the dishes, etc. She asks them to raise their hands if they've done of any of these things. She says that this, at a certain level, helps them commit themselves to the time dollar program in principle.

Third, she explains that all they would do in the time dollar program is the same sort of thing they already do for family and friends, but for a *new friend*. This addresses the common fear that they won't know what to do, since they're already doing it. It also helps make the point that the time dollar program will help members expand and renew their circle of friends.

SAMPLE INFORMATION FORM

Time Dollar
Member Information

For Official Use Only:

Organization _____
Recruiter ID _____ Site ID _____
Date enrolled _____ RSVP Y___ N___
Forms signed Y___ N___
Full particp'n/Recip'nt only F___ R___
Donor/Beneficiary D___ B___
If beneficiary, ID _____ % Transferred ____ %

First _____ Last _____ Nick name _____
Addr _____ City _____ State _____
Zip _____ Phone (h) _____ Phone (w) _____

Birthday _____ Emergency contact/Relationship/Phone #

_____ / _____ / _____

ETHNICITY: ❑ White ❑ Black ❑ Hispanic ❑ Asian ❑ Native American ❑ Other

LIVES: ❑ Alone ❑ With spouse ❑ With family ❑ Other

WHERE: ❑ Adult congr living facility ❑ Senior house ❑ Hotel ❑ House/apt.

Doctor _____ Phone _____

Car? ❑ Y ❑ N/Dr Lic #/ST _____ PUBLIC TRANS: ❑ Bus ❑ Metro ❑ Taxi ❑ Other

Smoker? ❑ Y ❑ N Smoke tolerance? ❑ Y ❑ N Mobility prob? ❑ Y ❑ N If YES, explain in COMMENTS.

Have you ever volunteered in the past? ❑ Y ❑ N Are you volunteering now? ❑ Y ❑ N

AVAILABILITY:

	Mo	Tu	Wd	Th	Fr	Sa	Su
Morn							
After							
Eve							

FLEXIBLE: Time of day _____ Day of week _____

LANGUAGES:

- ❏ English
- ❏ French
- ❏ Italian
- ❏ Signing
- ❏ Other _____
- ❏ Spanish
- ❏ Creole
- ❏ Braille
- ❏ Yiddish

SPECIFIC SKILLS OR SERVICES:

- ❏ 44. Administration
- ❏ 45. Adult day care
- ❏ 46. Adult literacy
- ❏ 47. Advocacy
- ❏ 48. Alzheimer's Care
- ❏ 49. Baby sitting
- ❏ 50. Child day care
- ❏ 51. Clerical
- ❏ 52. Companionship
- ❏ 53. Dressing assist.
- ❏ 54. Errands
- ❏ 55. Escort
- ❏ 56. Food & clothes distribtn.
- ❏ 57. Fund raising
- ❏ 58. Garden & yard
- ❏ 59. Home repair
- ❏ 60. Home mgmt/Bills
- ❏ 61. Homeless program
- ❏ 62. Hosp/Med referral
- ❏ 63. Hosp visiting
- ❏ 64. Laundry & ironing
- ❏ 65. Leisure & recreation.
- ❏ 66. Letter writing
- ❏ 67. Light housekeeping
- ❏ 68. Meal delivery
- ❏ 69. Meal preparation
- ❏ 70. Meal site aid
- ❏ 71. Pet care
- ❏ 72. Referral advocacy
- ❏ 73. Religious service escort
- ❏ 74. Respite care
- ❏ 75. Sewing & mending
- ❏ 76. Shopping
- ❏ 77. Special friend prgrm
- ❏ 78. Team leadership
- ❏ 79. Telephone assurance
- ❏ 80. Translation
- ❏ 81. Transportation
- ❏ 82. Tutoring
- ❏ 83. Other _____

Comments _____

_____

_____

Member's Signature _____

RIGHTS AND RESPONSIBILITIES OF THE TIME DOLLAR VOLUNTEER

RIGHTS

To Learn

To receive the training necessary to

- help others
- meet the challenge of new situations
- deal with emergencies

To Give

To do service that is comfortable and satisfying to the volunteer.

To Earn

To earn one Time Dollar for every hour he or she spends on assignment helping another member of the program.

To Save

Each Time Dollar is banked in the member's personal Time Dollar account, available to be used when the member wants or needs a service the program provides. These savings are inflation-proof. One Time Dollar will always equal one hour of service.

To Donate Your Time Dollars

Members can donate their Time Dollars:

- to a family member or friend
- to a charitable organization that belongs to the Time Dollar program
- to the program itself, to be used to help members unable to earn Time Dollars

To Spend Now . . .

. . . on any service the program offers.

To Be Valued

To receive recognition for their valuable service to the program and the community.

To Be Treated Fairly

Any dispute, complaint, or misunderstanding arising out of involvement with the program will be resolved promptly.

RESPONSIBILITIES

Training

Complete required training.

Job Requirements

1. Maintain service recipient confidentiality.

2. Observe the Code of Ethics.

3. Be prompt and keep scheduled commitments.

4. Accept supervision.

5. Keep monthly time sheets and hand them in.

RIGHTS OF THE TIME DOLLAR SERVICE RECIPIENT

To Be Treated with Dignity, Care, and Respect

When you receive service under a Time Dollar program, you are NOT receiving charity. Someone along the line, you yourself, a friend, an anonymous donor, or a loved one worked hard for the Time Dollars you are now spending for important services.

Confidentiality

All volunteers in the Time Dollar program are held to a strict Code of Ethics. A volunteer can be dismissed from the program for violating this Code. Volunteers are prohibited from disclosing information about the people they serve except to their immediate supervisor.

Guaranteed Price

One Time Dollar buys 1 hour of service. The price is guaranteed.

LIMITATIONS OF THE TIME DOLLAR PROGRAM

While a version of this particular statement of limitations is used by the Friend-to-Friend Time Dollar consortium in Miami, it can easily be adapted for use by a stand-alone program, or any other program configuration.

This program has been undertaken as a pilot program. All participating agencies are committed to making the program a permanent one. At present, Time Dollars have no expiration date and are intended to be good for the foreseeable future. This is subject to change, but no change will take place without a minimum of six (6) months of advance notice to all holders of service credits. If a change is necessary, the program will make adequate provision so that at least a portion of the credits earned can be used.

The agency with which a volunteer serves has primary responsibility for ensuring that all Time Dollars earned are honored. This assurance is backed by a good-faith pledge by the entire [*name of consortium*] network to see to it that all credits are honored.

Time Dollars have no cash value and are not redeemable for cash or credit. They may only be used for exchange transactions within the [*name of consortium*] system.

DOS AND DON'TS FOR THE TIME DOLLAR VOLUNTEER

Do . . .

1. When accepting an assignment, write down the name, place, date, and period of time that the assignment is expected to last.

2. Be on time to the Respite site . . . 5–10 minutes *early* is even better.

3. Know the service recipient's name, and be sure he or she knows yours.

4. Wear practical clothing.

5. Ask to be shown the layout of the house; anything unusual or potentially dangerous (like a steep staircase or a loose step); location of all doors, telephones, light switches, first-aid cabinet, fire extinguishers, etc.

6. Find out the numbers for a family member or friend, doctor, police, fire department, etc.

7. Find out who (if anyone) should be admitted to the house.

8. Follow all directions regarding the assignment explicitly.

Don't . . .

1. Don't give medication.

2. Don't lift, toilet, or bathe the care recipient. Remember, if you do so, you are fully liable.

3. Don't cancel at the last minute.

CODE OF ETHICS FOR THE TIME DOLLAR VOLUNTEER

The Time Dollar volunteer shall NOT:

1. Breach the service recipient's privacy or confidentiality.

2. Pressure the service recipient to accept his/her religious beliefs or political viewpoint.

3. Bring friends or relatives to the service recipient's home.

4. Solicit or accept money, gifts, or tips from the service recipient.

5. Consume the service recipient's food and drink.

6. Smoke in the service recipient's home, unless prior approval has been given by both the service recipient and the family caregiver.

7. Use the service recipient's telephone for personal calls.

8. Use the service recipient's car.

However, the Time Dollar volunteer MAY eat his or her personal lunch in the service recipient's home and use the recipient's bathroom facilities.

Index

A

Aaron, Henry, 3
Accounting
    of monetary transactions, 39
    in Time Dollar programs, 6, 7,
      38–39
      social value of, 12
ACTION, 202
Aging. *See also* Elderly
    of Americans, 4, 5
    of Swedes, 166, 167
Agreements
    memorandum of
      understanding, 230–35
    sample sponsorship, 230
Agriculture, economics and, 40
American Red Cross, 62, 65, 172
Americans
    aging of, 4, 5
    consumption by, 22
    financial status of, 22–23
    indebtedness of, 21
Axelrod, Robert, 185, 186
Ayers, Richard, 187
Azzai, Rabbi Ben, 81, 85

B

Baker, Russell, 15
Barter
    in early 1980s, 77
    IRS and, 77–79
    money and, 26, 27
Behavior, consequences of, 184–85,
    189
Berea College, 180
Bergman, Shimone, 80
Berry, Eric, 7, 64, 152, 254
Blacks, volunteerism by, 111
Borysenko, Joan, 88

Brochure coverage and layout,
    sample, 242–43
Brooklyn, Time Dollar program in,
    44–46, 47–56
Budget
    federal, problems with, 3–4,
      7, 8
    preparation, 205–7
    sample, 238
Bureaucracy
    in Florida, 96–97, 100–103,
      104–5, 107
    social welfare and, 74
Bush, George, 63
Business
    community and, 17, 18–19, 20
    international movement of, 187
    in 1980s, 133–34
Buyer's Up, 136

C

Care, community and, 19–20
Care shares. *See* Time Dollar(s)
Carnegie, Andrew, 18
Case management, 155
Cash crops, 40
Centro San Vicente, 142–50
    program handout from, 239–40
Charity
    dignity and security vs., 65–66
    Time Dollar programs vs.,
      54–55, 63, 65–66
Child care programs, 181, 195
    in Miami, 132–33, 137–41
Children, service to, 194
Child support payments, 182
Cigarettes, as currency, 39–40
CIMA, 213
Cities, social disconnection in, 188

Colgate-Palmolive, 164
College alumni, as social force, 136
Communism, decline of, 168
Community. *See also* Neighborhood
 breakdown of, economics and,
  22, 23
 business and, 17, 18–19, 20
 care and, 19–20
 division of labor and, 27–28,
  29
 economics and, in early U.S.
  history, 17–18
 economic value of, xi, xii
 professional services and, 126
 from Time Dollar programs,
  36, 64, 71
Community needs, 194
Community service, required by
 government, 169, 174
Community values, 163–64
Compleat Time Dollars Kit, 200,
 201
Computers and software, for Time
 Dollar programs, 201, 204–5,
 226
Conservatives, 163
Consumer debt, 21
Consumption, social interaction
 and, 20
Contracts
 barter, 79
 money and, 41–42
 trust vs., 80, 81–82
Conversation, in family, 15–16
Corporate Insurance Management
 Associates (CIMA), 213
Corporations, mobility of, 187
Cousins, Norman, 87
Crime prevention, 176

D

Daughters of Charity, 142, 143, 147
Day care programs, 181, 195
 in Miami, 132–33, 137–41
Democrats, 162–63
Depression, Great, 26, 48
DeVito, Carolee, 7, 66, 67, 129,
 131
Dignity, charity vs., 65–66

"Disabling professions," 121, 122,
 123–124, 126
Disease, money and, 88
Division, of labor, reduced
 socialization from, 27–28, 29, 122
Duggar, Margaret Lynn, 99–100,
 103, 104, 105, 106

E

Economics
 agriculture and, 40
 community and, in early U.S.
  history, 17–18
 conventional, limitations of, 9
 early history of, 23–24
 family and community
  breakdown and, 22, 23
 money and, 27, 32
 price and, 37–38
 sexism and, 67–68
 view of humans in, 42–43
Economy
 market vs. nonmarket, 182–83
 money-driven, 26
 physical health and, 87–88
 society and, 24
 women and, xi
Education, professionals and, 175
Educational services, 194
Elderly. *See also* Aging
 abuse of, 101
 appeal of Time Dollars to, 71
 in Florida, 97–98
 Health Maintenance
  Organization for (*see*
  Elderplan)
 hospitals and, 129
 needs of, 49–50, 53
 peers preferred by, 50–51
 relating to their children, 51,
  52–53
 self-esteem of, 52–55
 services for, 10, 194
 social workers and, 127
 telephone reassurance to, 55
Elderplan, 44–46, 47–56, 178
 concept of, 47
 sample flyer, 244–47
 worker profile, 56–61

El Paso, Time Dollar program in,
142–50
Emotional problems, caring for, 54
Employee Time Dollar programs,
218–20
Employment benefits, Time Dollars
as, 178
Entrepreneurs
in 1980s, 133–34
social, 134, 135–36
Etzione, Amitai, 30
Expertise, purchase of, 123

F

Fair, T. Willard, 111, 116
Family
breakdown of, economics and,
22, 23
conversation in, 15–16
division of labor and, 27–28, 29
economic value of, xi, xii
professional services and,
125–26
Family Assistance Act of 1988, 181
Feder, Judith, 11
Federal budget problems, 3–4, 7, 8
Federal deficit, 21, 77
Federal Deposit Insurance
Corporation, 41
Federal Reserve Board, 3, 77
Financial aid, for students earning
Time Dollar credits, 175, 180–81
Financial survival, of Time Dollar
programs, 220–28
Florence Burden Foundation, 110–11
Florida. *See also* Miami
bureaucracy in, 96–97,
100–103, 104–5, 107
elderly in, 97–98
Time Dollar legislation in, 99
Time Dollars rejected in, 95,
96–97
Florida bar association, 128
Florida Office of Aging, 96
Flyer, sample, 244–47
Fox, Roberta, 99, 100
Frankl, Viktor, 89
Frontier life, community and, 64
Frontier spirit, 134

G

Gatto, John Taylor, 124
General Accounting Office, 130
Giving, health and, 86–87, 89
GNP, 24, 31, 183
Goodwill, changing definition of,
18–19
Government
increased social demands to, 23
role in Time Dollars, 173–83
in Sweden, 166–67
Grace Hill Neighborhood Services,
153–58
Great Depression, 26, 48
Gross national product (GNP), 24,
31, 183

H

Habitat for Humanity, 136
Health
economy and, 87–88
giving and, 86–87, 89
Health care, in El Paso, 142–50
Health insurance, purchased with
Time Dollars, 45, 175–76
Health Maintenance Organizations
(HMOs), 46–47
for elderly. *See* Elderplan
social, 47–48
Helping, health and, 86–87, 89
HMOs. *See* Health Maintenance
Organizations
Holmes, Oliver Wendell, 42
Holt, John, 125
Home-care providers, activities of,
120–21
Homeless persons, 180
Hospitals
elderly care and, 129
as program sponsors, 197–98
volunteers in, 66–67
Household economy, xi

I

Illich, Ivan, 123–24
INA, 213
Industry. *See* Business
Inflation, in early 1980s, 77

Information form, sample, 256–57
Information package, 208–9
In Search of Excellence, 133, 156
"Inside Edition," 115, 117–18
Insurance, for givers and recipients, 213, 226
Insurance Company of North America (INA), 213
Insurance premiums, paid in Time Dollars, 178
Internal Revenue Service (IRS), x, 39, 76–80, 81–82

J
Jobs, Stephen, 133
Johnson, Lyndon, 46
Juvenile justice, 175

K
Kennedy, John F., 134
King, Martin Luther, Jr., 218
Kirtland Community College, VISCAP program, 242–43
Kitchen table, as symbol of social cohesion, 15–16

L
Labor, division of, reduced socialization from, 27–28, 29, 122
Landsman Schaften, 48–49
Law. *See also under* Florida; Michigan; Missouri
federal tax, 77, 79–80
Lawyers
legal problems and, 125
legal services and, 128
Legislative support, for Time Dollar programs, 222–27
Liability, caregiving and, 130–31
Liberals, 162–63
Local program, sample handout for, 239–40
Long-term considerations, in Time Dollar programs, 216–28
Ludd, Ned, 123
Luddites, 123
Lynd, Robert and Helen, 19

M
Market economy, as determinant of social welfare, 24–25
Marshall, John, 75–76
McCarthy, Colman, 89
McClelland, David, 43
Media coverage, of Time Dollar programs, 213–14
Medicaid, 154
Medical care, costs of, 46
Medical problems, caring for, 54
Medical professions
disease and, 125
elderly care and, 129–30
Medicare, 46
Meek, Carrie, 98, 99, 100, 111, 112–15
Megatrends, 98
Member information form, sample, 256–57
Member Organized Resource Exchange (MORE), 156
Member-to-Member program, 45, 49–50
Memorandum of understanding, 230–35
Men, volunteer work by, 11, 68
Miami. *See also* Florida
child care in, 132–33, 137–41
ethnic groups in, 111, 114
images of, 97
Time Dollar program in, 9–10, 116–19
manager profile, 72–74
start-up of, 110–16
Michigan. *See also* Berry, Eric
Time Dollar legislation in, 152
Time Dollar program in, 151–52
Minding the Body, Mending the Mind, 87
Missouri
monetary experiments in, 75
St. Louis, Time Dollar program in, 152–58
service credits guaranteed by, 158
Time Dollar legislation in, 76–77, 80, 151, 224

Mobility
   of money, 34–35
   social, 188–89
Money
   barter and, 26, 27
   as commodity, 39–40
   contracts and, 41–42
   disease and, 88
   division of labor and, 27–28
   economics and, 9, 27, 32
   as inadequate exchange
      medium, 31
   incentive of, 42–43
   limitations of, xii, 25, 30–43
   mobility of, 34–35
   monopoly of, challenge to,
      7–8
   purchasing possibilities with,
      36–37
   shortage of, 3
   social bonds and, 187, 188,
      189–90
   time as, xi, 6
   Time Dollars vs., 184, 190
   as transaction medium for
      strangers, 35–36
   trust in, 40–41
MORE, 156, 157

N
Nader, Ralph
   foreword by, ix–xiii
   Miami program and, 115
   as social entrepreneur, 135–36
   video segment introduced by,
      201
Naisbitt, John, 98
National Alliance for Business, 179
National Commission to Reduce
   Infant Mortality, 130
Nation of Strangers, A, 188–89
Needs, basic, purchased with Time
   Dollars, 175
Needs identification, 193–95
Neighborhood. *See also* Community
   economic value of, xi, xii
   social support from, 4, 5–6,
      108–9
New Deal, 20

Newsweek, Time Dollars mentioned
   in, 145
North Miami Foundation, 104–5

O
O'Hara, John, 18
Organizational charts, 203
   sample, 236–37
Organizational considerations,
   195–200
Organizations, as sponsors, 197–98
Ornish, Dean, 87

P
Pacific Presbyterian Medical Center,
   San Francisco, VIP program at,
   65, 71
Packard, Vance, 188
Parenting, women in industry and,
   30–31
Paso a Paso, 145
Peace Corps, 69, 134
Perot, H. Ross, 46
Peters, Thomas J., 133
"Phil Donahue Show," Time Dollar
   coverage on, 83–84, 86
Political Left, 162–63
Political Right, 24, 163–64
Polowy, Joanne, 151, 152–53, 158
Prices
   economics and, 37–38
   lack of, in Time Dollar
      programs, 37–38
Prisoner's Dilemma, The, 185
Procedures manual, 200, 201
Professionals
   dependency on, 123, 124, 125
   exclusivity of, 121–22
   helpers threatened by, 127–28
   as outsiders, 126–27
   problems created by, 124–25
   tax on services of, 177–78
Progress, concepts of, 123
Project Independence, 240–41
Project Rainbow, 132–33, 137–41
Promotional pitch, 209–11
   sample, 251–55
Promotional reprint, sample,
   248–50

Public sector support, for Time Dollar programs, 227–28
Public Service Corps, 178

Q

Questions and answers, sample, 240–41

R

Reader's Digest, promotional reprint from, 248–50
Reagan, Ronald, 20, 77
Reagan administration
    Florida elderly and, 97–98
    personal bankruptcies during, 21
    reduced social care funding by, 4
    STAES funding and, 155
    wealth and, 133
Reciprocity, in Time Dollar programs, 63–64, 69–71, 217–18
Record keeping, 204–5. *See also* Accounting
Recruits, 211
Red Cross, 39, 62, 65, 172
Rehabilitation, community service as, 174
Religious organizations, as program sponsors, 198
Request for proposals (RFPs), 223
Respite care, 241
Rewards, society and, xi-xii
RFPs, 223
Robert Wood Johnson Foundation, 7, 10, 11, 96, 111, 114, 156
Roosevelt, Franklin Delano, 35
RSVP, 69

S

St. Louis, Time Dollar program in, 78, 152–58
Sales pitch, 209–11
    sample, 251–55
Samuelson, Paul A., 26–27, 28–29
Sears World Trade, 77
Security
    charity vs., 65–66
    from Time Dollars, 81

Self-sufficiency, encouraging, 29
Seniors. *See* Elderly
Service credits. *See* Time Dollar(s)
Service recipients
    rights of, 259–60
    in Time Dollar programs, 211–13
Sexism, economics and, 67–68
Shriver, Sargent, 162
Smith, Adam, 23–24, 27, 28
Social HMOs (SHMOs), 47–48
Social programs
    costs of, quantification of, 183
    federally funded, 4
Social support, health and, 88
Social welfare, bureaucracy and, 74
Social workers, as outsiders, 126, 127
Society. *See also* Community
    "burdens" to, as producers, 8–9
    economy and, 24
    rewards and, xi-xii
South Shore Hospital (Miami), Time Dollar program at, 108, 115, 179
Specialization, of labor, reduced socialization from, 27–28, 29, 122
Sponsors, program, 197–98
Sponsorship agreement, sample, 230
Sports, money and, 34–35
STAES, 154, 155
Staffing, 201–3
Stanley Tool, 187
Steinbrenner, George, 35
Step by Step, 145
Students, financial aid to, 175, 180–81
Sweden, Time Dollars studied by, 166–68, 168–69, 171–72
Swedish Red Cross, 172
System to Assure Elderly Services (STAES), 154, 155

T

Taxation
    of professional services, 177–78
    social needs met by, 175, 176–78
    in Sweden, 166, 167

of Time Dollar credits, x, 39,
76–80, 226–27
in Time Dollars, 170–71
Taxes, paid in Time Dollars,
176–77
Television, family interaction and,
20–21
Third world, cash crops in, 40
Time, as wealth, xi, 6
Time Dollar(s)
accounting for, 6, 7, 38–39
social value of, 12
appealing across political lines,
162–63, 164
benefits purchased with, 12
conventional economics and, 9
credits and IRS, 78–79
criticisms of, 13, 32–34
demographics, 171
as entrepreneurialism, 137
government role in, 173–83
idea explained, ix-x, 6–7, 192
international interest in, 165
in money-driven market, 29
public status from, 176
reciprocal exchange with,
63–64, 69–71, 217–18
Swedish interest in, 166–68,
168–69, 171–72
Time Dollar credits
government guarantee of, 171,
225–26
in Missouri, 158
transfer of, 225
Time Dollar programs
base of operations, 195–200
constituency, 196
logistics, 195–96
one organization vs.
coalition, 196–97
philosophy, 196
sponsors, 197–98
strengths, 198–200
benefits of, 216–17
budget preparation, 205–7
charity vs., 54–55, 63, 65–66
community from, 36, 64, 71
costs of, 10–11, 205–6
demanding cases in, 57–58
directors of, 202

drop-out rate in, 67
financial survival of, long-term,
220–28
cash raised by volunteers,
221–22
institutionalizing program,
220–21
legislative or public sector
support, 222–28
informational package, 208–9
insurance arrangements, 213
launching, 208–15
limitations of, 260
long-range developments,
217–20
employee programs,
218–20
generating reciprocity,
217–18
media coverage, 213–14
needs identification, 193–95
network planning, 191–215
personal rewards of, 11, 14, 43,
45, 55–57, 69–71
policies and procedures,
200–201
record keeping, 204–5
recruits, 211
sample, 239–40
service recipients, 211–13
rights of, 259–60
staff, 202–3
start-up tools, 229–62
sustaining, 216–28
training and assignments,
214–15
volunteerism and, 62–74
work culture of, 68–69
Training, in Time Dollar programs,
214–15
Trump, Donald, 133
Trust, in Time Dollar programs, 41,
80–81, 82, 119

U

Unions, 178, 180
United States
early history of, community and
economy in, 17–18
economic condition of, 41

United States *(continued)*
  economies of, xi
  immigrants to, in 1920s, 48, 58
  lack of community in, 188
  medical costs in, 46
  national debt of, 40
U.S. Congress, federal budget and, 3
U.S. Department of Health and Human Services, 130

V

Values, traditional home and community, 163–64
VIP program, at Pacific Presbyterian Medical Center in San Francisco, 65, 71
VISCAP, 242–43
VISTA, 114, 116, 134, 179
  volunteer grants from, 202–3, 223
Volunteerism
  health and, 86–87, 89
  Time Dollar programs and, 11, 62–74
Volunteers
  cash raised by, 221–22
  code of ethics for, 262
  dos and don'ts for, 261
  humiliating perception of, 66–67

rights and responsibilities of, 258–59
in Time Dollar vs. other programs, 54–55
Volunteers in Service to America (VISTA), 114, 116, 134, 179
  volunteer grants from, 202–3, 223

W

Wages, Time Dollars as, 179
War on Poverty, 154, 162
Washington, D.C., Time Dollar program in, 3–7, 8, 12, 13–14
Waterman, Robert H., 133
Wealth. *See* Money
Wealth of Nations, The, 24, 27
Women
  economy and, xi
  as heads of households, 181–82
  in industry, parenting and, 30–31
  recognized for volunteer work, 67
  as service program participants, 8
Work ethic
  in Sweden, 166, 167–68
  in Time Dollar programs, 68–69
Working Assets, 134

The Compleat Time Dollar Kit

Take 25 percent off with this coupon when you order the entire kit.
A $97.00 value for $72.75!

The kit includes:

"How to Grow Time Dollars," a full manual $15.00

A systems and procedure manual. Available in
your choice of hard copy or diskette
(in WordPerfect 5.0) 10.00

Grantsmanship manual 15.00

A 10-minute video 12.00

A computer program with forms for keeping
records, making and tracking assignments,
and compiling reports 45.00

Cost of Kit	97.00
Less 25 Percent Discount	24.25
Total Cost of Kit	$72.75
Plus Shipping and Handling	6.00

TOTAL $78.75

NOTE: Individual items may be ordered at prices listed above. Include a shipping and handling charge of $2 for each item ordered.

NAME ————————————   STREET ————————————————

CITY ————————————————   STATE ———— ZIP ————

DESCRIPTION OF ITEMS ORDERED	QTY.	COST

Send check or money order to: Shipping and Handling
   Time Dollars
   P.O. Box 19405   Total Enclosed
   Washington, DC 20036